主办方
Co-organized by

希腊文化部 希腊文物及文化遗产总局
Hellenic Ministry of Culture
General Directorate of Antiquities and Cultural Heritage

HELLENIC REPUBLIC
Ministry of Culture
General Directorate of Antiquities and Cultural Heritage

希腊伊拉克利翁考古博物馆
Hellenic Archaeological Museum of Heraklion

ΑΡΧΑΙΟΛΟΓΙΚΟ ΜΟΥΣΕΙΟ ΗΡΑΚΛΕΙΟΥ

故宫博物院
The Palace Museum

故宫博物院
THE PALACE MUSEUM

联合推广方
Jointly Promoted by

CHOW TAI FOOK
周 大 福

Legends of Crete

DAEDALUS

Compiled by the Palace Museum and the Hellenic Archaeological Museum of Heraklion

代达罗斯

希腊克里特岛的神话

故宫博物院
希腊伊拉克利翁考古博物馆
编

故 宫 出 版 社
The Palace Museum Press

图书在版编目（C I P）数据

代达罗斯：希腊克里特岛的神话 / 故宫博物院，希腊伊拉克利翁考古博物馆编. 北京：故宫出版社，2025. 4. -- ISBN 978-7-5134-1678-8

Ⅰ. K885.450.2

中国国家版本馆CIP数据核字第20250AM034号

代达罗斯

希腊克里特岛的神话

故宫博物院　希腊伊拉克利翁考古博物馆 编

出 版 人：果美侠

责任编辑：方　妍　李园明

装帧设计：耕莘文化

责任印刷：常晓辉　顾从辉

出版发行：故宫出版社

地址：北京东城区景山前街4号　邮编：100009

电话：010-85007800　010-85007817

邮箱：ggcb@culturefc.cn

制版印刷：北京雅昌艺术印刷有限公司

开　　本：889毫米×1194毫米　1/16

印　　张：19

版　　次：2025年4月第1版

2025年4月第1次印刷

书　　号：ISBN 978-7-5134-1678-8

定　　价：320.00元

目录

CONTENTS

祝辞

“代达罗斯：希腊克里特岛的神话”展览是希腊文化部与故宫博物院深度合作的重要成果，为中国观众开启一扇了解距今三千多年前克里特文明非凡科技成就的窗口。这个以创造力、创新精神与工程技术闻名于世的古老文明，其遗产至今仍在启迪后世。

展览以神话中的建筑师、发明家与匠心象征——代达罗斯为灵感源泉，将古代克里特技术呈现为整合实用知识、环境适应与实验探索的有机体系，而非遥不可及的奇观。米诺斯文明及其后的克里特文明突破神话与艺术表达的局限，在建筑、水利、冶金与运输领域创造出超前解决方案。这些技术不仅精准回应社会需求，更展现出对天然材料与结构设计的深刻认知。

通过精选文物、精细复原模型与多媒体演示，观众将深入探索古代克里特文明如何建造抗震建筑、管理水资源、精密铸造工具武器，甚至开创早期自动化装置。这些成就不仅彰显技术智慧，更表明古代克里特文明中，创新精神已渗透于城市规划、农业生产、宗教仪式与工艺制造等日常生活。

古代中国文明与古代希腊文明都曾为人类历史作出长远贡献。此次展览既是中希两国文化合作的重要里程碑，也是两国保护、研究与弘扬古代文明的直接体现。在故宫博物院的殿宇之中呈现古希腊技术遗产，这不仅促成两大文明超越地理阻隔展开深度对话，更是让二者对匠心精神、传统守护与卓越追求的价值共鸣在此交相辉映。

我们诚挚感谢故宫博物院的鼎力支持，并向所有促成此次展览的机构与个人表示感谢。在此，我们特别感谢伊拉克利翁考古博物馆及希腊文化部的策展人和学者们。他们不仅展示出专业素养，还具备卓越的学术远见。同时，我们向参与这一复杂项目、具有精湛技艺的技术团队、文物保护专家和设计师致以崇高的敬意。此外，我们也衷心感谢本图录的权威撰稿人。

我们衷心希望本次展览不仅成为认知古代克里特技术成就的窗口，更成为激发创新精神的源泉，提醒世人发明创造是人类跨越时空的永恒追求。

莉娜・门佐尼

希腊文化部部长

2025 年 4 月

Preface

The exhibition *Daedalus: Legends of Crete* is the result of a close and fruitful collaboration between the Hellenic Ministry of Culture and the Palace Museum. It offers Chinese audiences a rare opportunity to engage with the remarkable technological achievements of ancient Crete, a civilization that flourished over 3,000 years ago and whose legacy continues to inspire through its creativity, innovation, and engineering skill.

Drawing inspiration from the mythical figure of Daedalus – architect, inventor, and symbol of ingenuity – this exhibition presents ancient Cretan technology not as a distant curiosity, but as a dynamic and integrated system of practical knowledge, adaptation, and experimentation. Far from being limited to myth or artistic expression, the Minoans and later ancient Cretans developed advanced solutions in architecture, hydraulics, metallurgy, and transportation. These technologies met the real needs of their society and demonstrate a sophisticated understanding of natural materials and structural design.

Through selected artifacts, detailed reconstructions, and multimedia presentations, visitors are invited to explore how ancient Cretans built earthquake-resistant structures, managed water resources, crafted tools and weapons with precision, and even created early forms of automation. These achievements are not only technologically impressive, but they also reflect a worldview in which innovation was woven into everyday life – from urban planning and agricultural production to ritual practice and craftsmanship.

The exhibition's organization in China is an important milestone in the cultural cooperation between our two countries. It reflects a shared commitment to the preservation, study, and promotion of our ancient civilizations – both of which have made lasting contributions to human history. This presentation of ancient Greek technological heritage in the historic halls of the Palace Museum invites a rich and meaningful exchange between two great cultures that, despite geographical distance, have always valued ingenuity, tradition, and the pursuit of excellence.

We extend our sincere thanks to the Palace Museum for its collaboration and hospitality, and to all those whose dedicated efforts made this exhibition possible. Special acknowledgment is due to the curators and scholars from the Heraklion Archaeological Museum and the Hellenic Ministry of Culture for their expertise and vision, to the technical teams, conservators, and designers who worked to bring this complex and ambitious project to life, as well as to the distinguished authors of the present catalogue.

We hope this exhibition will serve not only as an introduction to the technological achievements of ancient Crete, but also as a source of inspiration – reminding us that the spirit of invention is a universal and timeless human trait.

Dr. Lina Mendoni
The Minister of Culture of the Hellenic Republic
April 2025

祝辞

故宫博物院，这座承载中华五千年文明的精神家园，在 2025 年迎来建院百年华诞。值此历史性时刻，“代达罗斯：希腊克里特岛的神话”展览于神武门展厅隆重启幕，不仅彰显了故宫博物院守护人类文明的永恒使命，更谱写了中希两大文明古国促进文明交流互鉴的时代新篇。当克里特岛米诺斯文明的璀璨遗产与紫禁城的金瓦红垣交相辉映，两座文明丰碑在当代语境中激荡出超越时空的精神共鸣，为构建人类命运共同体提供了深刻启示。

作为地中海文明的曙光，克里特岛孕育的米诺斯文化以其独特的艺术创造与精神追求，在人类文明星空中绽放永恒光芒。本次展览以神话工匠代达罗斯为精神意象，通过希腊国宝级文物与学术研究成果的系统呈现，引领观众探寻爱琴文明在物质创造、艺术审美与人文精神层面的不朽价值，同时回望了同时代的中华文明。展览突破传统文明叙事的单一维度，以平等对话的姿态构建起东西方文明互通的桥梁，在当代语境中重新诠释人类早期海洋文明的智慧遗产。

此次合作标志着中希文明对话迈入新境界。故宫博物院与希腊文博界将以此次展览为起点，持续深化战略协作，共同探索文化遗产价值传播的创新路径。我们期待在代达罗斯的匠心智慧与紫禁城的营造哲学之间，在米诺斯文明的航海精神与东方“和合共生”理念之间，构建起更具深度的文明对话机制，让不同文明在相互映照中实现创造性转化、创新性发展，为当今世界注入更多的思考与活力。

六百载宫阙见证文明交融，一百年守正开启新的征程。值此百年华诞，我们以这场跨越东西的文明对话，向故宫博物院承载的包容精神致敬，向全球文明互鉴的时代命题致意。展览将成为唤醒文明记忆的时空之门，让智慧之光指引人类文明永续发展；故宫博物院将以海纳百川的胸怀，在人类文明的长河中续写交流互鉴的璀璨篇章。

故宫博物院院长

2025 年 4 月

Preface

The Palace Museum, home to the essence of the 5,000-year-old Chinese civilization, is celebrating its centennial anniversary in 2025. At such a historic moment, the exhibition *Daedalus: Legends of Crete* will be staged in the Gate of Divine Prowess Exhibition Hall as a witness to the Palace Museum's perpetual mission as a guardian of human civilization, writing a new chapter in cultural exchanges and mutual learning between China and Greece, contemporary representatives of two ancient civilizations. As the brilliant cultural heritage of the Minoan civilization is put on show in the Forbidden City, two civilizations resonate across time and space in a contemporary context, shedding light on our efforts to build a community with a shared future for mankind.

As the dawn of the Mediterranean civilization, the Minoan civilization of the Island of Crete shines with eternal radiance with its unique artistic creations and spiritual pursuits. This exhibition centers on the mythological craftsman Daedalus and leads visitors into the Aegean civilization through a systematic presentation of national treasures of Greece and relevant research findings, revealing timeless value of the material creations, aesthetics, and humanism represented by this ancient civilization. As cultural treasures of the Chinese civilization from the same period in history are also on display, the exhibition goes beyond the traditional approach of telling stories of one civilization alone to enable a dialogue between the East and the West on equal footing. As such, it provides a new perspective for visitors to understand the wisdom and heritage of an early maritime civilization in a contemporary context.

This collaboration marks the beginning of a new chapter in the dialogues civilizations between China and Greece and more in-depth strategic cooperation will follow between the Palace Museum and museums in Greece so as to jointly explore new approaches to the communication of the value of cultural heritage. It is our expectation that when craftsmanship of Daedalus collides with the architectural philosophy of the Forbidden City and when the maritime spirit of Minos meets the Eastern concept of harmonious coexistence, the dialogue between civilizations can deepen and new creations can come out, contributing more wisdom and vitality to the development of the human world today.

Over its 600-year history, the Forbidden City has witnessed how cultures meet and mingle. At its 100th anniversary, the Palace Museum embarks on a new journey while upholding its time-honored fundamental principles. To mark this special occasion, we hereby present this event of dialogue of civilizations between the East and the West as a tribute to inclusiveness and to mutual learning between civilizations, which are both important themes of our time. The exhibition, hopefully, will revive our memories of the past and enable ancient wisdom to shed light on sustainable development of humanity today. The Palace Museum will remain inclusive as it has always been and embrace more cultural exchanges and mutual learning, aspiring to a brilliant future for mankind.

Wang Xudong
Director of the Palace Museum
April 2025

祝辞

创新常被视为现代社会的标志，但创造性思维、技术智慧与攻坚克难的种子，在人类历史长河中早已生根发芽。在神话的暗影与发明的光辉交织下，本次“代达罗斯：希腊克里特岛的神话”展旨在揭示克里特岛上想象力与创造力之间的永恒互动。

本次展览以希腊神话中传奇的发明家、建筑师及工匠代达罗斯为灵感之源，举办地点位于故宫博物院庄严的殿堂之中。传说中，代达罗斯为克诺索斯国王米诺斯建造了囚禁米诺陶洛斯的迷宫。他曾雕刻出栩栩如生的雕像，甚至还用蜂蜡与羽毛制成翅膀，携其子伊卡洛斯逃离囚牢。古希腊人将他的名字赋予了智慧、技艺与创造力等诸多美德。透过他的故事，我们得以窥见人类创造力与文明塑造力量之间的深刻关联。在古希腊人的想象中，代达罗斯不仅是神话人物，更是他所涉足领域中创作者的化身。这些融合历史与寓言的故事，两千余年来始终启发着哲学家、诗人、艺术家与工程师。

克里特岛坐落于东地中海交汇处，曾是文化交流与技术发展的中心。岛上的工匠在建筑、冶金、陶艺与机械装置等领域展现出非凡的智慧。这些成就不仅服务于日常生活，更体现出对材料、设计与功能的深刻理解。

本次展览汇集伊拉克利翁考古博物馆的多件珍贵文物，这些器物均为首次向中国公众呈现，时间跨度从米诺斯文明早期一直到罗马时代。从工具器皿到仪式器物，这些展品见证了古代克里特人卓越的智慧和技艺，折射出跨越时空的灵感延续。通过精心策划的主题、多媒体诠释与沉浸式设计，代达罗斯展引领观众在回望历史的同时与之对话。

代达罗斯的形象贯穿展览始终。尽管属于神话，其故事仍折射出古代社会的真实价值追求，即希望以智慧与技艺创造、革新并解决问题。通过将神话与历史证据并置，本次展览能够引发人们对想象力与实践知识关系的思考，而这种关系至今仍具现实意义。在当今技术剧变的世界，代达罗斯提出的问题依然警示着我们。从人工智能到生物工程，从全球通信到气候适应，人类创造力的辉煌与困境无处不在。回溯古代的智慧典范，或许能让我们更深刻地理解当下。

我们非常荣幸于故宫博物院呈现此展，并衷心感谢中国的同仁与合作伙伴，正是他们的慷慨与协作，搭建起这座跨越大陆的文化之桥。希望本次展览不仅可以深化对克里特文明的理解，更能以神话与历史的丝线，通过共同的求知欲、尊重与探索精神，再次织紧希腊与中国人民之间的纽带。

史黛拉·克莱索拉克

希腊伊拉克利翁考古博物馆馆长

2025 年 4 月

Preface

Innovation is often regarded as the hallmark of the modern age. Yet the seeds of creative thinking, technological ingenuity, and problem-solving were sown long ago in human history. In the shadow of myth and the light of invention, the exhibition *Daedalus: Legends of Crete* seeks to illuminate the timeless interplay between imagination and creation, as it unfolded on the island of Crete.

This exhibition, hosted within the venerable halls of the Palace Museum, draws its breath from the figure of Daedalus. As the legendary inventor, architect, and artisan of Greek mythology, Daedalus was said to have built the Labyrinth for King Minos of Knossos, where the Minotaur was confined, crafted lifelike statues, and even constructed wings of wax and feather for himself and his son Icarus to escape captivity. In his name, the ancient Greeks gathered all the virtues of intelligence, skill, and invention; and through his story, we glimpse the powerful bond between human creativity and the forces that shape civilizations. In the ancient Greek imagination, Daedalus was not simply a mythical character. He was a symbol – perhaps even a prototype – of the creator in all his complexity. These tales – part history, part allegory – have inspired philosophers, poets, artists, and engineers for over two millennia.

Crete, situated at the crossroads of the Eastern Mediterranean, was a center of cultural exchange and technical development. The island's artisans demonstrated exceptional ingenuity in many fields, from architecture and metallurgy, to pottery and mechanical devices. These achievements not only served the needs of daily life but also reflected a deep understanding of materials, design, and functionality.

This exhibition brings together precious artifacts of the Archaeological Museum of Heraklion, spanning millennia – from the early Minoan period to the Roman era – and presents them to the Chinese public for the very first time. These objects, ranging from tools and vessels to ritual artifacts, are testament to the persistent brilliance of ancient Cretan minds and hands, reflecting a continuity of inspiration that bridges distant lands and ages. Through carefully curated themes, multimedia interpretation, and immersive design, *Daedalus* invites visitors not merely to witness the past, but also to converse with it.

The figure of Daedalus serves as a guiding thread throughout the exhibition. Although mythical, his story reflects real values and concerns of ancient societies: the desire to create, to innovate, and to solve problems through intelligence and craftsmanship. By placing myth alongside historical evidence, the exhibition encourages reflection on the relationship between imagination and practical knowledge – a relationship that remains relevant today. The questions Daedalus raises remain with us today, as we navigate a world shaped by rapid technological change. From artificial intelligence to bioengineering, from global communications to climate adaptation, we are surrounded by the triumphs and dilemmas of human inventiveness. By reflecting on ancient models of ingenuity, we may better understand our own.

We are proud to present this exhibition at the Palace Museum, and we warmly thank our colleagues and partners in China, whose generosity and collaboration have allowed this cultural bridge to span continents. May this exhibition not only deepen our understanding of the Cretan world but also reaffirm the ties between the peoples of Greece and China – ties woven, like the threads of myth and history, through shared curiosity, respect, and wonder.

Dr Stella D. Chrysoulaki
General Director of the Archaeological Museum of Heraklion
April 2025

31

代达罗斯：
彰显古克里特的技术创新与独创性

卡特琳娜・阿塔纳萨基、
乔治娅・弗拉达、迪米特里斯・斯法基纳基斯
伊拉克利翁考古博物馆

展览导言

故宫博物院组织的此次展览聚焦代达罗斯（Daedalus），这位古希腊神话中集发明家、建筑师、能工巧匠、雕塑大师与创新工具制造者等身份于一身的传奇人物，同时也是克里特多元神话谱系的核心象征。在古希腊文献传统中，史前克里特文明（后世以克诺索斯传奇国王米诺斯 [Minos] 之名命名，称之为“米诺斯文明”）的诸多技术创新皆被归功于这位标志性匠人。因其颇负盛名，甚至公元前 1000 年的艺术成就也被认为出自他手。秉承这些观念，本次展览将主题定为“代达罗斯”，精选多件古克里特文物首度亮相中国，重构这位神话先驱如何在米诺斯世界叙事与古希腊思想体系中获得如此象征地位。展览旨在拓展中希两国文明对话渠道，进一步巩固两国人民深厚的友谊。

神话传统中的代达罗斯

古代文献记载的代达罗斯神话主要围绕两大经典叙事展开：

（一）迷宫与米诺陶洛斯（Minotaur）：米诺斯王延请知名建筑师代达罗斯设计囚禁牛首人身怪物米诺陶洛斯的迷宫。迷宫错综复杂，任何进入者都将迷失其中。

（二）代达罗斯与伊卡洛斯（Icarus）的飞翔悲剧：为逃离克里特岛的囚禁，代达罗斯以羽毛和蜂蜡为材料，为自己与儿子伊卡洛斯打造飞行翼。代达罗斯虽警告其子勿近烈日，伊卡洛斯仍一意孤行。因飞临太阳过近致使蜡翼融化，伊卡洛斯最终坠海殒命。

故宫博物院本次展览以第一则神话为叙事主轴，借助文物展陈与多媒体装置，凸显代达罗斯精神特质的普适性——其创新性、独创性与创造力，将其作为发展的动力源泉，推动技术、经济、政治及社会生活多层面的发展变革。同时，展览亦引导观众深思古今“创新”活动蕴含的哲学与伦理命题：这位集大成的发明家、匠人、艺术家与建筑师，终为自身的创造力付出代价，沦为悲剧性的存在。

展览理念概览

此次展览以打造多层次教育互动体验为核心目标，旨在激发各年龄段观众的探究热情，促进思辨对话与主动参与。展览致力于引导观众深入了解文物承载的文化意义及其考古与历史背景，同时能够理解器物本身也是文化变革的推动者。

展览围绕代达罗斯神话的多元维度，设置六大主题展区，以这位神话匠人为展览的叙事脉络，串联各件展出文物。

展览精选涵盖标志性器物与日常器物的考古文物，配合文本资料、视觉与多媒体元素，令观众可以从多个维度探索这位神话人物。这种复合式展陈既能够将文物与知识呈现给所有观众，也能够帮助观众欣赏代达罗斯的创造智慧，体悟创新、创造在人类历史中的永恒价值。

代达罗斯与古克里特技术

从博物馆学视角出发，本次展览借助上下三千年的各类艺术成就，着力揭示古克里特技术文明中创新、创造活动的重要地位。克里特独特的物质文化自然源自其岛屿特性与得天独厚的地理区位。作为东地中海中枢，克里特坐拥欧、亚、非三洲海路交汇之利，始终发挥着人文与思想传播的枢纽职能[1]。凭借其在海上航线与贸易中的优异地位，克里特人不仅成功引入了艺术和技术创新，更是积极转化由埃及、安纳托利亚及近东等繁荣邻域文明传入的先进科技成果。

因此，尽管本次展览的灵感源于克诺索斯宫廷背景下的代达罗斯神话，但展品全景展示了米诺斯文明，涵盖米诺斯早期至罗马时期（公元前3000年至公元200年）。这一点通过开篇“神话”展区与“拟人化雕塑”专题来实现，代达罗斯被认为推动了古风时期早期雕塑革新运动，因而这类雕塑后被命名为“代达罗斯式”。“神话”展区同时重构了古代匠人行动的社会环境：米诺斯宫廷建筑作为强势中央权威的象征，管控着一般性的技术创新实践。

据狄奥多罗斯·西库卢斯（Diodorus Siculus）记载的神话版本，代达罗斯之父为墨提翁（Metion），一位“善发明者”，其祖父为欧帕拉摩斯（Eupalamos），亦为“巧手之人”[2]。西库卢斯将代达罗斯塑造为技艺超群、备受信赖的匠人典范，以非凡创

1 Chaniotis 2004, 9-15; Bennet 2013, 103-104; Rethemiotakis 2024, 14.

2 Diodorus Siculus, *Historical Library*, book 4, chapter 76, 1,1.

造力破解每一项技术难题[3]。通过神话传说及其在建筑、制陶、冶金、雕塑与航海领域的独特作品，代达罗斯的独创性举世闻名，深深植根于古希腊集体记忆。在希腊神话思想史上，这位工匠大师首次以作品与艺术的卓越性，跻身克诺索斯宫廷统治精英之列，甚至被赋予独立意志、话语权与决策权。这位最伟大创造者的无匹之作，既提升了日常生活品质，更以技术创新巩固了克诺索斯王室的威望与统治力。

代达罗斯的主要事迹牵扯到王后帕西法厄（Pasiphae）与公主阿里阿德涅（Ariadne），尤其是罗马时期文献证实的传奇迷宫建造事件。下令建造迷宫的米诺斯王对代达罗斯态度的矛盾性亦由此可解：米诺斯王作为推动“神话”发展的主要决策者，对代达罗斯时而极尽尊崇，时而生恐匠人背弃承诺以致王权失控。正如奥维德（Ovid）《变形记》（*Metamorphoses*）（第八卷）所述，代达罗斯甚至以智谋策划携子伊卡洛斯飞离克里特，此举直接触怒国王。

尽管如此，对代达罗斯崇拜的最早证据可追溯至史前时期。出土于克诺索斯王宫的泥板可追溯至公元前 14 世纪（公元前 1400 ~ 前1300 年），这也是最早的欧洲破译文本。这些泥板以形音并存的线形文字 B 这项米诺斯文明最重要的发明，记载了以代达罗斯命名的神庙。虽然具体神庙位置已不可考，但这些证据暗示着米诺斯历史上可能存在一位与代达罗斯相关的神祇[4]。因此，一些关键泥板记录了克诺索斯宫廷向神庙献祭之事，其最终目的地便是“Daedalion”（da–da–re–jo–de，Daidaleion–de）。一件泥板上记载有一个众神体系，另一件则提到了 da–pu–ri–to–jo po–ti–ni–ja（迷宫的女主人，公元前 14 世纪的崇拜对象），这两块泥板上都提到“Daedalion”一词，由此可将其与供奉代达罗斯的露天神龛或神庙关联起来。

据历史文献传承的神话所述，代达罗斯以铁匠学徒的身份出道，师从雅典娜女神，并首开神明塑像之先河[5]。公元前 6 至前 5 世纪的文字记载尤为凸显其雕塑家身份。相关文献记载，代达罗斯通过分离雕像双腿为跨步姿态、将手臂与躯干解离，首次为僵硬的躯干赋予“动态感”。这些革新被视为古风时期雕塑的重大成就，展览中以克里特普莱索斯城出土的陶制青年雕像三维数字复制品（约公元前 575 年）为典范呈现[6]。此外，代达罗斯更以多元材料组装的精妙器物闻名，其多项技术成就在米诺斯文明均属首创，包括速转陶轮、锯与钻具的发明、船帆的运用、克诺索斯迷宫建筑群的设计，乃至武器的制造。

代达罗斯神话在各个历史时期被赋予政治意涵：克诺索斯城将米诺陶洛斯与几何化迷宫图案铸为钱币象征；克里特南部强邦斐斯托斯则选用代达罗斯所造带翼巨人塔罗斯（Talos）形象作为钱币正面标志。

3 Frontisi-Ducroux 1970; Morris 1992, 259-260.

4 Ruipérez-Melena 1996, 244; Duhoux-Morpurgo Davies 2008, 257-61; Gulizio-Nakassis 2014, 122-24; Rizza 2015, 213-14; Judson 2017, 57-62.

5 Graves 1955, 270.

6 D. Sfakianakis in Mandalaki (ed.) 2019, 90.

因此，展览其余主题单元围绕雅典神话版本固化的代达罗斯核心成就展开，塑造这位匠人的多重身份特质：

1）创新工具制造者与使用者（石匠）：提升生产效率与工艺品质，诸如速转陶轮、锯具、用于硬质石材加工的水平钻或玉石车床。

2）“迷宫”建筑群的创造型建筑师：通过呈现米诺斯宫廷建筑核心特征的展品来进行阐释，包括“迷宫式”空间布局、木石建筑的和谐组合、“纪念性壁画”的运用以及“建筑雕塑装饰”体系。同时，呼应了神话记载的“阿里阿德涅的舞场”，展现空间中社会仪式的展演维度。

3）多元材料组装制作匠人、人形及兽形雕塑大师：展品系统呈现克里特拟人雕塑的演变轨迹，展示从最初的小型雕塑到大型立体造型艺术的发展历程，时间跨度从前王宫期延伸至多个历史时期（公元前 3000 年至公元 200 年）。

4）举世无双的发明家和现有技术革新者：通过发明帆具优化海上航行效能。这项技术强化了米诺斯文明的对外辐射力，使其在史前爱琴海区域占据了主导地位，并在地中海东部形成显著影响力。

鉴于此，展览以克里特史前时期丰沛的物质生产与金属工艺为核心叙事。自旧王宫期初期（约公元前 1900 年）速转陶轮发明后，传统泥条盘筑制罐技艺逐渐式微，仅用于大型贮藏器与丧葬陶瓮制作[7]。这种旋转器械推动制罐流程标准化，催生出诸多仿金属器形制的优雅器物。在此类器物中，宴饮场景中高频使用的“卡马雷斯彩绘风格”陶杯最具代表性，其繁复多彩的纹饰体系堪称米诺斯陶艺典范。

同时展出的还有公元前 2000 年的青铜工具，包括两类基本凿器、双刃斧、扁斧等类别，配合其铸造的石模实物，系统揭示工具的多种人体工学功能与用途。其中，两人操作的巨型解木锯最具米诺斯技术象征意义，此类工具为大型建筑群营造提供了关键技术支撑[8]。该展区还将展示祭祀用双刃斧、手斧、剑、开放式容器等宫室制品，以及用线形文字 A 与 B 书写生产记录的泥板[9]。

聚焦石容器制造技术的展品群，通过原料加工至成品的技术链实证，凸显米诺斯技术发明的物质印记。代表性展品包括造型复杂的祭酒器“来通杯”，包括特里同螺、牛首等精雕形制，凝结着米诺斯石作工艺的巅峰技艺。

本次展览特设独立单元呈现印章雕刻艺术。这门微型艺术在米诺斯时期臻至精妙绝伦之境：早至公元前 3000 年，克里特便与近东地区展开工艺交流，吸纳了使用印章印记代表个人或机构这一象征用法。在旧王宫期（公元前 1900 ~ 前 1700 年），印章多以软质石材制成，采用手持钻具进行雕刻。公元前 18 世纪末玉石车床的出现，使得在硬质半宝石材料上雕刻成为可能，由此催生出

7 关于米诺斯陶工首次使用陶轮的方式，请参见Jeffra (2013) 及先前讨论。

8 相关讨论见Evely (1993), 31, Type 3和34。

9 有关线形文字A和B的简短介绍，见Flouda (2015); Pratt (2025), 5-7。

印面更为精致的印章。此时已能在一枚印章上组合使用实心钻与筒形钻技术。伴随技术进步，长型三棱/四棱柱印章、带繁复钮饰的石质/金属图章，以及盘形、矩形、透镜状印章也纷纷问世。新王宫期（公元前1700~前1450年），印章雕刻术达到鼎盛，其应用范围扩展至资源管理及其他行政事务。印章纹饰囊括动物图景、人神互动场景、宗教符号等具象主题，同时出现复杂装饰纹样与几何构图，表明此时已发明多种金属钻头，以满足不同雕刻需求。

公元前1600至前1400年制作的金质印章戒指，以程式化仪式内涵的叙事场景为特征。此类彰显精英身份的器物常与各类精工首饰共出，多发现于米诺斯墓葬遗存。黄金作为贵重资源于公元前3000年初传入克里特，公元前17世纪后逐渐普及。通过熔铸入模技术，耳饰、手镯、项链串珠、戒指等饰物得以批量生产。金箔贴金、凸纹工艺、绞丝金片、多型链饰及造粒加工等技法，共同印证克里特工匠在金器工艺上的精进过程。

最后，聚焦纪念性雕塑历史的主题单元将集中展示“石首石肢木身（Acrolithic）雕塑”（肢体由不同材质组合成型）的实物例证。展品包括克诺索斯大型木雕的石质发饰模型、各地出土的陶制足部构件、可能与雕像有关的青铜发束等，系统展现通过材料组合塑造人体形态的艺术成就。除可能属于大型雕像的残件外，米诺斯时期唯一存世的大型石制简化人形雕像与巨型陶制人像亦同场展出，共同勾勒出米诺斯文明在纪念性雕塑领域的成就。

代达罗斯展将引领观众欣赏这位传奇匠人的多维遗产，激励他们在各自领域传承创新与创造精神。

From "Daedalus" to Innovation and Ingenuity in Ancient Cretan Technology

Katerina Athanasaki, Georgia Flouda,
Dimitris Sfakianakis
Archaeological Museum of Heraklion

Introduction to the exhibition

The exhibition organized at the Palace Museum explores the legacy of Daedalus, a universal character of ancient Greek mythology, known for his remarkable abilities as an inventor, architect, ingenious craftsman, peerless sculptor and innovative tool maker. It is remarkable that Daedalus is also a leading figure in the multifaceted Cretan mythological cycle. Most of the technological innovations of the prehistoric Cretan civilization, which today we conventionally call "Minoan" after the name of Minos, the legendary king of Knossos, were associated by the later ancient Greek philological tradition with the name of this iconic craftsman. Moreover, his fame was so great that even the artistic conquests of the 1st millennium BCE were attributed to Daedalus and his worthy hands. Following these notions, the exhibition "Daedalus" reconstructs the ways in which this pioneering mythical figure achieved such an emblematic position in the narratives for the Minoan world and in the thinking of ancient Greeks, presenting selected ancient Cretan works to the Chinese public for the first time. The primary aim of the exhibition initiative is to extend the communication channels between the two countries and, also, to strengthen the enduring and longstanding friendship among the people of China and Greece.

The mythological tradition on the mythical craftsman

Daedalus is mostly associated with the following two myths, which are handed down from the ancient written sources:

a. The myth of the labyrinth and of the Minotaur: In this mythological story, Daedalus was commissioned as a famous architect by King Minos to design and construct the labyrinth to contain the Minotaur, a monstrous creature with the body of a man and the head of a bull. The Labyrinth was designed to be so complex that anyone who entered would become hopelessly lost.

b. The myth of Daedalus and his son Icarus, who attempted to fly: Daedalus crafted a pair of wings for himself and his son, Icarus, made from feathers and wax, in order to help them escape imprisonment on Crete. However, Daedalus warned Icarus not to fly too close to the sun because the heat would melt the wax. Icarus ignored the warning and, tragically, fell into the sea when his wings disintegrated due to the sun's heat.

The exhibition at the Palace Museum specifically builds upon the first myth. Through the combination of ancient objects and multimedia material, it aims to highlight the universality of the characteristics of Daedalus: creation, ingenuity and inventiveness, as dynamic drivers of development that can trigger developments and changes at multiple levels (technology, economy, politics and social life). At the same time, however, it aspires to allow visitors to explore philosophical and ethical issues related to "innovation" in both the ancient and modern world, given that Daedalus, in addition to being a great inventor, craftsman, artist and architect, is also known as a tragic figure, as he himself paid the consequences of his own innovations.

Concept and overview of the exhibition

The design of the exhibition aims to create a rich educational and interactive experience to engage visitors of all ages, to encourage questions, discussions and active participation. Moreover, it aims to provide visitors with a deep understanding of the cultural significance of the artifacts and their archaeological and historical context and, at the same time, to understand artifacts as agents of cultural change.

The exhibits have been arranged into six thematic sections, which are dedicated to specific themes covering many aspects of the myth of Daedalus. As the main theme that ties together the artifacts and provides a narrative thread for the exhibition is used the mythical figure itself.

The selected archaeological artifacts comprise iconic pieces and "everyday" items, combined with textual information, visual and multimedia elements, allowing visitors to explore the mythical figure from different perspectives. The aim of this combination is to make the objects accessible and educational for visitors of all ages and also to help visitors appreciate the ingenuity of Daedalus and the enduring value of innovation and creativity in human history.

Daedalus and ancient Cretan technology

From a museological perspective, the main aim of the exhibition is to highlight the importance of innovation and ingenuity in ancient Cretan technology, as shown by a wide field of arts developed across three thousand years of history. Naturally, Cretans owe their distinctive material culture to insularity and to their advantageous geographical setting. Set in the centre of the eastern Mediterranean, at the crossroads of the sea routes between three continents of Europe, Asia and Africa, the island has always been a hub for the network connecting people and ideas.[1] Through their prominence in sea routes and commerce, Cretans have managed not only to introduce artistic and technological innovations, but also to adapt advanced technology transmitted to them by neighboring cultures that flourished in Egypt, Anatolia and the Near East.

Thus, although the exhibition is inspired by the myth of the inventive Daedalus, who is directly related to the palatial environment of Knossos, the exhibits offer a panorama of Cretan creation from the early Minoan to the Roman period (3rd millennium BCE to the 2nd century CE). This is achieved through the first section on "Myth", which introduces the exhibition, as well as the section of anthropomorphic sculpture, since Daedalus was associated with the movement of the early statues of the archaic period which were

1 Chaniotis 2004, 9-15; Bennet 2013, 103-104; Rethemiotakis 2024, 14.

subsequently called "Daedalic". The exhibit on "Myth" also functions as a framework for the social environment of action of the ancient craftsman, which is identified with the strong central authority of the Minoan palaces or "court-centered buildings" that regulated the adoption of innovative practices in general.

According to the version of the myth written by Diodorus Siculus, Daedalus, son of Metion ("inventive") and grandson of Eupalamos ("whose hands grasp")[2], represents the accomplished and trusted craftsman, who skillfully resolved every technical challenge assigned to him with outstanding creativity.[3] Through mythical tradition, his proverbial ingenuity was established in the consciousness of people with distinctive works in the fields of architecture, ceramics, metallurgy, sculpture, and navigation. For the first time in Greek mythical thought, a master craftsman took a prominent position with his work and art next to representatives of the select group that ruled over the palace of Knossos and, thus, acquired a personal opinion, will, and determination. The unparalleled works of this greatest mortal creator enhanced and upgraded the quality of everyday life, while his ingenuity primarily guaranteed the prestige of the royal house of Knossos and the consolidation of its power in the eyes of the people. Daedalus emerged as a protagonist together with the royal wife (Pasiphae) and the royal offspring Ariadne through the challenges that arose from his innovative works of art, especially the mythical Labyrinth that is attested to in written sources of the Roman period. It is therefore no coincidence that King Minos, the main operator of the decisions that motivate the "myth", treats Daedalus sometimes with the deepest respect and sometimes with fear in the face of the possibility of the relaxation of his commitment and power over him. After all, according to one version of the myth recounted by Ovid's *Metamorphoses* (Book 8), Daedalus' intelligence allows him to even attempt to escape from Crete with his son Icarus, thus provoking the king's wrath.

Nonetheless, the earliest evidence for a sanctuary named after Daedalus comes from proto-history, as it is encountered in Linear B tablets, the oldest texts written in a logosyllabic form of Greek that constitutes the most important Cretan invention *per se*. These clay Linear B tablets come from the palace of Knossos and represent the most ancient deciphered European texts, as they date back to the 14th century BCE (1400-1300 BCE). Although the sanctuary cannot be located archaeologically, these early testimonies possibly suggest a latent historical reality regarding the existence of a Minoan deity associated with the person of Daedalus.[4] Thus, important tablets record offerings from the palace of Knossos to sanctuaries of deities which are destined for "Daedalion" (*da-da-re-jo-de*, Daidaleion-de). The association of this particular term with an open-air shrine or sanctuary dedicated to Daedalus is mainly reinforced by its appearance on a tablet referring to a pantheon of deities and on another with a reference to the "Lady of the Labyrinth", *da-pu-ri-to-jo po-ti-ni-ja*, who was worshipped during the 14th century BCE.

Following the myth passed down through written sources of the historical period, Daedalus began his career as a blacksmith, apprenticed to the goddess Athena herself, and was the first to make statues of gods.[5] Daedalus is particularly attested as a sculptor from the 6th or 5th century BCE. According to the relevant written testimonies, he was the first to "give movement" to the rigid torso by separating

2 Diodorus Siculus, *Historical Library*, book 4, chapter 76, 1,1.

3 Frontisi-Ducroux 1970; Morris 1992, 259-260.

4 Ruipérez-Melena 1996, 244; Duhoux-Morpurgo Davies 2008, 257-61; Gulizio-Nakassis 2014, 122-24; Rizza 2015, 213-14; Judson 2017, 57-62.

5 Graves 1955, 270.

the legs of the figures into a stride and also detaching the arms from the torso. These innovations are considered achievements of Archaic sculpture, which is represented in the exhibition by the 3D digital copy of a clay kouros from the Cretan city of Praisos (Ca. 575 BCE).[6] At the same time, though, the creator is credited with various diverse artifacts that required the successful assembly of different materials, as well as a series of technical achievements which first appeared in Minoan Crete, such as the invention of the fast potter's wheel, the saw and the drill, the use of sails for ships, the architectural Labyrinth of Knossos, as well as the manufacture of military weapons.

On a political level, the myth of Daedalus was consolidated in historical times, when the city of Knossos chose the Minotaur and various geometrical renderings of the Labyrinth as symbols for its coinage. The powerful city of Phaistos in southern Crete also adopted the winged giant Talos, a creation of Daedalus, as the symbol for the obverse of its coins.

Consequently, the rest of the thematic units of the exhibition focus on those episodes that highlight Daedalus' achievements, as they are handed down by the crystallized Athenian version of the myth. In particular, the craftsman emerges as a figure with the following qualities:

1) As an innovative manufacturer and user of tools (*mason*) that improve the efficiency and quality of production, such as the fast potter's wheel, the saw and the horizontal drill or lapidary lathe used for processing hard stones.

2) As an inventive architect and builder of the "Labyrinth" building complex. Particular reference to this aspect is made through exhibits related to key aspects of Minoan palatial architecture, such as the "labyrinthine" design and the harmonious combination of cut-stone structures, timber and rubble construction, "monumental wall painting" and the use of "architectural sculptural decoration". At the same time, an allusion is made to the performance of social rituals in space, as reflected through the "Ariadne dance hall" reported by the myth.

3) As a skilled craftsman in the assembly of different materials and in the production of refined works from a variety of materials, but also as a bold sculptor in the representation of animal and human figures. The exhibits stress the evolution of Cretan anthropomorphic sculpture from the first steps of small-scale sculpture to large-scale plastic arts and over a wide chronological range from the Prepalatial period to historical times (3rd millennium BCE to the 2nd century CE).

4) As an unparalleled inventor who enhanced the dynamics of existing applications, for instance he improved sea navigation through the invention of sails; this invention strengthened the extroversion of Minoan Crete and gave it a strong lead in the prehistoric Aegean and a marked presence in eastern Mediterranean.

Accordingly, a prominent place in the exhibition is held by the rich production of prehistoric Crete and metalwork. After the invention of the fast potter's wheel at the beginning of the Protopalatial period (around 1900 BCE), the handmade technique of making vases with the addition of clay coils gradually declined and was limited to the manufacture of large storage vessels and funerary clay urns.[7]

6 D. Sfakianakis in Mandalaki (ed.) 2019, 90.

7 On the manner in which Minoan potters first employed the pottery wheel, see Jeffra 2013 with previous discussion.

The rotary movement of the advanced potter's wheel led to the standardization of the vase-making process and the achievement of elegant artifacts which in many cases imitate metallic vessels. Small drinking cups of the so-called "Kamares or Polychrome Style", mostly used for feasting, especially stand out for their complex colourful patterns and feature among the most characteristic clay products of the Minoan civilization.

Also presented are bronze tools dating from the 2nd millennium BCE, such as chisels of two basic types, double-edged axes, adzes, etc. These categories of tools as well as the corresponding stone moulds used for their production demonstrate a wide range of ergonomic functionality and use. This is particularly attested by the huge, two-man, timber-ripping saws, which have been credited to Minoan technical know-how and were essential for building the large architectural complexes of the Minoan period.[8] Moreover, selected products of the mainly palatial craft productionin metals are represented by ceremonial double axes, hand-axes, swords, closed and open vessels, while written testimonies documenting their production in the Linear A and B scripts are also presented.[9]

The exhibits displaying the technology of stone vessel manufacturing highlight the material imprints of technical inventions and focus on the sequence of technical operations that transform raw materials into final products. They also comprise emblematic Minoan stone artifacts, such as impressive libation vessels, called "rhyta", which were carved into intricate shapes including triton shells or bull's-heads.

A special thematic unit has also been dedicated to seal engraving. This art in miniature reached spectacular intricacy during the Minoan period, as Cretans were in contact with relevant production in the Near East by the 3rd millennium BCE and adopted the symbolic use of seal imprints for representing personal or institutional agency. Seals were made of soft stones and carved using hand-drills throughout most of the Protopalatial era (1900-1700 BCE). The appearance of the lapidary lathe at the end of the 18th century BCE meant that hard semi-precious stones could now be engraved, producing seals with refined sealing surfaces. Solid and cylindrical drills could also be used in combination on the same seal. Following this developed technology, long three- or four-sided prisms, stone and metal signets with elaborate handles, discoid, rectangular and lentoid seals were developed. Seal engraving reached its peak in the Neopalatial era (1700-1450 BCE), when seals were more widely employed for the administration of resources and other bureaucratic purposes. The seal motifs included pictorial themes, such as scenes involving animals, human or fantastical figures, and religious symbols. At the same time, compositions of complex decorative or geometric patterns also appeared, which suggest the invention of different metal drill bits for seal engraving.

Gold signet rings created from 1600 to 1400 BCE demonstrate figural scenes with a codified ritual meaning. These rings functioned as objects of elite display such as the various fine jewelry pieces, which have been mainly recovered from Minoan burial contexts. Gold was a luxury resource that was imported to Crete since the early 3rd millennium BCE and became widespread only after the 17th century BCE. It was melted and poured into a mould, facilitating the mass production of earrings, beads for bracelets and necklaces and rings.

8 See Evely 1993, 31, Type 3, and 34 for discussion.

9 For short introductions into the Linear A and B scripts, see Flouda 2015; Pratt 2025, 5-7.

Techniques, such as gilding with gold leaf, repoussé, the use of twisted and wounded foil, various forms of chains, and granulation attest to the diachronic mastery of Cretan craftsmen.

Last but not least, the thematic unit devoted to the birth of monumental sculpture includes various testimonies of "acrolithic" sculpture, namely works with limbs moulded or carved from different materials. These include the stone coiffure model from a large wooden statue from Knossos, clay feet from various locations, bronze hair-locks that were probably also associated with a statue etc., which testify to the achievements in assembling the plastic human form from different materials. Alongside the fragments of possible large statues, the only large-sized stone schematic figurine of the Minoan period and large-scale clay figurines are also exhibited in order to illustrate Minoan achievements in monumental sculpture.

The Daedalus exhibition invites visitors to contemplate the multifaceted legacy of Daedalus and also to carry forward the spirit of creativity and innovation in their own endeavors.

Bibliography

Bennet, J. "Minoan Crete: People in a World of Objects and Places." In: Galanakis, Y. (ed.), *The Aegean World. A Guide to the Cycladic, Minoan and Mycenaean Antiquities in the Ashmolean Museum*, Athens, 2013, 103-117.

Chaniotis, A. *Das antike Kreta*. Munich, 2004.

Duhoux, Y., and A. Morpurgo Davies, eds. *A Companion to Linear B: Mycenaean Greek Texts and Their World. 1*. Louvain-la-Neuve, 2008.

Evely, R.D.G. *Minoan Crafts: Tools and Techniques. An Introduction*. SIMA 92.1. Göteborg, 1993.

Flouda, G. "The Invention of Writing and Sealing." In: Mandalaki, S. and Rethemiotakis, G. (eds.), *Minoan World. Journey to the Origins of Europe*. Heraklion, 2015, 63-93.

Frontisi-Ducroux, F. "Dédale et Talos. Mythologie et histoire de techniques." *Revue Historique* 243 (1970): 281-296.

Graves, R. *The Greek Myths*. Baltimore, 1955.

Jeffra, C. "A Re-examination of Early Wheel Potting in Crete." *The Annual of the British School at Athens* 108 (2013): 31–49.

Judson, A. "The Mystery of the Mycenaean 'Labyrinth': the Value of Linear B *PU2* and Related Signs", *Studi Micenei ed Egeo-Anatolici* N.S. 2 (2017): 53-72.

Mandalaki, S., ed. *Δαίδαλος. Στα ίχνη του μυθικού τεχνίτη*. Heraklion, 2019.

Morris, S.P. *Daidalos and the Origins of Greek Art*. Princeton, 1992.

Pratt, C.E. "Economy and Commodity Production in the Aegean Bronze Age", *Elements in The Aegean Bronze Age* (2025), Cambridge: Cambridge University Press. doi: 10.1017/9781009454681.

Rethemiotakis, G. *Discovering Ancient Crete through the Archaeological Museum of Heraklion*. Heraklion, 2024.

Rizza, G. "Dedalo e le Origini della Scultura Greca." In A. Pautasso and O. Pilz, eds. *Πήλινα Ειδώλια. New Perspectives in Cretan Coroplastic Studies (13th-7th Cent. B.C.), Bilateral Workshop Italy-Germany, Catania, 19-21 Settembre 2013. Creta Antica* 16 (2015): 203-237.

Ruipérez, M.S. and J.L. Melena. *Οι Μυκηναίοι Έλληνες*. Αθήνα, 1996.

前言

海皇挥舞三叉戟劈开爱琴碧波，浪花飞溅处诞育三千岛屿，宛若美神阿芙洛狄忒抛下的璀璨宝石。克里特，正是那永恒生辉的祖母绿。

它风光旖旎，被视作众神之王宙斯的故乡；它玄秘莫测，萌生出代达罗斯修建迷宫的奇想。瑰丽神话，驱使考古学家用鹤嘴镐击碎时光岩壁；不懈努力，让失落已久的史前遗迹重现容颜。

听啊！闪烁荣光的文明清泉从克里特及周边岛、陆汩汩涌出，汇聚成河，于公元前三千纪冲破青铜时代的闸关。冒险者以舟为箭射穿海上迷雾，为贸易远涉四方眺望星汉。

视野开阔的岛民熔炼外域文化，制作了精美器皿，营建起壮伟宫殿，创造出瑰丽艺术。一个崇尚自然、多姿多彩、兼收并蓄的文明在欧、亚、非三洲交汇处绽放绚烂，为古希腊文明结成夏果献上第一波春日芳妍。

当神话挣脱虚幻的桎梏，便化作鎏金密钥，去开启尘封已久的历史匣龛。

欣逢故宫博物院百年华诞，这里展示来自希腊伊拉克利翁考古博物馆的珍贵文物，让克诺索斯王宫的柱廊与紫禁城的丹墀互映辉光，向您解读代达罗斯神话背后的古希腊之源，昭示伟大文明间应有的和合之美、交流互鉴。

Foreword

Poseidon, wielding his trident, parts the azure waves of the Aegean, where the splashing spray gives birth to a myriad of islands, like the dazzling gems cast by Aphrodite. Crete, among all of them, shines eternally as an emerald.

With its enchanting landscapes, Crete cradled the infancy of Zeus, the king of the gods. Its mysteries inspired the legendary architect Daedalus to conceive the labyrinth. Myths drove archaeologists to shatter the hard walls of time with their picks, bringing long-lost prehistoric ruins back to light at last.

Hark! The glorious springs of civilization gush from Crete and its surrounding islands, converging into a river that burst open the gates of the Bronze Age in the third millennium BCE. Pioneering Minoans sailed the seas under the guidance of stars, venturing far and wide for trade.

The islanders with expansive vision assimilated foreign cultures into their own essence, crafting exquisite vessels, erecting magnificent palaces and creating splendid art. At the crossroads of Europe, Asia and Africa blossomed a vibrant civilization that cherished nature, celebrated diversity, and embraced all influences, representing the first fragrant bloom that would mature into the golden fruit of Greek civilization.

Myths, no longer confined to the realm of fantasy, become keys unlocking the treasure chest of history.

To commemorate the centennial anniversary of the Palace Museum, we are privileged to showcase artifacts from the Hellenic Archaeological Museum of Heraklion, creating a dialogue between the majestic colonnades of the Minoan palace and the imperial stairways of the Forbidden City, a resplendent meeting of civilizations across time and space. This exhibition aims to interpret the origins of Greek mythology behind the tales of Daedalus for our audience, showcasing the beauty of exchange, mutual learning, and harmony between great civilizations.

图版目录

第一单元　神话

代代相传

寻踪溯源

第二单元　迷宫

第三单元　青铜

第四单元　巧匠

彩陶绘奇趣

金饰竞辉光

美石琢巧器

小印钤万方

第五单元　雕像

第六单元　远航

List of Plates

Unit 1 Myth

Passed Down Through Generations

Tracing the Origins

Unit 2 Labyrinth

Unit 3 Bronze

Unit 4 Craftsman

Painted Pottery: A World of Fantasy

The Radiance of Gold Ornaments

Exquisite Stone Vessels

Small Seals, Big World

Unit 5 Statue

Unit 6 Voyage

I - II - III - I

V – V – VI

图 版

Plates

古希腊神话中，克里特岛是众神之王宙斯的故乡。他化身银蹄踏浪的白牛，引诱腓尼基公主欧罗巴至此，诞下米诺斯、拉达曼提斯和萨尔珀冬。这片土地便随之有了代达罗斯修造迷宫，米诺牛食人嗜血，忒修斯杀牛除害的动人传说。

欢迎来到美丽的克里特岛，您不仅能触摸到掩埋在古老地层里的神话烙印，更将透过悠久的历史、精彩的文物解读镌刻在西方文明源流处的基因密码。

In ancient Greek mythology, Crete was the birthplace of Zeus, the king of the gods. Disguised as a silver-hoofed bull, he lured the Phoenician princess Europa to this island and gave birth to Minos, Rhadamanthys and Sarpedon, leading to the legends of Daedalus constructing the labyrinth, Minotaur devouring humans, and Theseus slaying the beast to end its terror.

Welcome to the beautiful island of Crete, a place where ancient myths echo through history and artifacts reveal the roots of Western civilization.

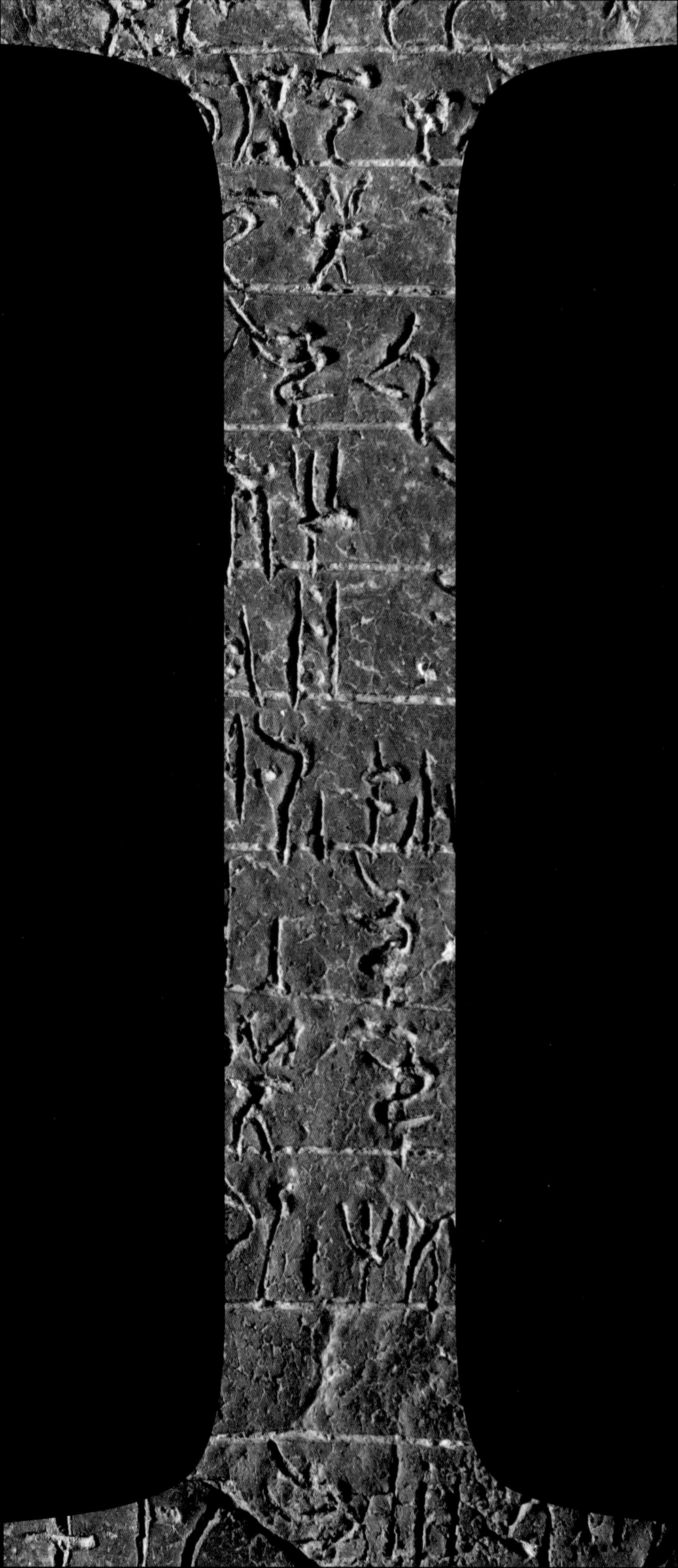

独特的地理隔绝性与史前文明断层，为克里特岛蒙上神秘面纱，成为孕育神话的天然沃土。

自荷马史诗至奥维德《变形记》，代达罗斯神话历经八百年传诵淬炼。希腊罗马作家们以克里特岛为叙事背景，将能工与巧匠的智创、凡人与神祇的博弈、迷宫与飞翔的奇观，绘制在壮阔史诗画卷上。这些故事不仅承载着对智慧与勇毅的永恒礼赞，更在代际传唱中沉淀为西方文明的基因片段。

当神话迷雾遇见考古炬火，虚实交织的历史密码终现端倪。19 世纪末，伊文思等考古学家踏着史诗指引的方向登陆克里特岛。克诺索斯王宫遗址的惊世出土，不仅印证了青铜时代米诺斯文化的辉煌，更让代达罗斯建造迷宫的传说得到历史真相的回响——那些错落层叠的宫室、繁复华美的壁画，恰是几千年前“迷宫”原型最有力的物证。

The island of Crete's remote location and ancient history have given an air of mystery that inspires infinite reverie.

From Homer's epics to Ovid's *Metamorphoses*, the myths of Daedalus evolved through eight centuries of oral transmission and literary refinement. With Crete as their setting, Greek and Roman writers wove tales of ingenious craftsmanship, mortal-deity interactions, marvels of labyrinths and human flight into the grand tapestry of epic poetry. The stories celebrate timeless virtues of wisdom and courage, and have ultimately crystallized into foundational elements of Western civilization.

When the mist of myth met the torch of archaeology, the encoded interplay of legend and history finally came to light. In the late 19th century, Arthur Evans and his team followed epic tales to Crete. The groundbreaking excavation of the Palace of Knossos not only unveiled the splendor of Bronze Age Minoan culture, but also echoed the historical truth behind Daedalus' legendary labyrinth. The multi-tiered architecture and intricate frescoes stood as tangible proof of the prototype of the labyrinth from millennia past.

代代相传

古希腊神话中，代达罗斯作为绝世巧匠的形象最早可追溯至克里特本土传说：他奉米诺斯王之命建造迷宫，囚禁王后诞下的怪物米诺牛。随着公元前 8 世纪以后古希腊文明的勃兴，这段奇闻通过史诗传唱与戏剧演绎逐渐成形，在陶器彩绘与钱币纹饰中衍生出丰富变体。当历史长河流淌至罗马帝国，维吉尔、奥维德与普鲁塔克等人的经典著作，终将这些零散传说熔铸成体系完备的文学瑰宝。其中最为璀璨的篇章，当属雅典英雄忒修斯渡海斩魔的壮举。这位智勇双全的王子深入迷宫诛杀食人恶兽，将代达罗斯神话推向震撼人心的史诗高潮，最终成就了西方文明中代代相传的永恒经典。

Passed Down Through Generations

In Greek mythology, the archetype of Daedalus as the legendary artificer first emerged in Cretan legends, where King Minos commissioned him to build a labyrinth to imprison the Minotaur, a monstrous creature with bull head born from the cursed Queen Pasiphae. As Greek civilization flourished from the 8th century BCE onward, these narratives crystallized through epic recitations and theatrical performances, spawning artistic variations from vase paintings to coin motifs. Particularly during the Roman Empire, writers like Virgil, Ovid, and Plutarch compiled and refined the fragmented legends into a cohesive literary narrative. Among them, the saga of the Athenian hero Theseus remains one of the most radiant jewels. This prince of wisdom and valor penetrated the labyrinth and vanquished the flesh-devouring beast, elevating the Daedalus myth to a climactic grandeur. The legend crystallized into an eternal classic, its echoes resonating across generations in Western civilization.

1

斐斯托斯的斯塔特

希腊化时代（公元前 300 ~ 前 270 年）

银

直径 2.4 厘米，重量 11.55 克

1963 年出土于克里特岛哈拉卡斯钱币窖藏

希腊伊拉克利翁考古博物馆藏，编号 N2124

银币正面为长翅膀的巨人塔罗斯，面向右侧，准备投掷手中石块。铭文为T-AΛ-ΩN（“Talon”）；背面为一头在地面上向右奔跑的公牛。铭文为ΦAIΣTIΩ[N]（Phaistion，意为“斐斯托斯人的”）。

（克莱安西斯・希迪洛保罗斯）

1

Stater of Phaistos

Hellenistic period (300-270 BCE)

Silver

Diam. 2.4 cm, weight 11.55 g

Charakas, coin hoard/1963

Archaeological Museum of Heraklion, N2124

Obverse: the winged giant Talos prepares to hurl stones he holds in his hands, to the right. Identifying inscription T-AΛ-ΩN (“Talon”).

Reverse: bull charging right, on ground line. Inscription ΦAIΣTIΩ[N] (Phaistion, “of the Phaistians”).

References

Oeconomides-Caramessini M.1981, 118, no.7. IGCH no.109/1963.

(Kleanthis Sidiropoulos)

2

克诺索斯的四德拉克马

希腊化时代（公元前 125 ~ 前 100 年）

银

直径 3 ~ 3.2 厘米，重量 15.1 克

1942 年出土于克里特岛克森尼索钱币窖藏

希腊伊拉克利翁考古博物馆藏，编号 N1375

银币正面为米诺斯国王头像，戴王冠，面朝右侧；背面为方形迷宫图案，环绕铭文为KNΩ/Σ-I/ΩN（Knossion，意为“克诺索斯人的”）。

（克莱安西斯·希迪洛保罗斯）

2

Tetradrachm of Knossos

Hellenistic period (125-100 BCE)

Silver

Diam. 3-3.2 cm, weight 15.1 g

Chersonessos, coin hoard/1942

Archaeological Museum of Heraklion, N1375

Obverse: Head of King Minos, diademed right.

Reverse: Square labyrinth; surrounding inscription KNΩ/Σ-I/ΩN (Knossion, “of the Knossians”).

References

Le Rider 1966, 271-72, no.3, pl.XXXVI,3. IGCH no.332/1942.

(Kleanthis Sidiropoulos)

兄弟头像（两件）
公元前 50 ~ 前 10 年
大理石
高 23 厘米 /18 厘米
发现于克里特岛
希腊伊拉克利翁考古博物馆藏，编号 Γ717 & Γ718+930

这是两件保存极为完好的稍小于真人比例的头像，来自一组表现两位年轻人的荣誉奉献雕塑群。虽然缺乏确切的来源证据，但由于风格、个体特征及保存状态都极为相似，可以断定两者来自同一组雕塑，是一对年龄存在明显差异的兄弟。雕塑对复杂发型和光滑皮肤进行了精细刻画，连同理想化的面部特征以及表现出的一种介于庄重与哀伤之间的氛围，成功地传递出他们已获得的英雄地位。

两件雕塑的头部都保留有用于佩戴花冠的环形凹槽，从遗存痕迹可推测花冠为金质或镀金。在克里特岛上，同一家族的两位成员都获得体育竞赛的胜利并因此获得荣誉的情况极为罕见，但这一场景是否真实尚存疑问。目前，这两件头像的具体身份仍未确定。

这对雕像是首次以组合形式展出并公开发表。

（克莱安西斯・希迪洛保罗斯）

3

Heads of two brothers

50-10 BCE

Marble

H. 23 cm & 18 cm

Crete

Archaeological Museum of Heraklion, Γ717 & Γ718+930

Two extraordinarily well-preserved heads at a slightly smaller than life-size scale, from an honorary votive complex of statues representing two youths. Although the precise evidence of their provenance is lacking, the similarities in their style, their individual characteristics and their comparable current state of preservation leave no doubt that they come from the same sculptural composition of – at least – two brothers, with a clear age difference. The meticulous work in modelling the elaborate hairdos and smooth skin, together with the fine, idealised features and the atmosphere they exude, somewhere between seriousness and sadness, successfully conveys that they have acquired heroic status.

Both preserve a peripheral groove round the head for the placing of a wreath, which seems to have been gold or at least gilded, as shown from some of its remains. It is rare in Crete to find two illustrious members of the same family who had received such an honour as victors, actual or conventional, in sporting competitions. The identification of the portraits remains an unsolved problem for the time being.

They are exhibited and published together here for the first time.

References

Lagogianni-Georgarakos 2002, 56, Nr.12, Taf.13 (only 717, dated to the end of the 1st c. BCE). Λαγογιάννη-Γεωργαράκου 2006, especially 117-121, pl.1-2. (only 718, dated to the end of the 2nd c. BCE).

(Kleanthis Sidiropoulos)

4

阿斯克勒庇俄斯头像

约 150 年

大理石

高 29.5 厘米

发现于克里特岛戈尔蒂斯

希腊伊拉克利翁考古博物馆藏，编号 Γ151

这件精美的医神阿斯克勒庇俄斯头像原本为真人尺寸雕像的独立部件，如今雕像主体虽已遗失，但仍可通过头像佩戴的独特冕状饰物（corona tortilis）来辨认其身份。雕像的头发和胡须雕刻工艺极为精细，原本涂有色彩的部分使光影效果更加突出，与半透明白色大理石的冷峻面容形成鲜明对比。鼻子为单独制作的部件，用铁钉固定于雕像上，目前铁钉仍然保存完好。

这件头像模仿了公元前 4 世纪早期的雕像风格，可能出自戈尔蒂斯的工坊。戈尔蒂斯的雕塑作品在罗马繁荣的成熟时期曾远销至北非。

（克莱安西斯・希迪洛保罗斯）

4

Head of Asclepius

Ca. 150 CE

Marble

H. 29.5 cm

Gortys

Archaeological Museum of Heraklion, Γ151

Excellent quality head of the god of medicine worked as an independent component to be fitted to a life-sized statue, now lost. He is identifiable from the characteristic diadem (*corona tortilis*) he wears. The particularly elaborate work of the hair and beard, the play of light and shade of which would have been accentuated even more by the painted colouring they certainly bore, is in severe contrast to the stark white face in translucent marble. The nose, made of a separate piece of material, was fixed in place with the surviving iron peg.

Copying a statuary type of the early 4th century BCE, the work is probably from a Gortynian workshop, whose products reached as far as North Africa, in the mature years of Roman prosperity.

References

Romeo-Portale 1998, 165-169, no.41.

(Kleanthis Sidiropoulos)

5

沉睡的厄洛斯浮雕

公元 2 世纪

大理石

高 18 厘米，长 41 厘米，宽 26 厘米

发现于克里特岛克诺索斯

希腊伊拉克利翁考古博物馆藏，编号 Γ281

这件浮雕描绘了厄洛斯（爱神丘比特）小睡的情景。他躺在半展开的双翼和斗篷上，一只手托着头部，另一只手拿着两枝枯萎的罂粟花。他的箭袋背带斜跨胸前，箭袋的尖端露出在头部后方，身体前方侧边放着未使用的弓。厄洛斯的脚边趴着一只象征着生命的蜥蜴。

浮雕的形式、与冥后珀耳塞福涅相关的葬礼罂粟花，以及疲惫的爱神在静谧睡眠中的悲伤面容，都清晰地表明这是一件青年男子的墓碑。这名男子在爱神降临前便已被死神夺去生命。

这是一件经典主义风格的优秀复制品，其原型可追溯至公元前 1 世纪。

（克莱安西斯·希迪洛保罗斯）

5

Relief with sleeping Eros

2nd c. CE

Marble

H. 18 cm, l. 41 cm, w. 26 cm

Knossos

Archaeological Museum of Heraklion, Γ281

The little Eros (Cupid), asleep on his half-spread wings and mantle, supports his head with one hand and holds two withered poppies in the other. Across his chest runs the strap of his quiver, the tip of which is visible behind his head, while beside and in front of him lies the inactive bow. Near the feet of the figure moves a lizard, as a sign of life.

The form of the sculpture, the funerary poppies of Persephone, the sadness on the face of an exhausted god in the stillness of sleep, clearly show that we are dealing with the funerary monument of a young man whom Death took before Love could.

Good Classicising copy of a prototype dated to the 1st century BCE.

References

Platon 1958, 172, No.281. Söldner 1986, 643, Nr.86.

(Kleanthis Sidiropoulos)

6

阿芙洛狄忒躯干雕像

公元 1 世纪

大理石

高 26 厘米

发现于圣尼古拉奥斯（古卡马拉）

希腊伊拉克利翁考古博物馆藏，编号 Γ291

这件小型雕像以小比例复刻了一个非常著名的雕像类型，该类型在多种材质、不同尺寸和品质的作品中均有体现。阿芙洛狄忒正脱下她左脚的凉鞋准备入浴，这也是她身上最后一件衣物。这一造型的原作为青铜材质，创作于约公元前 200 年。这件高质量装饰性复制品制作于公元 1 世纪，出自一座城市豪宅。

阿芙洛狄忒是掌管爱情、生育和婚姻的女神，也是掌管女性美貌和美德的女神。在罗马世界，没有哪位奥林匹斯神比她更受崇拜。这类小型雕像通常置于富裕家庭中，与家庭生活息息相关，同时也常被视作嫁妆的一部分，赠与年轻的新娘，象征着她新生活中的陪伴与保护者。

（克莱安西斯・希迪洛保罗斯）

6

Headless torso of Aphrodite's statuette

1st c. CE

Marble

H. 26 cm

Agios Nikolaos (ancient Kamara)

Archaeological Museum of Heraklion, Γ291

The sculpture reproduces on a small scale the statuary type very well known from many examples in various materials, at different sizes and of varying qualities – of Aphrodite preparing for her bath by removing the sandal from her left foot – the last bit of clothing on her body. Its bronze original dates to around 200 BCE. This is a good-quality, decorative replica from a 1st century CE urban mansion.

Aphrodite, as the goddess of love, fertility and marriage, as well as of female beauty and virtue, was worshipped in the Roman world like no other Olympian goddess. The position given to smaller statuettes of this type in wealthy homes in the context of family life could also confirm the view that such sculptures were presented to young maidens as part of their dowries, as a companion and protector in their new life.

References

Lexicon Iconographicum Mythologiae Classicae II-1, 1984, s.v. Aphrodite (A. Delivorrias), 57-59, no.462-481. Sporn 2018.

(Kleanthis Sidiropoulos)

7

阿波罗躯干雕像

125～150 年

大理石

高 45 厘米

发现于克里特岛克诺索斯

希腊伊拉克利翁考古博物馆藏，编号 Γ292

这件裸体神像是对弹奏七弦琴的阿波罗雕像的再次创作，而这种原型本就罕见。雕像借鉴了希腊化时期的雕塑风格，这一点在其生动的形态和裸体上体现得淋漓尽致。

神像呈现出鲜明的“对立式平衡”姿态，右腿支撑身体重量，左腿向前伸展。双臂则呈相反的姿势：右臂弯曲，手持低垂的拨片；左手则高举七弦琴（琴身少见地由悬挂带固定）。

雕像背面制作较为粗糙，表明或为桌腿的主要装饰元素。

这类雕像通常被认为起源并流行于奥古斯都时期的罗马，因此从这件作品中，我们也可以看到克诺索斯朱利亚贵族殖民城自建立之初便具有的强烈罗马色彩。

（克莱安西斯・希迪洛保罗斯）

7

Headless torso of Apollo's statuette

125-150 CE

Marble

H. 45 cm

Knossos

Archaeological Museum of Heraklion, Γ292

This type of statue of the naked god is an unknown variant on the already unusual original of a kithara-playing Apollo. This piece depends on a Hellenistic model, as is particularly demonstrated by its animated rendition and nudity.

The god is portrayed in a sharp contrapposto pose, with his weight on the right supporting leg and his left one extended, with counter-positions taken by the arm – the right one, no doubt bent, holding the plectrum in a lowered position, while in the left he holds the kithara (lyre) aloft with the unusual dangling strap by which it is secured.

The poor standard of work on the reverse suggests that it is probably the main decorative element of a table-support.

The genesis and popularity of the statuary type is thought to be associated with Augustan Rome itself, so that the piece here reminds us of the strongly Roman character of Colonia Julia Nobilis Cnossus from its foundation.

References

Lexicon Iconographicum Mythologiae Classicae II-1 1984, s.v. Apollo (O. Palagia), 211-213, no.219-238. Flashar 1992.

(Kleanthis Sidiropoulos)

寻踪溯源

千百年来，实证的缺乏导致人们难以判断代达罗斯与迷宫故事的虚实，神话终归是神话，一切都停留在梦境般的幻想中。直到英国考古学家亚瑟·伊文思等人拉开史前考古大幕，神话的奥秘才逐步破解。尽管我们无法知晓这些传说的最早起点，却能在克里特岛的上古遗物中窥见蛛丝马迹。代达罗斯神殿之名赫然书写在线形文字泥板上，牛首雕塑暗示人们所说的迷宫怪物并非空穴来风，舞蹈陶俑的动感仿佛闪烁出王家庭院的喧嚣残影。诸多证据表明，公元前 14 世纪左右的青铜时代末期，代达罗斯神话可能已有轮廓，故事内容也大概来源于现实生活。

Tracing the Origins

For thousands of years, the lack of evidence made it difficult to discern the truth behind the tales of Daedalus and the labyrinth. Myths remain myths, confined to the realm of fantasy. It was not until British archaeologist Arthur Evans and others unveiled the curtain of prehistoric archaeology that the mysteries began to unravel. Although we cannot pinpoint the exact origins of these legends, traces of their existence can be glimpsed in the ancient legacies of Crete. The name of a shrine of Daedalus is inscribed on Linear B tablets, bull-headed sculptures hint that the labyrinth's monstrous creature was not merely a figment of imagination, and the dynamic poses of dancer figurines seem to echo the lively remnants of the royal courtyard. Numerous pieces of evidence suggest that by the end of the Bronze Age, around the 14th century BCE, the myth of Daedalus had likely taken shape, with its narrative possibly rooted in reality.

8

写有线形文字 A 的泥板

米诺斯晚期 I B（公元前 1500 ~ 前 1450 年）

陶土

最大高度 8.5 厘米，宽 5.8 厘米

发现于克里特岛圣特里亚达的皇家别墅

希腊伊拉克利翁考古博物馆藏，编号 Π－N 19

这是一块刻有未解读的形音并存线形文字 A 文本（GORILA HT 31）的泥板。这块重要的泥板记录了各类封口和敞口式容器的信息，包括三足锅具、双耳瓶以及其他不同器形的敞口容器。清单中列出了容器的名称，其中至少有五处名称附有“连字符”，即在标音符号上叠加了一个表意符号。此外，另有两个条目未附表意符号，但可能也指代容器名称。这些容器名称仅在线形文字 A 语料库中出现过一次。泥板上的第二个词，根据线形文字 B 的语音值推测，可以转写为“PU-KO”，有学者认为在线形文字 A 中可能意为“青铜”。按照这一解释，清单可能记录了一件或多件珍贵的青铜容器。

（乔治娅・弗拉达）

8

Linear A tablet

Late Minoan I B (1500-1450 BCE)

Clay

Max. h. 8.5 cm, w. 5.8 cm

Hagia Triada, Royal Villa

Archaeological Museum of Heraklion, Π-N 19

Clay tablet inscribed in the undeciphered logo-syllabic Linear A script (GORILA HT 31). This important tablet represents an inventory of closed and open vessels including tripod cauldrons, amphoras and different examples of open shapes. These are listed with their name which is accompanied in at least five cases by a “ligature”, a composite sign consisting of a logogram with phonetic signs over it. Two more entries which are not followed by a logogram may also refer to vase names. All these vase names are encountered only once in the Linear A corpus. The second word of the tablet, which according to the phonetic values of Linear B could be hypothetically transcribed as PU-KO, has been suggested as possibly meaning “bronze” in Linear A. Following this interpretation, the inventory may list one or more valuable vessels in bronze.

References

Duhoux 2000-2001. Montecchi, 2019. 188-194.

(Georgia Flouda)

9

写有线形文字 B 的泥板

米诺斯晚期ⅢA2（公元前 1375 ~ 前 1300 年）
陶土
最长 8.1 厘米，最宽 2.5 厘米
发现于克里特岛克诺索斯王宫
希腊伊拉克利翁考古博物馆藏，编号 Π-N560

克诺索斯王宫发现的线形文字 B 泥板属于会计记录，表明宫廷官僚机构设有一套复杂的生产管理控制系统。泥板列出了剑、箭和战车等众多武器，表明宫殿可能控制着战士阶层并为其提供补给。这些武器装备既用于展示力量，也是提升军事能力的手段。

现存泥板未提及金属工匠的具体制作工艺，也未像近东地区文献一样记录有合金配方。不过，根据成品记录可知，当时的工匠技术已呈现出高度的专业化。残缺的棕榈叶形泥板 Ra(1) 1541 中使用了“phasgana”一词来记录成品刀剑，这一术语也出现在后来的荷马史诗中。剑的原始数量记录未能保存下来。此外，文本中还提到了“ka-si-ko-no”这一词汇，其词源存疑，可能用于指代在克诺索斯和皮洛斯制作青铜剑的工匠。

（乔治娅・弗拉达）

9

Linear B tablet

Late Minoan Ⅲ A 2 (1375-1300 BCE)
Clay
Max. l. 8.1 cm, max. w. 2.5 cm
Knossos, palace
Archaeological Museum of Heraklion, Π-N 560

The clay tablets with Linear B inscriptions from the palace of Knossos are accounting records that reveal a complex system of administration and control of production by the palace bureaucracy. Among other things, the tablets list a multitude of weapons, swords, arrows and chariots, evidence that the palace possibly controlled and supplied a warrior class. This armament was a means of displaying strength and developing military prowess.

The surviving tablets do not mention the details of the metal-worker's craft, as they do not record recipes for making alloys, like the texts found in the Near East. The record of the finished products, however, reveals a high level of specialisation. The fragmentary palm-leaf tablet Ra(1) 1541 records swords that have already been produced, using the term *phasgana*, which is also found in the later Homeric epics. The original number of swords has not been preserved. The text also includes the name *ka-si-ko-no*, of dubious etymology, which is used to refer to the artisans involved in the production of bronze swords in both Knossos and Pylos.

References

CMIK II, 164 (Ra(1) 1541). Michailidou 2008. Morpurgo Davies 1975.

(Georgia Flouda)

10

写有线形文字 B 的泥板

米诺斯晚期ⅢA1（约公元前 1390 ~ 前 1375 年）
陶土
长 9.1 厘米，高 2.7 厘米
发现于克里特岛克诺索斯王宫的战车泥板房间
希腊伊拉克利翁考古博物馆藏，编号 Π–N243

这是一块残缺的棕叶形泥板，记录了一套盔甲、一辆组装完整的战车以及一匹马的分配情况，但接收者的姓名未被记录下来。这块泥板出土自“战车泥板房间”，是克诺索斯最早的线形文字 B 记录之一。这些记录具有重要意义，反映了米诺斯行政系统（使用线形文字 A 和克里特象形文字）向高度中央集权的官僚体系的过渡，而这种体系是以希腊大陆的迈锡尼中心为标准。战车部队的维护是克诺索斯行政体系的主要关切之一，因此相关工作有专门的文书部门负责记录。

（乔治娅・弗拉达）

10

Linear B tablet

Late Minoan ⅢA1 (Ca. 1390-1375 BCE)
Clay
L. 9.1 cm, h. 2.7 cm
Knossos, palace, Room of the Chariot Tablets
Archaeological Museum of Heraklion, Π-N243

Fragmentary clay palm-leaf tablet, which registers the distribution of a suit of armour, a fully assembled chariot and a horse to a man whose name is not preserved. It belongs to the earliest group of Knossian Linear B records from the Room of the Chariot Tablets. These are very significant, as they document the transition from a Minoan administration employing the Linear A and Cretan Hieroglyphic scripts to a highly centralised bureaucracy that follows the standards known from the Mycenaean centres of the mainland. The maintenance of organised chariot forces was one of the main concerns of the Knossian administration and of specific scribal departments specialising in recording various types of military equipment.

References

Driessen 1996, 483, 489-491. Driessen 2000.

(Georgia Flouda)

11

写有线形文字 B 的泥板

米诺斯晚期ⅢA2（公元前 1375 ~ 前 1300 年）

陶土

高 12.6 厘米，最大宽度 6.7 厘米，厚 1.3 厘米

发现于克里特岛克诺索斯王宫的“陶土箱”

希腊伊拉克利翁考古博物馆藏，编号 Π–N 97 [KN Fp(1) 1]

克诺索斯线形文字 B 泥板上的相关书面记载可以追溯到公元前 14 世纪，代达罗斯的神话因此获得了历史层面的证实。编号 Fp(1) 1 的泥板上提到了“Daidaleion”（da–da–re–jo–de）一词，这类泥板是克诺索斯宫行政流程中的典型账目清单。这块泥板是 Fp 系列中关于宗教供奉的重要记录之一，其记载了公元前 14 世纪克里特岛上所崇拜的神系。“致众神”（πᾶσι θεοῖς）这一短语后列出了具体的神名，如狄克特的宙斯、厄里尼厄斯以及可能起源于米诺斯文化的神祇 pa–de 和 qe–ra–si–ja。这些大小神明都被记录为接收了来自克诺索斯王宫的橄榄油供奉，这些供奉物是在“Deukios”月由克诺索斯王宫运送到特定地点。

除了“Daidaleion”（参见本书图版 12），泥板中还提到了阿姆尼索斯（Amnisos，这一地名也见于荷马的《伊利亚特》），以及另一个未确认的地名。研究者认为这些地名可能指代三个不同的祭祀地点，这一观点因泥板上“致众神”这一表述重复出现以及两行记录的橄榄油数量不同而得到佐证。另一项记录显示，需要向“风之女祭司”（a–ne–mo i–je–rē–ja）分发大量橄榄油，这是祭司阶层的一位重要人物。这些记录进一步支持了“Daidaleion”是宗教圣所或献给代达罗斯的神庙这一推测，表明其可能是前希腊时期一个重要的宗教中心，至公元前 14 世纪时仍存世。泥板最后记录了所分配橄榄油的总量。

（乔治娅·弗拉达）

11

Linear B tablet

Late Minoan ⅢA2 (1375-1300 BCE)
Clay
H. 12.6 cm, max. w. 6.7 cm, th. 1.3 cm
Knossos palace, "Clay Chest"
Archaeological Museum of Heraklion, Π-N 97 [KN Fp(1) 1]

The myth of Daedalus surprisingly acquires a mantle of historical validation and an even greater historical depth, thanks to the first relevant written testimonies of the Knossos Linear B tablets that date to the 14th century BCE. The word "Daidaleion" (*da-da-re-jo-de*) is mentioned on the summarising page tablet Fp(1) 1, a typical accounting list serving the bureaucratic process centred on the palace of Knossos. It is one of the most important tablets of the Fp series on the subject of religious offerings, since it refers to the pantheon of deities worshipped in Crete during the 14th century BCE. The expression "to all the gods" (πᾶσι θεοῖς) is accompanied by the names of Dictaean Zeus, Erinys and the deities *pa-de* and *qe-ra-si-ja*, who were probably of Minoan origin. All these major and minor gods are identified as recipients of quantities of olive oil sent in the month of "Deukios" from the palace of Knossos to specific destinations.

In addition to the "Daedaleion" (see also Cat. no. 12), the place-name Amnisos (*a-mi-ni-so-de*), also known from the *Iliad* of Homer, is mentioned, together with another toponym of uncertain identification. Researchers argue that these are three different places of worship, a probability that is strengthened by the repetition of the expression "to all the gods" and the recording of different amounts of oil in two rows on the tablet. Another entry involves the distribution of a large quantity of oil to the "Priestess of the Winds" (*a-ne-mo i-je-rē-ja*), a distinguished member of the priesthood. This supports the possibility that the "Daidaleion" is a religious temenos or sanctuary dedicated to Daedalus, probably the centre of an important pre-Hellenic cult still surviving in the 14th century BCE. The tablet concludes with the total quantity of olive oil distributed.

References

Adrados 1964, 134. DMic I, 148-49. CMIK I, 1. Ruipérez-Melena 1996, 244. Duhoux-Morpurgo Davies 2008, 257-61. Gulizio-Nakassis 2014, 122-24. Rizza 2015, 213-14. Melena-Firth 2019, 166, 577.

(Georgia Flouda)

12

写有线形文字 B 的泥板

米诺斯晚期ⅢA2（公元前 1375 ~ 前 1300 年）

陶土

高 2.5 厘米，最大宽度 7 厘米

发现于克里特岛克诺索斯王宫

希腊伊拉克利翁考古博物馆藏，编号 Π–N484（KN X723）

在克诺索斯王宫各区域发现的数千块泥板上书写着线形文字 B，这是一种由线形文字 A 发展而来的形音并存的文字系统。这些泥板是现存最早的希腊文字文本。编号 X723 的棕榈叶形泥板残片仅可辨认出重要词汇“da–da–re–jo–de”，音译为 Δαιδάλειον-δε（Daidaleion–de），可能记录的是向“Daedaleion”运送物品的情况。Fp(1) 1 号陶土板提到了众神体系，其上同样有“Daedaleion”一词，由此进一步证实该词可能指代供奉代达罗斯的神庙或圣所。此外，KN Gg(1) 702 号泥板则通过间接提及迈锡尼人对“迷宫”（该词源自罗马时期的历史文献）的表达，即“da–pu–ri–to–jo po–ti–ni–ja”（迷宫的女主人）这一短语，为这一关联提供了进一步的支持。

（乔治娅 · 弗拉达）

12

Linear B tablet

Late Minoan ⅢA2 (1375-1300 BCE)

Clay

H. 2.5 cm, max. w. 7 cm

Knossos, palace

Archaeological Museum of Heraklion, Π-N484 (KN X723)

The thousands of clay tablets found in various parts of the palace of Knossos are written in the logo-syllabic Linear B script, which is a development from Linear A. They represent the earliest texts written in a Greek script. The fragmentary palm-leaf tablet X723 preserves only the important word *da-da-re-jo-de*, transliterated as *Δαιδάλειον-δε* (Daidaleion-de), and probably documented the transfer of goods to the "Daedaleion". The association of the term with a place of worship, a shrine or sanctuary dedicated to Daedalus, is reinforced by the appearance of the name on tablet Fp(1) 1 which refers to a pantheon of deities. It is further supported by tablet KN Gg (1) 702 with its indirect reference to the Mycenaean rendering of the word "Labyrinth" (known from historical sources of the Roman period) in the phrase *da-pu-ri-to-jo po-ti-ni-ja*, the Lady of the Labyrinth.

References

CMIK I, 274 (X723). DMic I, 148-149, 156-157. Melena-Firth 2019, 336, 644.

(Georgia Flouda)

484

13

公牛首形来通杯

米诺斯晚期 I B（约公元前 1500～前 1450 年）

绿泥石

高 15 厘米（不含牛角部分）

发现于克里特岛扎克罗斯王宫的西翼采光井

希腊伊拉克利翁考古博物馆藏，编号 Λ2713

器物由软绿色石材雕刻而成，形似牛首，整体由两个雕刻部分构成：一个是面部特征精致且带颈部的较大中空兽首，另一个则是带有凹陷边缘的平坦背板，与颈部接合。器物的牛角和嵌入式牛眼已遗失，但已参照其他牛首形器的样式进行了修复。此外，面部左下方和鼻口部也存在缺失。牛首的毛皮既使用浮雕手法雕刻，也以刻线方式刻画。毛发纹理表明这可能是一头牛犊，其浓密的波浪状毛发覆盖了头顶、前额和面部，一直延伸至鼻部。两眼间的旋涡状毛发尤为显眼；在其他类似器物中，这种图案通常代表花结，也有观点认为此处纹路与天体有关。牛首上有两个孔洞，较大的一个位于后颈，较小的一个在颅顶左侧靠近牛角的位置，这些孔洞用于倒入液体；来通杯的次级开口位于鼻尖，用于倾倒液体。

“来通杯”（Rhyton）一词来源于希腊语动词“流动”，是许多古代文明的主要奠酒器。这种器物的造型多样，主要为圆锥形，偶尔也会制成兽首状。来通杯的关键特征是杯身上有一个次级开口，用于倾倒液体；注入口和倾倒口通常位于器物两端。

牛首形来通杯材质多样，是青铜时代爱琴海地区最为精致的器物类型之一。这种象征威望的器物常被用作统治者之间进行外交交流的礼品。在希腊大陆发现的石质牛首形奠酒器数量极少，而在埃及第十八王朝法老墓室的壁画中，克里特人（Keftiu，即米诺斯人）手持此类器物的形象表明，这种器物可能在克里特岛与东地中海其他势力的外交关系中发挥了重要作用。

这件器物的破碎情况至今仍是考古学界未解之谜。大多数碎片是在中央圣殿采光井区域发现的，分布零散。尽管考古人员尽力寻找，但始终未能找到牛首的其他部分。值得注意的是，在这座宫殿的这一区域发现的其他石器几乎完好无损，唯独这件牛首形来通杯残缺不全。许多学者认为，这实际上是一种象征性的“肢解”行为，即用器物代替真实的牛进行祭献。进行此种祭献时，可能会抛撒“献祭牛”的碎片，而仪式参与者也可能会带走这些石质碎片。

作为克诺索斯权力的象征，牛的意象在新王宫期的最后阶段（公元前 15 世纪）得到了显著拓展。猎牛、捕牛、斗牛，特别是“跳公牛”等人牛互动的场景均起源于克诺索斯。这一表现形式反映了克诺索斯精英阶层向岛上其他宫殿中心进行政治宣传的意图。正因如此，在克里特东部港口城镇扎克罗斯的宫殿珍宝库中发现的这件器物具有极其重要的意义。

（迪米特里斯·斯法基纳基斯）

13

Bull's-head libation vessel ("Rhyton")

Late Minoan IB (Ca. 1500-1450 BCE)

Chlorite

H. 15 cm (without horns)

Zakros, palace, lightwell of the West Wing

Archaeological Museum of Heraklion, Λ2713

Made of soft greenish stone in the shape of a bull's head, this vessel consists of two carved parts: the larger hollow protome with the sculpturally rendered facial features and the neck, and the flat back plate cut with a recessed border fitting into the neck. The horns and inlaid eyes are missing; the vessel is restored according to the form of other bull's-head vessels. Many parts of the lower left portion of the face and parts of the muzzle are also missing. The hide is both carved in relief and incised. The hairy head probably indicates a young animal: bushy wavy locks cover the top of the head, the forehead and parts of the face down to the nose. The swirling tuft of hair between the eyes is noteworthy due to the symbolic meaning of the rosette on the forehead of other examples; this circular sign between horns is thought to be connected to celestial bodies. Two holes, the wider on the nape and the narrower on the left side of the top of the head close to the horn, are the openings for pouring in the liquid; the secondary perforation of the libation vessel, through which the liquid flowed out, is at the tip of the muzzle.

The rhyton, a name derived from the verb "to flow", was the main libation vessel of many ancient civilisations. Rhytons were produced in several shapes, chiefly conical, and occasionally in the shape of an animal's head. The main feature that defines a vessel as a rhyton is a secondary opening in the body for pouring libations; the filling and pouring holes are normally located at opposite ends.

Bull's-head rhytons are among the most elaborate vessels sculpted in various materials in the Aegean Bronze Age. As a prestige object, this kind of vase was used as an exchange gift for diplomatic purposes by the rulers of the island. The small number of stone bull's-head vases in mainland Greece, and the depictions of Keftiu (Cretans/Minoans) bearing such vessels on the walls of tombs of pharaohs of the 18th Dynasty, imply that this practice played a part in the island's relations with other powers of the East Mediterranean.

The fragmentation of the object is still an unanswered archaeological riddle. Most of the fragments were found scattered in the lightwell area of the Central Sanctuary. Despite their efforts, the excavators were unable to find any other part of the bull's head. The fragmentary state of the find is noteworthy, since the stone vases in this part of the palace were uncovered almost intact. Many scholars argue for a kind of symbolic dismemberment and scattering of the image of the bull in place of the sacrifice of the actual animal. This action was combined with the scattering of the fragments of the "sacrificed bull" and the appropriation of those stone fragments by the participants in the ceremony.

As a symbol of Knossian power, the iconography of the bull expanded significantly during the last period of the Neopalatial era (15th century BCE). Many scenes including both humans and bulls (bull-hunting, capturing, fighting and particularly bull-leaping, etc.) are believed to be of Knossian origin. This representation reflects the political propaganda of the Knossian elite towards the other palatial centres of the island. The presence of the stone bull's-head rhyton in the Treasury of the palace of Zakros, the eastern harbour town of Crete, is therefore highly significant.

References

Hallager-Hallager 1995. Πλάτων 1974, 150-2. Koehl 2006. Rehak 1995, 440, 443, 459, no.21, pl.51 a-c.

(Dimitris Sfakianakis)

14

公牛陶塑

米诺斯晚期ⅢC 至后王宫期（公元前 1200 年以后）

陶土

高 35 厘米（不含牛角部分）

发现于克里特岛斐斯托斯的米诺斯王宫

希腊伊拉克利翁考古博物馆藏，编号 Π1763

这件陶塑的躯干和头部分别制作，采用类似于陶器轮制的工艺。中空的圆柱形躯干带凸起脊梁，而臀部和胸部则通过手工塑造而成；中空的圆锥形头部连接到躯干前方的颈部凸出部分。牛角、生殖器和喉部垂肉等细节也得到特别凸显。牛角前倾明显，并饰以绳索状彩绘线条和网状图案，额头上刻有三角纹路。碟形鼻端有一个单独塑形的环，连接穿孔的左鼻孔和嘴部的水平切口。大而圆的眼球和牛角下的耳垂则通过浮雕表现，并涂有彩绘。红棕色的线条装饰覆盖全身，并伴有纵向的纹饰区，其中许多纹饰标示着动物的肌肉部位。

在米诺斯文明漫长的历史中，牛在宗教与祭祀活动中一直占据着重要地位。牛的形象频繁出现在米诺斯文明的平面和立体艺术中，显示出牛在米诺斯文明中的核心地位，这在古典时期的米诺斯神话体系中也有所体现。无论是早期的实心牛形陶塑还是后期的中空牛形陶塑，都是米诺斯神庙中极为常见的物品。在宫殿中心遭遇大规模破坏后约两个世纪里，大型中空牛形陶塑成为建于旧米诺斯宫殿遗址上的露天神庙中最常见的祭祀供品。

在这一时期，斐斯托斯宫殿遗址上也建立起一处露天神庙。人们认为，在遗址上建立神庙既是对辉煌过往的缅怀，也带有一种神圣感。在这座神庙中发现的轮制中空牛形陶塑属于宴饮器，是克里特岛中部最精美的器物代表作之一。

在斐斯托斯陶塑所属的时期，克里特岛和希腊本土的轮制牛形陶塑产量激增。这一现象与宗教活动的转变有关；牛形塑像可能被用于替代真实祭品。斐斯托斯陶塑的许多特征都暗示了这一点，如鼻部的“链环”，额头上刻画并彩绘的“网状”装饰，以及牛角上的绳索状线条；牛身上的实体彩绘区域甚至可能代表着被屠宰动物的各个部位。综上所述，斐斯托斯牛形陶塑是克里特岛青铜时代末期米诺斯牛崇拜存续的有力见证。

（迪米特里斯·斯法基纳基斯）

14

Bull figurine

Late Minoan III C – Postpalatial era (after 1200 BCE)
Clay
H. 35 cm (without horns)
Phaistos, Minoan palace
Archaeological Museum of Heraklion, Π1763

The body and probably the head are made of separately modelled pieces, similarly to vase-throwing on the potter's wheel. The hollow cylindrical torso features a spine ridge and hand modelling of the animal's haunches and chest; the hollow conical head joins the neck, attached to a forward projection of the body; various anatomical details such as the horns, genitals and dewlap are emphasised. The horns, sharply tilted forward are distinctive, with painted ropelike lines and a net pattern between them with an incised triangle on the forehead; there is a modelled hoop in the disc-shaped muzzle which connects the perforated left nostril with the horizontal incision of the mouth. The large eyeballs and the ear flaps beneath the horns are rendered in relief and painted. Reddish-brown linear decoration covers the body, accompanied by solid vertical fields; many of these mark the muscles of the animal.

The bull played a crucial part in Minoan religion and cultic practices throughout the long history of Minoan culture. The frequent representation of the animal, in almost every form of two- and three-dimensional art, demonstrates the key status of the Minoan bull, a fact that is subsequently reflected in the Minoan mythological circle of classical antiquity. Clay bull figurines, solid in early periods or hollow in later periods, are a very common find at Minoan sanctuaries. Almost two centuries after the great destruction of the palatial centres, large hollow bull figurines became the most frequent votive offering in open-air sanctuaries built on the sites of the old Minoan palaces.

One of these open-air sanctuaries was founded on the ruins of the palace of Phaistos during that period. The establishment of this kind of sanctuary is believed to be connected with the sanctity inspired by the ruins in the memory of a legendary past. The clay wheelmade hollow bull figurine from Phaistos found in a context of such a sanctuary, associated with feasting pottery assemblages, remains one of the finest examples in Central Crete.

The Phaistos figurine belongs to a period when a sudden growth in the production of terracotta wheelmade bull figurines, both in Crete and in mainland Greece, is clearly attested. This fact is related to a presumed shift in cultic activity. Bull figurines were probably used as substitutes for real sacrifices. Many characteristic features of the Phaistian bull indicate such a possibility: the "chain ring" in the nose, the incised and painted "net-like" decoration on the forehead, the rope-like lines on the horns; even the solid painted fields on the body might represent the parts of the slaughtered animal. In any case, the Phaistian bull is a typical witness to the durability and survival of the bull cult during the final centuries of the Aegean Bronze Age in Crete.

References

Pernier 1902, 123 cf. fig.54. Kourou-Karetsou, 1997.

(Dimitris Sfakianakis)

15

舞蹈者与音乐家陶塑群像（4件）

米诺斯晚期ⅢA（公元前1400～前1300年）

陶土

高13厘米，现代底座直径24厘米

发现于克里特岛帕莱卡斯特罗（D区44号房间）

希腊伊拉克利翁考古博物馆藏，编号Π3903

这组陶塑群像由三位女性舞者和一位女性音乐家组成，呈现出圆舞的整体造型。女性人物造型统一，衣着均为中空钟形裙。裙子的弧形表面不仅有棕色彩绘，而且带波浪状边框，与形状类似的未彩绘区域相结合，表现出服装的丰富褶皱和层叠装饰。在裙子未彩绘的部分，以层层棕色线条表现裙摆的横向褶皱。女性们身系宽腰带，紧身上衣背部有纵向线条勾勒，胸口为角形开口设计。头发盘成圆形发髻高高束起。音乐家还佩戴了两串项链。她手中的乐器被认为是七弦琴，但其造型仅为示意，未表现琴弦，琴头两端为S形天鹅头装饰。

舞者站在一个圆形的舞蹈场地上，手臂水平伸展，与肩齐高，并未交叠。该组陶塑通常被置于一个实心的圆形平台上，音乐家位于舞蹈的中心。舞者中空裙边的小凸起表明，这些陶塑原本被固定在一个环形底座上，这种底座在同一神庙内也有发现。音乐家的裙边没有类似的凸起，表明她可能是通过其他方式支撑。音乐家也可能是一尊独立陶塑，通常放置在舞圈之外，而非主要群像的中心位置。

在米诺斯宫殿西侧庭院及周边聚落的特定空间中进行的舞蹈活动，让人联想到荷马提到的“阿里阿德涅的舞场”。这一舞场是代达罗斯为米诺斯国王之女阿里阿德涅在克诺索斯建造的杰作。

（斯特拉·曼达莱基）

15

Figurine group of dancers and a musician

Late Minoan ⅢA (1400-1300 BCE)

Clay

H. of figurines 13 cm, diam. modern base 24 cm

Palaikastro (Room 44 of Block D)

Archaeological Museum of Heraklion, Π3903

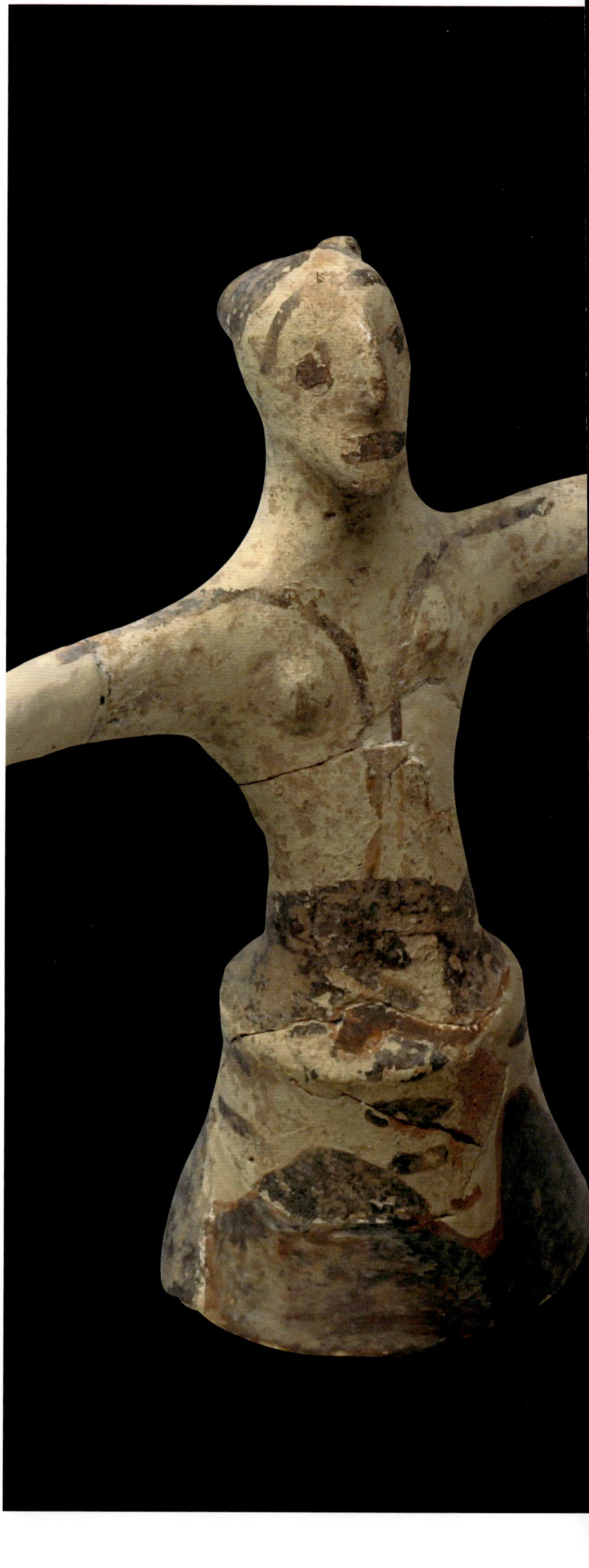

Three figurines of female dancers and one of a female musician form part of a single circle-dance composition. The female figures are uniformly rendered with hollow bell-shaped skirts. The painted brown curved surfaces with a wavy border, combined with the unpainted sections of similar shape, indicate the rich folds and flounces of the garments. Stacked brown lines within the unpainted sections of the skirt represent horizontal folds. The women wear a wide belt around the waist and fitted bodices marked by vertical lines on the back and an angular opening at the chest. The hair is drawn up into a circular bun on the head. The musician also wears two necklaces. The musical instrument, which is identified as a lyre, is rendered schematically without strings and with S-shaped, swan's-head finials.

The dancers have their arms extended at shoulder height, without interlacing them, and are standing on a circular dancing floor. They are usually placed on a solid circular platform with the musician in the middle. However, small protrusions on the edges of the dancers' hollow dresses indicate that they were originally attached to a ring base, similar to the one found in the same sanctuary. The absence of a similar protrusion on the edge of the musician's gown shows that the figurine must have been supported in a different manner. She may have been an independent figurine, set outside the dance circle rather than placed at the centre of the main composition.

The performance of dances in suitably designed spaces in the west courts of the Minoan palaces and in the surrounding settlements recalls Homer's reference to "Ariadne's dancing floor", the work of Daedalus undertaken for the daughter of King Minos at Knossos.

References

Dawkins 1903-04, 216-25, fig.6 (identifying the musician as a snake goddess). Xanthoudides 1905-06, 18. Bosanquet-Dawkins 1923, 88-91, fig.71 (restoration of the circle dance). PM III, 72-73, fig.41. Warren 1984, 318-19, pl.35a. Younger 1998, 23, 75 no.54, pl.1.

(Stella Mandalaki)

16

储物缸

米诺斯晚期 I（公元前 1600 ~ 前 1450 年）

陶土

高 110 厘米，最大口径 45 厘米，最大直径 60 厘米

发现于克里特岛伊拉克利翁的阿夫利

希腊伊拉克利翁考古博物馆藏，编号 Π19497

卵形储物缸，宽口，配两排纵向把手。缸体装饰有波状和水平凸起的条纹，还有雕刻图案以及同心圆印花。

这种中大型容器容量可观（200 ~ 300 升）且适宜长期储存，主要用于满足家庭食材存储所需。

这件储物缸出土于克里特岛中北部阿夫利的一座部分发掘的宅邸，其年代为米诺斯晚期 I（公元前 1600 ~ 前 1450 年）。在同一宅邸中还发现了其他储物缸的残片，表明该地区存在大量储物偏好。这种储物缸稳定性适中且便于搬运，能够通过较小的容器或舀勺轻松取用内容物。

宽口缸是米诺斯陶器中最具代表性的实用器形，主要用于存储农产品，如谷物、豆类、橄榄油和葡萄酒。考古证据表明，这种器物还有其他多种用途，例如用于盛接鲜榨橄榄油和葡萄酒，或者用作埋葬容器。

不同用途的储存容器在容量、便携性、易取程度和稳定性方面存在明显差异，能够真实反映克里特青铜文明时期社会各阶层的储物行为。从发现地点来看，宫殿发现的储物缸最多，其次是非宫殿聚落的中心建筑和富人宅邸，普通家庭发现的数量最少。

（卡特琳娜·阿塔纳萨基）

16

Storage jar (pithos)

Late Minoan I (1600-1450 BCE)

Clay

H. 110 cm, max. rim diam. 45 cm, max. diam. 60 cm

Avli, Heraklion

Archaeological Museum of Heraklion, Π19497

Ovoid pithos with a wide mouth and two rows of vertical handles. It is decorated with a series of wavy and horizontal raised bands, featuring incised patterns and concentric circle stamp impressions.

This medium to large-sized vessel offers considerable storage capacity (200-300 litres) and is ideal for long term storage, indented exclusively to meet household nutritional needs.

It was found in a partly excavated mansion at Avli, in north-central Crete, dated to the Late Minoan I period (1600-1450 BCE). Fragments of other pithoi were also found in the same mansion, indicating a broader pattern of bulk storage. It offers moderate stability and transportability with easy access to the contents, possibly by the use of smaller vessels or dippers.

The pithos is the most distinctive utilitarian form in the Minoan ceramic repertoire. It was primarily used for storing agricultural products such as cereals, pulses, olive oil and wine. Contextual evidence suggests that it also served various other purposes, frequently acting as a collector in wine and olive-press installations, or even as a burial receptacle.

Variations in functional attributes such as capacity, transportability, accessibility and stability suggest differences in the primary functions of these storage containers and reflect the storage practices adopted across various social sectors of Cretan Bronze Age societies. In terms of distribution, the largest percentage is found in palaces, a smaller proportion in central buildings of non-palatial settlements and wealthy mansions, and an even smaller number in simple domestic units.

References

Alexiou 1972, 621. Christakis 2008. Christakis 2011.

(Katerina Athanasaki)

17

王宫风格罐

米诺斯晚期Ⅱ（公元前 1450 ~ 前 1400 年）

陶土

高 50.7 厘米，口径 22 厘米，底径 19 厘米

发现于克里特岛克诺索斯的未发掘宅邸

希腊伊拉克利翁考古博物馆藏，编号 Π21168

陶罐肩部配三个纵向带状把手，平底。壶身表面饰有风格独特的百合图案，并以曲线作为填充。此陶罐属于典型的王宫风格，这一风格器物的特点为通体饰有独特的花卉和海洋风图案。

王宫风陶罐和双耳瓶往往制作工艺高超且装饰精美，通常被认为出自宫殿工坊。能在豪华宅邸和墓葬中觅得其踪，表明统治阶级也将这些器物视为奢华的陈列品。此件陶罐出土自克诺索斯未发掘宅邸上层房间，房内还藏有双耳浅口杯、杯和壶等大量精美华丽的陶器。

（艾琳·尼古拉科普卢）

17

"Palace Style" pithoid jar

Late Minoan Ⅱ (1450-1400 BCE)

Clay

H. 50.7 cm, diam. rim 22 cm, diam. base 19 cm

Knossos, Unexplored Mansion

Archaeological Museum of Heraklion, Π21168

Pithoid jar with three vertical strap handles on the shoulder and disc base. The whole surface of the body is decorated with waz-lilies with stylised flowers and curvilinear filling motifs. A representative example of the Palace Style, which depicted highly stylised motifs of the Floral and Marine Styles of the previous period, often in zones covering the whole surface of the vessel.

Due to their high quality of manufacture and decoration, Palace Style pithoid jars and amphorae are believed to be the products of palace workshops, while their discovery in luxurious residences and tombs shows that they were used by the ruling class as luxury display vessels. This particular jar comes from an assemblage in a room on the upper floor of the Unexplored Mansion at Knossos, which contained a large number of delicate, elaborately decorated vessels (kylikes, cups, jugs).

References

Popham et al. 1984, 36, H 181, pl.68a-b.

(Irene Nikolakopoulou)

Legend has it that the labyrinth built by Daedalus possessed an intricate layout and served as both a terrifying prison and a mysterious palace.

The British archaeologist Evans discovered the Palace of Knossos, which may have possibly inspired the mythical labyrinth described in the tales of Daedalus. The myth can be seen as a literary reflection of the architectural achievements of Minoan civilization. The ruins of the palace, with their winding corridors, indeed match the elusive descriptions of the story. In its prime, the palace must have been magnificent, with red columns, towering walls, colonnades, and courtyards, all speaking to its grandeur. Vibrant frescoes depicting serene flora, graceful princes, and elegantly dressed women add a divine charm to the palace.

Such architectural remnants scatter across Crete, dating from different eras of the Bronze Age civilization. These structures, which grew and evolved over centuries, were central to the lives of the Cretan people, marking the emergence of early states and serving as monuments to the Minoan civilization's dominance over the Aegean. Only a powerful and prosperous society could have achieved such awe-inspiring feats.

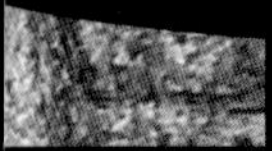

18

带浮雕装饰的建筑楣板（残片）

米诺斯中期ⅢB 至米诺斯晚期Ⅱ
（公元前 1650～前 1400 年）
绿片岩
长 23 厘米，宽 15 厘米，厚 5.5 厘米
发现于克里特岛克诺索斯王宫西廷房舍
希腊伊拉克利翁考古博物馆藏，编号 Γ270

建筑楣板残片，其上有浮雕装饰，中心为对称排列的半花形纹样，一端带有螺旋形纵向带状装饰，底部由一组平行凸起线条构成边界。在螺旋纹样旁的纵向带状装饰处，还可见打磨后的凸起与凹槽痕迹，揭示出下一对半花形纹样的起始位置。

类似的建筑檐饰残片在宫殿西南角和西北角可能存在的纪念性入口、西侧庭院以及通往西翼上层的前厅区域皆有发现，发掘地点位于伊文思标记的米诺斯中期ⅢB 地层。这类器物的主要特征便是带有半花形纹样浮雕和“三竖纹”装饰，或者带有完整的花形纹样浮雕。在米诺斯中期ⅢB 至米诺斯晚期ⅠB 的壁画和浮雕中也曾出现类似的建筑檐饰图案，表明克诺索斯工坊从新王宫初期便开始逐步发展建筑浮雕工艺。半花形纹样和“三竖纹”也被后来的迈锡尼人用于装饰宫殿和纪念性圆顶墓，并且普遍出现在迈锡尼图画作品中。也有观点认为，克诺索斯的这种建筑浮雕主题可能属于王宫期末期，是迈锡尼文化影响下的产物。

这些石质建筑浮雕发现于纪念性入口处，表明其最初为门楣檐饰，放置在石壁上的木质或金属托架中，以便有效支撑其重量。类似主题的木质装饰则用于低矮阶梯形栏杆的外墙。描绘相同图案的壁画也常用作墙壁底部装饰。

半花形纹样与“三竖纹”的组合，以及其与内凹祭坛形状的相似性，体现出一种宗教象征意义。此外，这一主题频繁出现在新王宫期与王宫期末期的壁画与印章中，表明其可能象征宫殿权威。

（斯特拉·曼达莱基）

18

Part of an architectural frieze with relief decoration

Middle Minoan ⅢB – Late Minoan Ⅱ (1650-1400 BCE)
Green schist
L.23 cm, w. 15 cm, th. 5.5 cm
Knossos, palace, West Court Houses
Archaeological Museum of Heraklion, Γ270

Part of an architectural frieze with a relief of opposed half-rosettes in the centre and a vertical band of spirals at one end. The composition is delimited at the base by a set of parallel ridges. Beside the vertical band flanking the spirals are traces of a smoothed ridge-and-groove, apparently indicating the start of the next pair of half-rosettes.

Many fragments of similar architectural friezes with relief decoration either of half-rosettes with "triglyph" or of full rosettes have been found in the presumed monumental entrances at the SW and NW corners of the palace, as well as in the West Court and in the area of the Propylaeum leading to the upper storey of the West Wing, in layers dated by Evans to MM Ⅲ. The early dating, which is consistent with the depiction of similar architectural friezes with this subject in MM ⅢB–Late Minoan ⅠB frescoes and reliefs, documents the development of architectural relief-work by the Knossian workshops from the beginning of the Neopalatial period. Later, the combination of half-rosettes with triglyphs was adopted by the Mycenaeans in the decoration of palaces and monumental tholos tombs, as well as in pictorial compositions in general. According to another theory, the architectural reliefs of Knossos with this particular theme are dated to the Final Palatial period and indicate a Mycenaean influence.

The discovery of the stone architectural reliefs in monumental entrances strengthens the hypothesis that they were originally located in friezes above doorways, set on a wooden or metal seating within the masonry, so as to effectively support their weight. In contrast, the representation of the same theme in wood is found in the façades of low, stepped balustrades. Frescoes with this motif also decorated the lower part of the walls immediately above the floor.

The similarity of the combination of half-rosettes and "triglyphs" to the incurved altar shape indicates a religious symbolism. Further, the frequent depiction of the theme in the frescoes and seals of the Neopalatial and Final Palatial periods is interpreted as a symbolic statement of palatial authority.

References

PM II, 162, 590-608, 696-97, 704; IV, 221-28, 919-20. Hägg 1987, 132 and n.21. Marinatos 2010, 27-29, 131-39. Soles 2016, 250, pl.LXXXII.

(Stella Mandalaki)

19

花形浮雕柱顶

米诺斯中期ⅢB 至米诺斯晚期Ⅱ

（公元前 1650 ~ 前 1400 年）

蛇纹石

高 13.5 厘米，宽 13.5 厘米，厚 10 厘米

发现于克里特岛克诺索斯王宫中央庭院通往主厅的柱廊楼梯附近

希腊伊拉克利翁考古博物馆藏，编号 Λ6152

花形浮雕柱顶，有三片花瓣。其背面平整，表明曾固定在石立面上。顶部中央有一个圆柱状凸起，可能用于连接上方的建筑构件。上表面留有因打磨加工而产生的同心刻线痕迹。

（斯特拉・曼达莱基）

19

Flower-shaped architectural relief capital

Middle Minoan ⅢB – Late Minoan Ⅱ (1650-1400 BCE)

Serpentinite

H. 13.5 cm, w. 13.5 cm, th. 10 cm

Knossos, palace, in the Central Court near the hypostyle staircase leading to the Piano Nobile

Archaeological Museum of Heraklion, Λ6152

Flower-shaped architectural capital in relief, with three petals. The flat back suggests it was attached to a stone façade. In the centre of the upper surface, a cylindrical protrusion is preserved, for the attachment of a superimposed architectural member. Concentric incised circles are also visible on the same surface, the result of smoothing actions.

References

PM II, 815, Suppl. Pl.XXX c, d, e.

(Stella Mandalaki)

20

莲花形浮雕柱顶

米诺斯中期ⅢB 至米诺斯晚期Ⅱ
（公元前 1650～前 1400 年）
蛇纹石
高 17 厘米，宽 13 厘米，厚 8.5 厘米
发现于克里特岛克诺索斯王宫中央庭院通往主厅的柱廊楼梯附近
希腊伊拉克利翁考古博物馆藏，编号 Λ6153

莲花形浮雕柱顶，其背面平整，表明曾固定在石立面上。顶部中央有一个圆柱状凸起，可能用于连接上方的建筑构件。

（斯特拉·曼达莱基）

20

Lotus-shaped architectural relief capital

Middle Minoan ⅢB – Late Minoan Ⅱ (1650-1400 BCE)
Serpentinite
H. 17 cm, w. 13 cm, th. 8.5 cm.
Knossos, palace, in the Central Court near the hypostyle staircase leading to the Piano Nobile
Archaeological Museum of Heraklion, Λ6153

Lotus-shaped architectural capital in relief. The flat back suggests it was attached to a stone façade. In the centre of the upper surface, a cylindrical protrusion is preserved, for the attachment of a superimposed architectural member.

References

PM II, 815, Suppl. Pl. XXX a,b.

(Stella Mandalaki)

21
灯
米诺斯晚期ⅠA（公元前1600～前1500年）
石材
高11厘米，直径24厘米
发现于克里特岛斐斯托斯王宫
希腊伊拉克利翁考古博物馆藏，编号Λ1515

低型无足石灯，其边缘饰有一圈凸出的锥形螺旋浮雕。灯体呈锥形，顶部挖有灯槽，边缘设有四个呈十字形排列的三角形灯嘴或灯芯座，底部有一个明显的圆盘状底座。灯嘴之间有三处高浮雕螺旋壳装饰。一侧灯嘴下保存有一个三角形“水滴”状提手。灯具整体呈半复原状态。

此类低型石灯以及带有细长圆柱形底座的高型灯，是多层宫殿建筑黑暗房间和走廊的主要照明方式。这些灯具通常以花卉或其他浮雕图案加以装饰，其中不乏宫殿作坊石匠的艺术杰作。这些精致的石灯可能摆放在宫殿内，供精英阶层在夜间进行祭仪或宴会活动时使用。

（迪米特里斯·斯法基纳基斯）

21
Lamp
Late Minoan ⅠA (1600-1500 BCE)
Stone
H. 11 cm, d. 24 cm
Phaistos, palace
Archaeological Museum of Heraklion, Λ1515

Stone lamp, low type without a foot, with a series of protruding conical spirals in relief on the rim. It has a conical body with a distinct, disc-shaped base, and a basin worked in the top, with four triangular nozzles or wick-holders set in a cross pattern on the rim; in the spaces between the nozzles are three conical spiraliform shells in high relief. In the preserved part, below one nozzle depends a lug-handle shaped like a triangular "drop". Half restored.

Such low lamps, as well as the tall ones on a slender cylindrical stem or foot, were the main means of lighting the dark rooms and corridors of the multi-storey palace complexes. Elaborately decorated with relief floral or other decorative motifs, they are sometimes true masterpieces of the stoneworker's art of the palace workshops. They are perhaps the most characteristic examples of the finely crafted vessels available to the members of the elite society who lived within the palace, extending their ritual or banqueting activities even into the dark night hours.

References
Pernier-Banti 1951, 385-6, fig.253. Warren 1969, 53.

(Dimitris Sfakianakis)

22

描绘迷宫的壁画残片

米诺斯中期Ⅲ（公元前 1700 ~ 前 1600 年）

壁画

50 × 60 厘米

发现于克里特岛克诺索斯王宫东翼

希腊伊拉克利翁考古博物馆藏，编号 T50

描绘迷宫的壁画残片，原壁画曾装饰在克诺索斯王宫东翼。制作时，首先需要在抹灰表面上刻线，然后用鲜红色颜料填充线条。白色背景上交错的回纹图案构成了一个装饰性迷宫。这一设计与埃及尼罗河三角洲泰尔达巴宫遗址中一处地板上的迷宫装饰高度相似，该地板曾用于呈现“跳公牛”场景。有学者认为，克诺索斯的这幅地板壁画出自同一批游走于爱琴海地区的艺术家之手，这些艺术家也在埃及创作了类似壁画。

（埃拉尼·齐拉基）

22

Fresco fragment depicting a labyrinth

Middle Minoan Ⅲ (1700-1600 BCE)

Fresco

50×60 cm

Knossos, palace, East Wing

Archaeological Museum of Heraklion, T50

A fragment from a floor painting depicting a labyrinth. This is part of a larger composition, which decorated the floor of the East Wing of the Minoan palace at Knossos. The design was made by incising lines into the surface of the plaster and ten filling the grooves with bright red paint. The linear grid of the interlocked meander pattern on a white ground makes a decorative maze design. It bears a striking resemblance to a floor from the Tell el Dab'a site, in the Nile Delta in Egypt, which functions as a backdrop to a bull-leaping scene. The Knossian floor painting is attributed to the same itinerant team of Aegean artists who created the corresponding fresco in Egypt.

References

Shaw 2012.

(Eleni Tziraki)

23

描绘“献祭之角”的壁画残片

米诺斯中期ⅢB– 米诺斯晚期ⅠA

（公元前 1650 ~ 前 1550 年）

石灰膏

高 7 厘米

发现于克里特岛克诺索斯王宫

希腊伊拉克利翁考古博物馆藏，编号 T.B44

23

Fresco fragment

Middle Minoan ⅢB-Late Minoan ⅠA (1650-1550 BCE)

Lime plaster

H. 7 cm

Knossos, palace

Archaeological Museum of Heraklion, T.B44

大致呈椭圆形的薄石灰膏残片，来自宫殿北入口上层墙壁的一幅小型壁画。从保存下来的画面中可以看到部分建筑外立面，可能是宫殿建筑或神庙的屋顶。画面展示了由两排等边排列方石块构成的石墙，上方饰有一排神圣的“献祭之角”，背景为红色。在石砌墙面下方，可以看到至少三个实心圆形图案，可能代表木梁的圆端。在画面顶部，可以模糊地分辨出至少两个矩形开口，可能为窗户。这块残片属于克诺索斯王宫中特有的“小型壁画”系列，其风格独特，与其他小型壁画的风格截然不同，展现出独特的艺术风格。

虽然画师精妙的笔触能够为房间增添壮丽与宏伟，但宫殿中的绘画往往并不仅仅用于装饰目的。在宫殿这一具有重要社会意义的地点，壁画应当描绘出每处场所的功能特点。这些壁画需要起到宣传作用，突出建筑本身蕴含的权力象征。形象化的绘画是新王宫期建筑的重要特征，在这一时期，壁画艺术家很可能是建筑团队中不可或缺的一部分。

（迪米特里斯・斯法基纳基斯）

Roughly ovoid fragment, of thin lime plaster, from a miniature fresco which once adorned a wall on the upper floors of the complex making up the North Entrance of the palace. In the surviving representation, part of an architectural facade can be seen, probably the roof of a palace building or a sanctuary. Two courses of dressed stone blocks, arranged in an isodomic layout, can be distinguished, crowned by a row of “horns of consecration”, all on a red background. Below the masonry at least three solid painted circles can be seen, probably representing the round ends of wooden beams. At the very top of the image, at least two rectangular openings, probably windows, can just be discerned. The fragment belongs to the group of “miniature frescoes” that come from this particular palace site and is unique in style, since it is not attributed to any of the hands detected in the other miniatures.

Painting in the palaces, in many cases, does not serve an exclusively decorative purpose, although this does not mean that the skilled painter’s ingenious brush did not add splendor and grandeur to the palace rooms. The repertoire of the wall paintings, set as they are in a building of particular importance for social organisation, depicts the functional features of the respective spaces. They serve the purposes of propaganda and reinforce the power-symbolism that the building itself expresses. Figurative painting is a characteristic feature of the architecture of the Neopalatial era, and the mural painters were probably an integral part of the team of engineers and builders responsible for Neopalatial architecture.

References

Cameron 1976, vol.I, 323-324, 690, 692, vol.II, 46 B.

(Dimitris Sfakianakis)

24
“城市马赛克”费昂斯板
米诺斯中期Ⅲ（公元前 1700 ~ 前 1600 年）
费昂斯
高 4.7 厘米，宽 3.2 厘米，厚 0.4 厘米
发现于克里特岛克诺索斯王宫西翼
希腊伊拉克利翁考古博物馆藏，编号 Y1/28

24
Faience plaque from the “Town Mosaic”
Middle Minoan Ⅲ (1700-1600 BCE)
Faience
H. 4.7 cm, w. 3.2 cm, th. 0.4 cm
Knossos, West Wing of the palace
Archaeological Museum of Heraklion, Y1/28

“城市马赛克”费昂斯板，这一名称由伊文思（A. Evans）提出，用于指代 20 世纪初克诺索斯发掘时出土的一组约 100 块费昂斯板。这些费昂斯板很可能曾镶嵌在某些木制品上作为装饰，主要表现建筑元素，包括房屋立面、几何图案、人物、动物、树木、植物、船只、武器，甚至水域。这块板描绘的是用规则石块砌成的立面，也包含木结构和其他建筑元素，窗户以红色表示。

虽然“城市马赛克”的解读仍存在争议，但它对我们了解米诺斯建筑具有重要意义，并且也是米诺斯奢侈品制造工艺、艺术创意以及多工艺协作的典型例证。此外，用费昂斯或象牙装饰景观场景可能受到了自然景观的启发，这既体现了米诺斯人对自然的热爱，也展示出小型艺术作品的象征力量。

（卡特琳娜·阿塔纳萨基，乔治娅·弗拉达）

A faience plaque with surface glaze, from the so-called “Town Mosaic”, a name that was given by A. Evans to a group of ca. 100 plaques that were found during the excavations at Knossos at the beginning of the 20th century. Most of the faience plaques, which were probably inlaid as a decoration in some wooden object(s), represent architectural elements, mainly house facades, geometric motifs, men, animals, trees, plants, boats, weapons and, possibly, also water. This particular example represents a façade with coursed ashlar blocks, timber framework and other structural elements, whereby the windows are rendered in red colour.

Although the interpretation of the “Town Mosaic” remains controversial, it is regarded as an important find towards our understanding of Minoan architecture and also a characteristic example of pyrotechnical skills, artistic creativity and cross-craft interconnections in the manufacture of Minoan luxury items. On the other hand, landscape scenes may have been the inspiration for decorative syntheses made of faience or ivory inlays and appliqués, thus attesting to the love of Minoans for nature and, also, to the symbolic power of small-scale art.

References

Blakolmer 2020, 74, 89 fig.2.20. Foster 2008. Poursat-Knappett 2022, 234.

(Katerina Athanasaki, Georgia Flouda)

25

房屋外墙模型

米诺斯中期ⅢA（公元前 1700 ~ 前 1650 年）
陶土
高 9.2 厘米
发现于克里特岛克诺索斯王宫
希腊伊拉克利翁考古博物馆藏，编号 Π2586

这件陶土制成的建筑模型表现的是一面墙壁，其上有一系列竖长矩形开口，中间间隔着明显的墙体分段。模型平面呈半矩形，可能是在展示一种矩形壁龛或圣墙的特征。该模型经过部分修复，总体保留了原始形式。一些观点认为这些开口是建筑上层的多对窗户，另一件同组模型也能为此提供佐证；也有观点认为这些开口象征宫殿建筑中的多开门入口，这种入口是新王宫繁荣时期宫殿建筑的典型特征。

从另一件保存完整的克诺索斯建筑模型中，可以辨认出一些独立的建筑结构元素，这些元素颜色不同，但排列和谐。其中一些元素可能代表门框的石材部分，另一些则代表木质构件，如框架或支撑梁的端部。石材与木材是新旧王宫过渡时期米诺斯建筑的两种主要建材。

这些陶土模型可能模仿了宗教砖石结构（如祭坛、围墙等），用于宫殿内外真实建筑的奠基仪式。

"建筑大师"代达罗斯在克里特–迈锡尼世界无人不晓，其在切割、建造和建材连接方面的精湛技艺深刻影响了爱琴海地区的抗震建筑设计。这位"迷宫"建造者的形象实际上代表了米诺斯宫殿所有工匠的智慧，是他们的巧思为宫殿内的建筑元素赋予了象征意义，展现出克里特文明鼎盛时期的辉煌。

（迪米特里斯・斯法基纳基斯）

25

Model of house façade

Middle Minoan ⅢA (1700-1650 BCE)
Clay
H. 9.2 cm
Knossos, palace
Archaeological Museum of Heraklion, Π2586

Clay model of an architectural feature, a wall with a series of long, vertical, rectangular openings with solid intervening walls with distinct courses. The piece is Π-shaped (semi-rectangular) in plan and probably presents the characteristics of a rectangular niche or sacred enclosure, while it is half restored, safely following its original form. The openings are sometimes interpreted as pairs of double windows in an upper storey of a building – an interpretation reinforced by another model in the set – and sometimes as representing the many-doored polythyron entrance to a room on a ground floor. The latter is a characteristic feature of the palatial architecture of the flourishing era of the New Palaces.

In the surviving parts of the other, complete, architectural model from Knossos, individual structural elements can be distinguished, differentiated in colour and harmoniously arranged. Some probably indicate the stonework of the door frames and others the wooden parts, such as frames and the ends of the supporting beams. Stone and wood are two of the most basic building materials of Minoan architecture at the transition from the Old to the New Palaces.

These clay models of religious masonry structures (altars, enclosure walls, etc.) may have been used as votive offerings in foundation ceremonies of the corresponding real structures, either within the palace environment or in outdoor spaces.

The "master mason" of the Creto-Mycenaean world, Daedalus, was famed for his technological ingenuity and skill in cutting, building and joining the architectural materials which were widely used in the anti-seismic architecture of the Aegean. The creator of the "Labyrinth" essentially stands for all those craftsmen of the Minoan palaces, to whose ingenuity is owed the embodiment of symbolic meanings within the structural elements of the prestigious architecture of an elite society in its heyday.

References

PM I, 220-21, fig.166 C.

(Dimitris Sfakianakis)

26

单柄带流杯

米诺斯中期Ⅱ至Ⅲ（公元前 1800～前 1600 年）
条纹大理石
高 10 厘米，最大直径 15 厘米
发现于克里特岛斐斯托斯王宫
希腊伊拉克利翁考古博物馆藏，编号 Λ193

半球形石杯，敛口，配纵向手柄（顶部有折角）以及从杯肩延伸出的管状流，杯底较窄。

这件器物的内外处理均极为精细，并且巧妙利用了石材的横向纹理，表明其加工技艺极高。不过，经过打磨和抛光，几乎完全抹去了先前加工步骤的痕迹。杯底和杯口经修复和复原。

（卡特琳娜·阿塔纳萨基）

26

Single-handled spouted cup

Middle Minoan Ⅱ–Ⅲ (1800-1600 BCE)
Banded marble
H. 10 cm, max. diam. 15 cm
Phaistos, palace
Archaeological Museum of Heraklion, Λ193

Hemispherical cup with a narrow base, inverted rim, a vertical handle with angled turn at top and a tubular spout from the shoulder of the vessel.

The excellent treatment, both externally and internally, as well as the exploitation of the stone's horizontal veining, indicate a high level of expertise in the art of stone-working. However, smoothing and polishing have removed almost all traces of previous manufacturing steps. Repaired and restored at base and mouth.

References

Pernier-Banti 1951, 391, no.60, fig.247a. Warren 1969, 48. Palio 2008, 37.

(Katerina Athanasaki)

193

27

球形容器

米诺斯晚期 I B（公元前 1500 ~ 前 1450 年）

蚀变辉长岩

高 4.8 厘米，最大直径 7 厘米

发现于克里特岛扎克罗斯王宫的 XLV 号房间

希腊伊拉克利翁考古博物馆藏，编号 Λ3077

扁球形容器，口沿略微外翻且平整，无柄，矮平底。整体保存完整，但有多处磕碰损伤。外部装饰有水平凹槽或棱纹，这些装饰可能是通过车床加工而成，石材本身自带的斑点纹理也具有高度装饰性效果。这件器物与其他一批石器一同出土于宫殿南翼的 XLV 房间，该房间已被证实进行过水晶切割等石材加工活动。

该器物属于米诺斯晚期 I B，这一时期石雕工艺迎来了新的繁荣，不仅生产水平大幅提高，也出现了新的器形。

（卡特琳娜・阿塔纳萨基）

27

Globular vase

Late Minoan I B (1500-1450 BCE)

Weathered gabbro

H. 4.8 cm, max. diam. 7 cm

Zakros, palace, Room XLV

Archaeological Museum of Heraklion, Λ3077

A handleless, depressed globular vessel with a low disc base and a slightly everted rim with a flat upper surface. Complete, but with chips in various places. The vase has a decoration of horizontal grooves/ridges on the outside, which were probably made using a lathe, while the choice of the speckled stone itself has a highly decorative effect. It comes, together with other stone vessels, from Room XLV in the south wing of the palace, where the existence of stone-processing activities, including rock-crystal cutting, has been certified.

The vase is dated to Late Minoan I B, a new floruit in the craft of stone-carving, with an increase in production levels and the creation of new types.

References

Πλάτων 1968, 147, pl.129 a.

(Katerina Athanasaki)

28

球形壶

米诺斯晚期Ⅰ/Ⅲ至ⅢA1

（公元前1450～前1375年）

大理石

高20.8厘米，最大直径20厘米

发现于克里特岛克诺索斯王宫

希腊伊拉克利翁考古博物馆藏，编号Λ50

球形壶，带有竖条式高把手和流，内外均可见抛光痕迹。这件石壶巧妙利用了石材纹理来达到高度装饰性效果，充分展示出工匠的高超技艺。

此器物仅见于宫廷场景，可能出自已经毁坏的宫殿遗址。石壶整体完好，仅底部和流部有轻微的缺损和修复痕迹。

（卡特琳娜·阿塔纳萨基）

28

Globular jug

Late Minoan Ⅰ/Ⅲ–ⅢA1 (1450-1375 BCE)

Marble

H. 20.8 cm, max. diam. 20 cm

Knossos, palace

Archaeological Museum of Heraklion, Λ50

Globular jug with high strap handle and spout with traces of polishing inside and out. This is an excellent example of the harmonious exploitation of the veining of the stone by a skilled craftsman, achieving a highly decorative end result.

It probably comes from the destruction layer of the palace; its use is considered to be restricted exclusively to the palatial environment. Intact, with small chips and repairs at the base and spout.

References

Zervos 1956, 494. Warren 1969, 47-48.

(Katerina Athanasaki)

29
桥形流储物缸
米诺斯中期ⅡB（公元前 1750 ~ 前 1700 年）
陶土
高 68.5 厘米，直径 50.5 厘米
发现于克里特岛斐斯托斯王宫（LXIV 号房间）
希腊伊拉克利翁考古博物馆藏，编号 Π10678

陶缸，器身呈卵形，带桥形流，配两个水平把手和一个与流相对的纵向把手。此器物用于储存液体，可能在宫殿宴会期间使用。缸身通过泥条盘筑法制作，然后在慢速陶轮上进行塑形。器物采用卡马雷斯陶器装饰风格，其图案以深色为背景，上面绘有白色、橙色和红色的多彩几何及抽象图案，其核心装饰为几乎覆盖整个器表的宽阔白色平行旋涡条纹。

（帕拉斯克维·斯塔马塔基）

29
Bridge-spouted pithos
Middle Minoan ⅡB (1750-1700 BCE)
Clay
H. 68.5 cm, diam. 50.5 cm
Phaistos, palace (Room LXIV)
Archaeological Museum of Heraklion, Π10678

Clay bridge-spouted pithos with ovoid body, two horizontal handles and one vertical handle opposite the spout. It was used for storing liquids, perhaps during palace banquets. The main body was built up from successive coils that were subsequently thrown on a slow potter's wheel. It bears Kamares Ware decoration, consisting of polychrome, geometric and abstract designs in white, orange and red on a dark ground, the central ornament here being a wide zone of parallel white running spirals that cover almost all of the exterior surface.

References
Betancourt 1985 94-101, pl.11E. Rethemiotakis 2024, 36-41. Walberg 1976.

(Paraskevi Stamataki)

30

桥形流罐

米诺斯中期ⅠB至ⅡA（公元前1900～前1750年）

陶土

高24.6厘米

发现于克里特岛斐斯托斯王宫（LXV号房间）

希腊伊拉克利翁考古博物馆藏，编号Π11196

陶罐呈卵形，带桥形流，配两个水平把手和一个与流相对的纵向把手，用于宫殿宴会期间临时存放液体。壶身由泥条盘筑法制作，最后在陶轮上塑形完成。此器物饰有卡马雷斯陶器装饰，以白色、橙色和红色的多彩几何及抽象图案绘于深色背景上。罐身上还有由细小陶土团块组成的浮雕花形图案，位于彩绘的同心圆内。这种装饰技术被称为“巴尔波丁装饰”，是米诺斯文明的一项独特工艺。

（帕拉斯克维·斯塔马塔基）

30

Bridge-spouted jug

Middle Minoan ⅠB–ⅡA (1900-1750 BCE)

Clay

Max. h. 24.6 cm

Phaistos, palace (Room LXV)

Archaeological Museum of Heraklion, Π11196

Clay bridge-spouted vessel with ovoid body, two horizontal handles and one vertical handle opposite the spout, used for the temporary storage of liquids during palace banquets. The main body was built up from successive coils that were subsequently thrown on the wheel to produce the final shape. It bears Kamares Ware decoration, which consists of polychrome, geometric and abstract designs painted in white, orange and red on a dark ground. It also features relief rosettes in the centre of painted concentric circles, created by adding fine lumps of clay, a Minoan decorative technique known as "barbotine".

References

Betancourt 1985, 83-85, 94-101. Levi 1976, 147-151, table 26a, 26c, plate XIa. Rethemiotakis 2024, 36-41. Walberg 1976.

(Paraskevi Stamataki)

31

宽口罐

米诺斯晚期 I（公元前 1600 ~ 前 1450 年）

陶土

高 22 厘米，口径 12.5 厘米

发现于克里特岛克诺索斯王宫的壁画厅

希腊伊拉克利翁考古博物馆藏，编号 Π7754

宽口罐，罐身饰以光亮褐彩绘制旋涡纹和带状图案。壶内可见制作时留下的指印，表明其制作过程采用了在快速旋转的陶轮上盘筑泥条并刮平修饰的技术。

（乔治娅·弗拉达）

31

Wide-mouthed jug

Late Minoan I (1600-1450 BCE)

Clay

H. 22 cm, diam. rim 12.5 cm

Knossos, palace, House of the Frescoes

Archaeological Museum of Heraklion, Π7754

Wide-mouthed jug with running spiral decoration and bands rendered in a glossy brown paint. In the interior are visible the finger-marks resulting from its creation, employing the technique of the successive addition of clay coils and then their smoothing on the fast potter's wheel.

References

PM II, 436-37. Hatzaki 2007, 152-53, fig.5.1B.

(Georgia Flouda)

32

海洋风格膏油瓶

米诺斯晚期 I B（公元前 1500 ~ 前 1450 年）

陶土

高 23 厘米，瓶身最大直径 15.4 厘米，

口径 9.8 厘米，底径 13.5 厘米

发现于克里特岛克诺索斯王宫北厅，位于未发掘宅邸以西

希腊伊拉克利翁考古博物馆藏，编号 Π24298

此类略高的膏油瓶，瓶口折沿、圆柱形瓶颈长度较短、底座宽而平，在米诺斯晚期 I B 颇为流行。这件膏油瓶采用典型的海洋风装饰。瓶身主要区域饰有海星图案，以中心“眼状”为核心向外辐射，周围是点状圆环，与独特的三角形岩石图案交替排列。瓶颈采用环状浮雕工艺，颈下饰有两条叶状纹带和一排蛇状标记。装饰图案的布局营造出流动的构图感，突出了海洋世界的氛围，但不像其他海洋风陶器那样以密集装饰填满空白处。

这件陶瓶出土于克诺索斯王宫西北一座由方石砌成的建筑物内，与其一同发现的还有约 24 件陶器。膏油瓶通常尺寸较小，瓶口狭窄且易于密封，由此推断，这类器物可能用于存储、运输和供奉贵重物品，如香氛油、酿造或蒸馏产品。此外，还有石膏油瓶，许多图像场景中都可见其身影。

（艾琳・尼古拉科普卢）

32

Clay alabastron in the Marine Style

Late Minoan I B (1500-1450 BCE)

Clay

H. 23 cm, max. diam. body 15.4 cm,

diam. rim 9.8 cm, diam. base 13.5 cm

Knossos, palace, North House, west of Unexplored Mansion

Archaeological Museum of Heraklion, Π24298

Vases of the tall alabastron type, with a wide flat base, low cylindrical neck and flaring rim, were particularly popular in the Late Minoan IB period. This alabastron is a typical example of the Marine Style of decoration. In the main zone of the body are starfish with multiple arms radiating out from a central "eye", surrounded by a dotted circle and alternating with stylised rocks with distinctive triangular outlines. The upper body, under the relief neck-ring, is adorned with two foliate bands and a row of adder marks. The arrangement of the decorative motifs gives the impression of a flowing composition, highlighting the sense of the marine world, without the horror vacui, the fear of empty space, indicated by the dense decoration of other vases in the same style.

This vase was found in a building with ashlar masonry northwest of the palace of Knossos, in a room containing an assemblage of around 24 vases. Judging from the particularly narrow, easily sealed mouth, and the small size of alabastra generally, these vessels may have been used for the storage, transportation and offering of goods considered valuable, such as perfumed oils or fermented, distilled or other products. Vases of the same shape were also made of stone, while they are also known from pictorial scenes.

References

Catling 1980, 49-50, fig.85.

(Irene Nikolakopoulou)

33

特殊王宫风格海洋生物纹扁壶

米诺斯晚期ⅠB（公元前1500～前1450年）

陶土

高27厘米，壶身直径23厘米，壶口直径5厘米

发现于克里特岛帕莱卡斯特罗

希腊伊拉克利翁考古博物馆藏，编号Π3383

扁壶出土于帕莱卡斯特罗，是米诺斯晚期IB最具代表性的“海洋风”陶器之一，也是米诺斯陶艺的集大成之作。壶身呈透镜状，壶颈及壶口较狭窄，配两个纵向短把手。壶身两侧绘有巨大章鱼图案，章鱼以正面姿态刻画，但似乎正朝对角线方向游动，其扭动的触手覆盖了整个壶面。触手之间点缀着各类海底元素，如海胆、特里同螺壳以及带海草的小岩石。

海洋风是特殊王宫风格的一支。海洋风陶器往往设计优雅，装饰主题能够完美契合并凸显器物形态。最为精美的特殊王宫风陶器很可能出自克诺索斯和克里特东部的宫廷工坊。这件来自帕莱卡斯特罗的陶壶与出自古尔尼亚和扎克罗斯的其他陶壶在风格和主题上高度相似，因此可以合理推测它们来自同一工坊，甚至可能出自同一位陶器画匠之手。

（艾琳·尼古拉科普卢）

33

Flask with Marine Style decoration of the Special Palatial Tradition

Late Minoan ⅠB (1500-1450 BCE)

Clay

H. 27 cm, diam. body 23 cm, diam. rim 5 cm

Palaikastro

Archaeological Museum of Heraklion, Π3383

This flask from Palaikastro is one of the most iconic vases of the Marine Style of the Late Minoan IB period and a masterpiece of the Minoan potter's art. It has a lentoid body, a narrow neck and mouth, and two short vertical handles. It is decorated with large octopuses on the two main sides, depicted frontally but appearing to be swimming diagonally, their writhing tentacles covering the whole surface of the flask. Among the tentacles are themes denoting the seabed, such as sea urchins, triton shells and small rocks with seaweed.

The Marine Style is one of the styles that make up the Special Palatial Tradition. The vessels in this style are elegant masterpieces, distinguished by the way in which the decorative themes are perfectly adapted to and highlight the shape of the vessel. The best examples of vases in the Special Palatial Tradition were probably produced by palace workshops, mainly those of Knossos and East Crete. The stylistic and thematic similarities between this particular vase from Palaikastro and other examples from Gournia and Zakros have led to the hypothesis that these vessels are products of the same workshop and perhaps even the same vase-painter.

References

Mountjoy 1984, pl.19a. Bosanquet-Dawkins 1923, pl.18a.

(Irene Nikolakopoulou)

34

开放式石模

米诺斯中期Ⅲ至米诺斯晚期Ⅰ

（公元前 1700 ~ 前 1450 年）

钙质砂岩

长 35.5 厘米，宽 12.5 厘米，厚 10 厘米

发现于克里特岛斐斯托斯王宫

希腊伊拉克利翁考古博物馆藏，编号 Λ234

粗加工三角形石模，模腔设计用于铸造一种长形凿器，所铸凿器尾端略凸，整体宽度逐渐增大至末端形成平直的切削刃。凿器成品长度为 31.5 厘米，最大宽度为 4 厘米。所铸工具结构坚固，表明其设计用途可能是石材加工。模腔内的黑色变色痕迹是高温熔融金属所致。

斐斯托斯及其他地区出土的开放式石模，被广泛用于制作各种长度和形状的凿器，以满足木匠和石匠的特定需求。熔融金属从模腔的一端倒入，而模具的其余部分表面会覆上盖子，以尽量减少金属与空气的接触。

（斯特拉·曼达莱基）

34

Open stone mould

Middle Minoan Ⅲ– Late Minoan Ⅰ (1700-1450 BCE)

Calcareous sandstone

L.35.5 cm, w. 12.5 cm, th. 10 cm

Phaistos, palace

Archaeological Museum of Heraklion, Λ234

Roughly worked triangular stone with one cavity for casting a long chisel with a convex butt, gradually increasing in width to end in a flat and straight cutting edge. The tool's length is 31.5 cm and its max. width 4 cm. The robust construction of the tool could possibly indicate its intended use in working stone structures. The black discolouring of the stone inside the cavity is due to the heat of the molten metal.

Open moulds, such as this one from Phaistos, were used extensively to make chisels of various lengths and shapes for specialised uses in wood and stone-working. Molten metal was poured into one end of the cavity, while the rest of the surface was covered with a lid to minimise exposure of the metal to the air.

References

Pernier-Banti 1951, 369 no.23, fig.235a. Branigan 1974, 77-80. Evely 2000, 353-56, 358 no.11, fig.142.

(Stella Mandalaki)

35

双面二片式模具（一半）

米诺斯中期Ⅲ至米诺斯晚期Ⅰ（公元前1700～前1450年）
绿色片岩
长16.3厘米，宽8.5厘米，厚3.8厘米
发现于克里特岛马利亚王宫的E号厅
希腊伊拉克利翁考古博物馆藏，编号Λ2473

这是一件几乎完整的矩形二片式模具的一半，其内侧用于铸造双刃斧，外侧则用于铸造匕首。模具长边顶部有两个深孔和一个未成型孔，用于连接模具的两部分。模具内侧有一个半圆形凹槽，用于放置斧眼芯。背面和窄边有深斜切痕及交叉切口，用于绑定两半模具。内侧铸造腔表面可以看到大面积的圆形磨损痕迹。模具外侧曲面被加工成开放式模具，用于铸造尖端呈锐角的小型三角形匕首，匕首长11.5厘米，宽3厘米。模具所有表面均有黑色变色痕迹。

此模具出土于宫殿外围的一座房屋遗址，表明马利亚王宫城镇周边还存在其他工坊。在新王宫期，这一地区的铜加工方式依旧延续了旧王宫期的传统。这种两用模具不仅有效节约材料，还方便金属工匠携带。

（斯特拉·曼达莱基）

35

Two-faced half of a two-piece mould

Middle Minoan Ⅲ– Late Minoan Ⅰ (1700-1450 BCE)

Green schistoid stone

L. 16.3 cm, w. 8.5 cm, th. 3.8 cm

Malia, palace, House E

Archaeological Museum of Heraklion, Λ2473

Almost complete half of rectangular two-piece mould for casting a double axe on the inside and a dagger on the outside. Two deep holes and one unfinished one along the top of one long side were used to join the two parts. On the inside here, a semicircular recess indicates the position of the tool's shaft-hole core. Deep, oblique and x-shaped cuts on the back and on the narrow edges are for the binding of the two halves. Extensive wear in a circular pattern can be seen on the surface of the inner casting cavity. The curved outer side of the half has been worked to be used as an open mould for casting a small triangular dagger with a pointed tip, 11.5 cm long and 3 cm wide. Black discolouring on all surfaces.

The origin of the mould from a house on the perimeter of the palace illustrates the operation of workshops within the wider urban environment of palatial Malia, where the earlier tradition of Protopalatial times in the processing of copper in this manner continues on in the Neopalatial era. The dual use of the mould – open for the manufacture of a dagger and closed for a double axe – serves to economise on material and assures the easy transportation of the basic equipment by the metalworkers.

References

Deshayes-Dessenne 1959, 137 no.16, pl.L3. Branigan 1974, 80-83. Evely 2000, 353-56, 360 no.25. Lowe-Fri 2011, 11-16. Poursat-Oberweiler 2011.

(Stella Mandalaki)

36

双面二片式模具（一半）

米诺斯中期Ⅲ至米诺斯晚期Ⅰ（公元前 1700～前 1450 年）

砂岩

长 13.5 厘米，宽 10.2 厘米，厚 5.4 厘米

发现于克里特岛斐斯托斯王宫

希腊伊拉克利翁考古博物馆藏，编号 Λ231

二片式模具，其内侧用于铸造双刃斧，外侧则用于铸造小型锤子。模具的长边边缘有两个孔，以便将模具两半连接起来使用。双刃斧形腔中央有一个明显的半圆形凹槽，用于放置斧眼芯。边缘和背面有切口，以便用金属线将两半模具绑定在一起。

模具外侧凸起，中央有一长形腔，深 1 厘米，用于铸造小型锤子（9 厘米长），矩形锤身向敲击端逐渐变细（从 1.9 厘米变为 1.3 厘米）。长形腔内的小方形凹陷标明锤眼芯的位置。锤眼更靠近锤身宽端，能够确保工具在使用时的平衡性。

所铸锤子尺寸较小，可能是为金匠或其他金属工匠打造。此模具的发现表明，在新王宫期，人们已经开始使用青铜锤来替代早先的石锤。

（斯特拉·曼达莱基）

36

Two-faced half of a two-piece mould

Middle Minoan Ⅲ– Late Minoan Ⅰ (1700-1450 BCE)

Sandstone

L. 13.5 cm, w 10.2 cm, th. 5.4 cm

Phaistos, palace

Archaeological Museum of Heraklion, Λ231

Half of a two-piece mould for casting a double axe on one side and a small hammer on the other external curved face. Two holes along the rim of one long side of the cavity for the double axe were used to join the two halves together when used as a two-piece mould. In the centre of the same side is a distinct semi-circular recess for the shaft-hole core of the double axe. Incisions and cuts made on the edges and on the back served to bind the halves together with metal "wires".

A long cavity 1 cm deep has been carved in the centre of the convex exterior surface to cast a slender rectangular hammer (9 cm long) tapering towards the striking end (from 1.90 to 1.30 cm). A small square depression within the oblong cavity indicates the location of the shaft-hole core for the hammer. Placing this shaft-hole closer to the broad end ensures a proper balance to the tool when in use.

The small size of the hammer probably indicates it was for a goldsmith or other metalsmith. This is a unique example in bronze of a particular tool type used during the Neopalatial era, probably in place of a similar item in stone as used in earlier periods.

References

Pernier-Banti 1951, 371, fig.235c. Evely 1993, 102, fig.45; 2000, 353-56, 360 no.27.

(Stella Mandalaki)

231.

第三单元　青铜

Unit 3 Bronze

克里特岛古老窑炉中偶然泛起的金属幽光，点燃人类冶金历史的第一簇星火。当青铜熔液在陶范中流淌，这里便奏响社会巨变的乐章。锻锤敲击出时代强音，把石质工具送入历史帷幕。那些曾被燧石限制的创造力，终于在冷峻光泽中喷薄绽放。

米诺斯匠人把金属魔法推向巅峰。他们以铆接技术解锁青铜奥秘，用柔韧板材锻造三足圣釜，让这些与金银争辉的器物，在棱镜中折射出阶级社会的光谱。甲胄流动着大海波纹，剑锋凝结着月华寒芒。神圣的双刃斧在祭坛劈开天地通灵之路，那弧线既昭示战争威仪，亦勾描仪轨轮廓。青铜的物理特性完美转化为权力的视觉语法，在克里特岛宫墙残垣间，留下跨越数千年的永恒封印。

The faint glimmer of metal in Bronze Age kilns at Crete ignited the first spark of human metallurgy. As molten bronze flowed into clay molds, the island began to play the symphony of transformation. The hammer's strikes heralded a new era, consigning stone tools to the annals of history. Creativity, once constrained by stone, now burst forth in the cool gleam of bronze tools.

Minoan craftsmen elevated metalworking to an art form. Through riveting techniques, they unlocked the secrets of bronze, forging tripod cauldrons that rivaled gold and silver in brilliance. These vessels, used in feasts, reflected the hues of a stratified society. Armor flowed with the waves of the sea, and sword blades gleamed with the cold light of the moon. The sacred double-headed axe, used in rituals, carved a path between heaven and earth, its curved blade embodying both the might of war and the solemnity of ceremony. The physical properties of bronze were masterfully transformed into a visual language of power, leaving an eternal imprint on the ruins of Knossos, a seal that transcends three millennia.

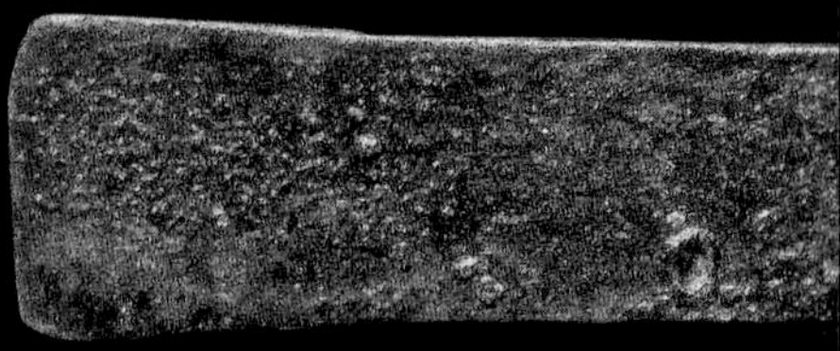

37

杆形凿器（7 件）

米诺斯晚期 I 至 II（公元前 1600 ~ 前 1400 年）

青铜

A) 长 39.5 厘米，最大宽度 3.5 厘米

B) 长 27 厘米，最大宽度 2 厘米，厚 1.4 厘米

C) 长 20.2 厘米，最大宽度 1.5 厘米，厚 1.3 厘米

D) 长 24.5 厘米，最大宽度 1.5 厘米，厚 1.2 厘米

E) 长 21.5 厘米，最大宽度 1.5 厘米，厚 1.1 厘米

F) 长 22 厘米，最大宽度 1.7 厘米，厚 1 厘米

G) 长 24.5 厘米，最大宽度 2 厘米，厚 1.2 厘米

发现于罗塔西的阿斯普罗利瓦达遗址

希腊伊拉克利翁考古博物馆藏，编号 X2472、X2475、X2481、X2476、X2480、X2479、X2477

这七件杆状（纺锤形）凿器长短不一，凿柄上下表面凸起，末端几乎收束，切削刃经过磨平形成直边，保存状况极佳。其中大多数凿器的末端平面因受到敲击工具（如木槌）的反复捶击，留下了明显的损伤痕迹。例如 C 上可见水平凹槽痕迹，D 和 E 表面凹凸不平，F 上有一个异常的圆形凹痕，G 的末端被削成斜角，中心有浅刻痕迹。不过，只有 B 和 F 存在明显的切削刃磨损痕迹。

这些凿器结构坚固且符合人体工学设计，表明它们主要用于雕刻石材。末端因连续敲击造成的严重损伤也佐证了这一用途。这些凿器既可用作劈开石块的楔子，也可用于修整石块表面。此外，它们可能也用于木工，在加工长木梁或木板时使用。

根据伊夫利（Evely，1993 年）的分类法，这些凿器可归入 2 型。罗塔西同时发现了三种不同类型的凿器（1 型、2 型和 3 型），这表明新王宫期的工具具有高度专业化的特点，也反映出当时米诺斯社会的复杂需求。

（斯特拉 · 曼达莱基）

37

Seven rod-shaped chisels

Late Minoan I – II (1600-1400 BCE)

Bronze

A) L. 39.5 cm, max. w. 3.5 cm

B) L. 27 cm, max. w. 2 cm, th. 1.4 cm

C) L. 20.2 cm, max. w. 1.5 cm, th.1.3 cm

D) L. 24.5 cm, max. w. 1.5 cm, th.1.2 cm

E) L. 21.5 cm, max. w. 1.5 cm, th. 1.1 cm

F) L. 22 cm, max. w. 1.7 cm, th. 1 cm

G) L. 24.5 cm, max. w. 2 cm, th. 1.2 cm

Rotasi, Asprolivada site

Archaeological Museum of Heraklion, X 2472, 2475, 2481, 2476, 2480, 2479, 2477

Seven strong rod-like (spindle-shaped) chisels of varying length, with the convex upper and lower surfaces of the shank almost converging at the two ends, and a flattened and straight cutting edge. Excellent state of preservation. Most show obvious traces of impacts on the initially flat butt end from successive blows of a percussion tool (mallet). On C. a horizontal gouge-mark can be made out, for D.-E. the surface is uneven, and in F. an abnormal circular depression is found; while in G. the butt end is chamfered with a shallow gouge in the centre. Clear traces of wear on the cutting edge can only be seen on B. and F.

The particularly robust construction and ergonomic design argue for the use of this particular type of chisel mainly in stone-carving. The strong damage to the end taking successive blows tells the same story. These chisels could be used both as wedges to split stone blocks or as tools to work their surface. They may also have been used in woodworking, especially in dealing with long beams or planks.

They belong to type 2 of Evely's (1993) typology. The coexistence of three different types of chisel (1, 2 and 3) in the same tool assemblage from Rotasi indicates the highly specialised nature of tools during the Neopalatial era, apparently echoing the similarly complex needs of Minoan society.

References

Unpublished. Cf. Πλάτων 1957, 339. 1958, 480; Shaw 1973, 70-75; Evely 1993, 2-19, especially 8 no.58-63.

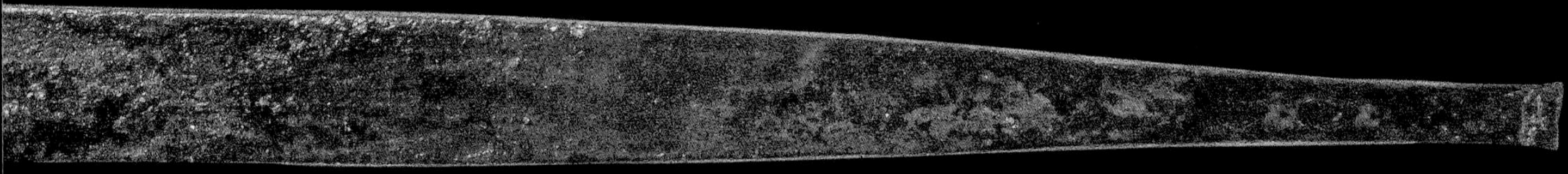

A

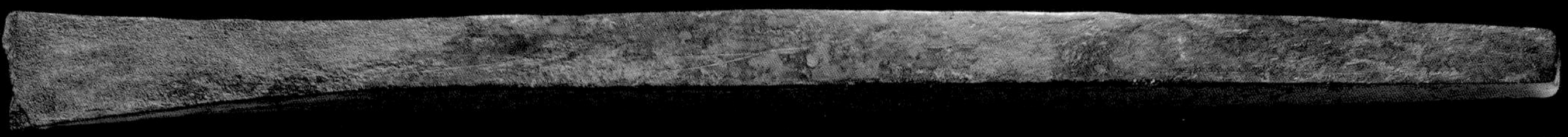

B

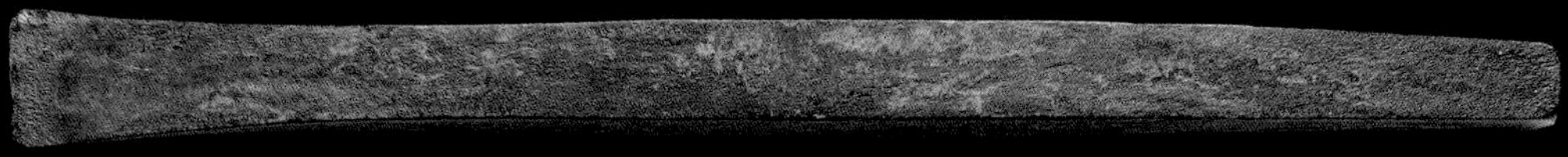

C

D

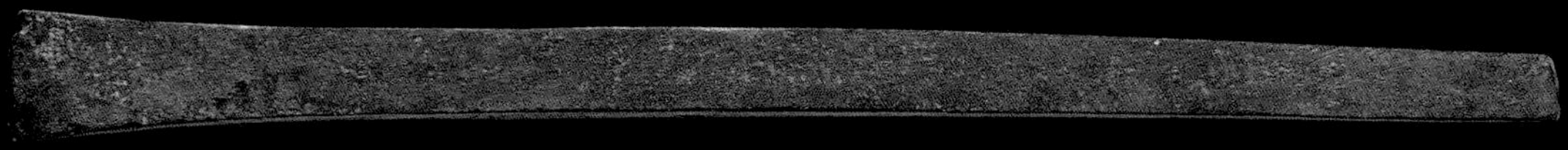

E

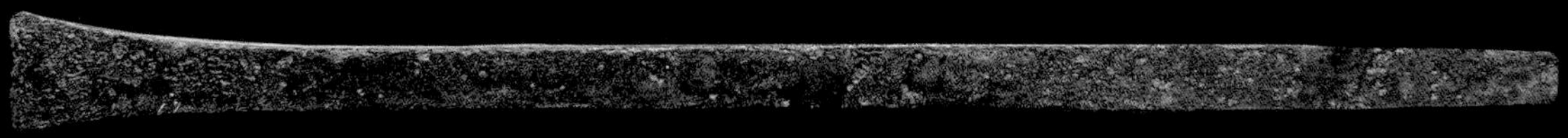

F

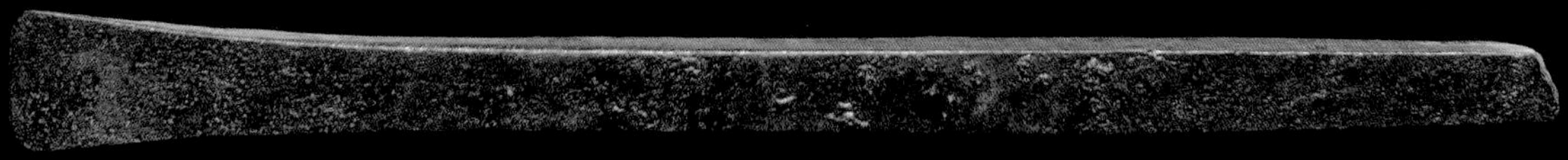

G

38

渐变柄宽凿器（两件）

米诺斯晚期Ⅰ至Ⅱ（公元前 1600 ~ 前 1400 年）
青铜
A) 长 23.8 厘米，最大宽度 1.8 厘米，厚 1.1 厘米；B) 长 40.5 厘米，最大宽度 4 厘米
发现于克里特岛罗塔西的阿斯普罗利瓦达遗址
希腊伊拉克利翁考古博物馆藏，编号 X2478、X2474

这两件青铜凿器制作工艺精巧，长度较长。凿器尾端柄部较窄，顺柄部朝凿器中心及切削刃方向，宽度共出现两次明显增大，使得凿器侧边略微呈波浪形。柄部中央厚 9 毫米；切削刃经过磨平形成直边，厚度仅为 2 毫米。B 号凿器的受击端可见磨损痕迹，上表面因重复敲击出现了斜角。下方出现的纵向缺口也可能是在使用过程中造成的损伤。

凿器是最常见的金属工具之一，是各类工坊不可或缺的工具，这种工具可追溯到米诺斯早期。在新王宫期，凿器长度有所增加，但通常不超过 34 厘米。该时期柄部和切削刃形状多样，整体造型也更为精细。这种改进不仅提升了工具性能，也方便工匠使用。

不同形制的凿器可用于加工木材、石材、象牙及金属等不同材质。许多工具切削或雕刻留下的痕迹都得以保存。在整块方石的切割表面上、锯齿的制作过程中、青铜工具铸造完成后的修整中、黄金片的切割和装饰中，以及其他许多场景中均可见凿痕。

这种凿器属于伊夫利（Evely，1993 年）划分的 3b 型，这种先进工具在新王宫期得到广泛使用。柄部靠近尾端处采用狭窄设计，以便嵌套木质柄套，方便使用者握持。

与这两件凿器一同发现的还有锯子、双斧，以及其他型号的凿器等。这批工具的出土表明阿斯普罗利瓦达遗址的米诺斯聚落存在工坊；同时，这也可能反映出拥有金属物品在当时具有重要的社会和经济意义。

（斯特拉·曼达莱基）

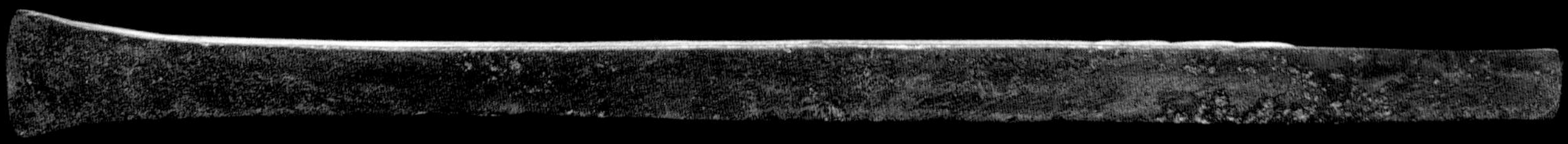

A

Two chisels with a variable shank width

Late Minoan I – II (1600-1400 BCE)

Bronze

A) L. 23.8 cm, max. w. 1.8 cm, th.1.1 cm, B) L. 40.5 cm, max. w. 4 cm

Rotasi, Asprolivada site

Archaeological Museum of Heraklion, X2478, 2474

Long chisels with a narrow width to the shank before the butt, which then increases noticeably towards the centre and again to the cutting edge, making a slightly wavy profile to the edge: all indicating a highly refined process of manufacture. The shank is 9 mm thick in the central section and tapers to 2 mm at the cutting edge, which is flattened and given a straight edge. Traces of wear from use can be seen on the struck butt of B, where the upper surface is chamfered, apparently from repeated strikes with the mallet or such. A vertical chip just below this may also be due to the tool's use.

Chisels in general are the most common metal tool encountered, being required in every sort of workshop. Although their manufacture goes back to the Early Minoan era, during the Neopalatial period they acquire a longer length that usually does not exceed 34 cm, with a variety of shapes for the shank and particularly the cutting edge, and careful shaping of the whole. This improved the technical performance of the tool and facilitated its use by craftsmen. The different types of chisel indicate specialised uses in working wood, stone, ivory and metals. Quite often traces left by the cutting or carving end of the tool are preserved: they appear on the surfaces of the cut blocks on ashlar façades, in the making of teeth on a saw, in the final working of bronze tools after their casting in moulds, in the cutting and decoration of gold sheet, and in many other cases.

This type belongs to category 3b of Evely's (1993) typology and is considered particularly sophisticated and popular during the Neopalatial era. The small width of the shank at the top of the butt allows the wooden sheathing of the tool here to provide a better grip for the user.

The finding of the chisels together with other tools (saws, double axe, chisels of different types), together constituting a hoard, indicates the existence of a workshop in the Minoan settlement located at the Asprolivada site; however, it may reflect the particular social and economic importance the possession of metal objects bestowed.

References

Unpublished. Cf. Πλάτων 1957, 339. 1958, 480; Shaw 1973, 70-75; Branigan 1974, 79-80; Evely 1993, 2-19, especially 10 no.123, Type 3b.

(Stella Mandalaki)

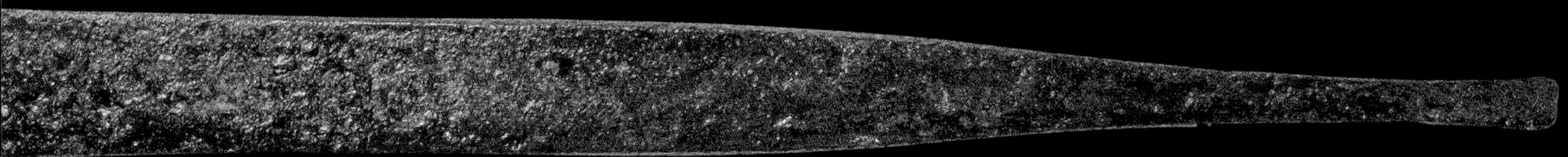

B

39

双刃斧

米诺斯晚期Ⅰ至Ⅱ（公元前1600~前1400年）

青铜

长17.5厘米，最大宽度5.5厘米，厚2.5厘米，斧眼直径1.9厘米

发现于克里特岛罗塔西的阿斯普罗利瓦达遗址

希腊伊拉克利翁考古博物馆藏，编号X2469

双刃斧整体及斧刃均呈简单的矩形，斧刃略弯，刃部锋利。斧刃边缘的一小部分磨损痕迹表明，该工具并未用于加工硬质材料，而可能是用于木工和日常家务。斧眼两侧有细长的深槽，铸造过程中，熔融金属可能从此流入模具。不过，这些凹槽也可能是为了嵌入木楔以增强斧头和柄部的稳定性。

（斯特拉·曼达莱基）

39

Double axe

Late Minoan Ⅰ–Ⅱ (1600-1400 BCE)

Bronze

L.17.5 cm, max. w. 5.5 cm, th. 2.5 cm, diam. shaft-hole 1.9 cm

Rotasi, Asprolivada site

Archaeological Museum of Heraklion, X2469

Double axe with a simple rectangular outline to the body and blades, the last being slightly curved, and sharp along the length of the cutting edges. Wear from use on a small part of the edges testifies that the tool was not used in the processing of hard materials, but probably in carpentry and for daily household needs. Elongated deep grooves on either side of the shaft-hole indicate either points where the molten metal entered the mould in the cast, or the fitting of wooden wedges to enhance the stability of head and handle.

References

Unpublished. Cf. Πλάτων 1957, 339. 1958, 480; Evely 1993, 41-55, especially 49 no.175-77; Lowe-Fri 2011, 110 no.156.

(Stella Mandalaki)

40

双刃斧

米诺斯晚期Ⅰ至Ⅱ（公元前1600～前1400年）

青铜

长20.2厘米，最大宽度5.9厘米，厚2.4厘米，斧眼直径2厘米

发现于克里特岛罗塔西的阿斯普罗利瓦达遗址

希腊伊拉克利翁考古博物馆藏，编号X2468

双刃斧整体轮廓近似矩形，刃部锋利。斧眼两侧各有一条与之相对的纵向凹槽，与斧刃走向一致。这些凹槽可能是在工具铸造过程中形成的，或许是为了嵌入木楔以加固木柄，从而增强工具的稳定性。另一种解释认为，这些凹槽是当时斧具制造工艺的产物，凹槽是纵向浇口的末端，熔融金属从陶坩埚中倒出后，会通过这些凹槽流入闭合的双片模具中。斧身两侧表面有许多细小圆形剥片痕迹，表明这件工具可能使用了双片砂模铸造技术。这类模具由有机材料制成，因此未能保存下来。具体而言，模具会用到两个木制半框架，框架内填充沙子，随后压入工具复制品进行印模。此外，还会在模具中设置木制通道，引导熔融金属流动。砂模铸造的双刃斧形态更为精致，而石模铸造的工具则通常较为厚重。

在罗塔西的米诺斯遗址中，同时发现了用于木工和石工的不同类型凿器以及实用型双刃斧，表明当时的人们已经能够组合使用各类工具加工多种材料。

（斯特拉·曼达莱基）

40

Double axe

Late Minoan Ⅰ–Ⅱ (1600-1400 BCE)

Bronze

L. 20.2 cm, max. w. 5.9 cm, th. 2.4 cm, diam. shaft-hole 2 cm

Rotasi, Asprolivada site

Archaeological Museum of Heraklion, X2468

Double axe with simple near-rectangular outline to body and blades with sharp cutting edges. On either side of the circular shaft-hole are two distinct opposed, longitudinal grooves running along the blade. These were created during the casting of the tool and probably served for the reinforcement of the wooden handle with lateral wedges of wood to provide better stability to the tool. According to another interpretation, the grooves along the blades are due to the manner of manufacture of the tool. In this case they are the ends of the vertical pouring gates through which the molten metal was poured from the clay melting crucible into the closed two-piece mould. The abundant microscopic circular flaking on the surface of both sides of the tool is probably an indication of it being cast using a two-piece sand mould. Moulds of this type have not survived, since they consist of organic materials: two wooden halves with sand inside, into which are impressed replicas of the tools to be cast, with wooden channels to assist the passage of the molten metal. Double axes made in sand moulds are more refined in form than those made in stone moulds, which come out thicker.

The coexistence of utilitarian double axes with chisels of different types, suitable for woodcutting and stonecutting, in the same "hoard" from the Minoan settlement at Rotasi, suggests the use of kit suited to the processing of different materials.

References

Unpublished. Cf. Πλάτων 1957, 339. 1958, 480; Evely 1993, 41-55, especially 49 no.175-77; Lowe-Fri 2011, especially 110 no.155.

(Stella Mandalaki)

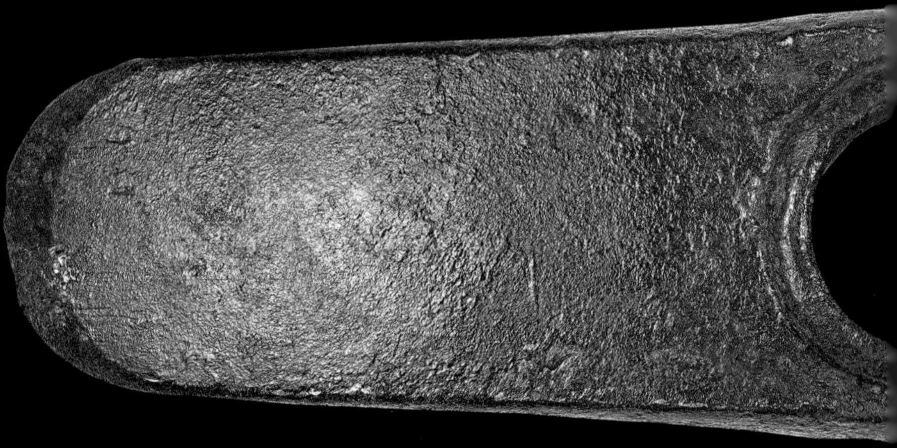

41

双刃扁斧

米诺斯中期Ⅲ至米诺斯晚期Ⅰ（公元前 1700 ~ 前 1450 年）

青铜

长 25.7 厘米，宽 4.7 厘米

发现于克里特岛克诺索斯王宫的西北厅

希腊伊拉克利翁考古博物馆藏，编号 X2080

长形、舌状的双刃扁斧，其两侧刃部尺寸略有差异，围绕中央圆形斧眼对称分布。扁斧在斧眼处略微外扩形成“肩部”，斧眼周围作了加固处理，上下方均有明显的凸出边缘。刃部末端非常圆润，弧度较大，横截面略微削薄，刃边因使用而出现轻微的卷边变形。

这种圆润刃部的设计引发了有关工具动力学和人体工学的讨论。这件器物与克诺索斯西北厅发现的其他青铜工具也有很大关联。如果圆边是因使用而变钝，那这件工具可能正处于维修或回收的状态，但较为对称的刃部弯曲程度又与这一观点相矛盾。如果圆润的刃部符合其功能性特点的话，那么这件工具可能是用于木工或者石工作业。其结构牢固、尺寸适中，还可能用于剥离软岩、采石或挖沟。

（迪米特里斯·斯法基纳基斯）

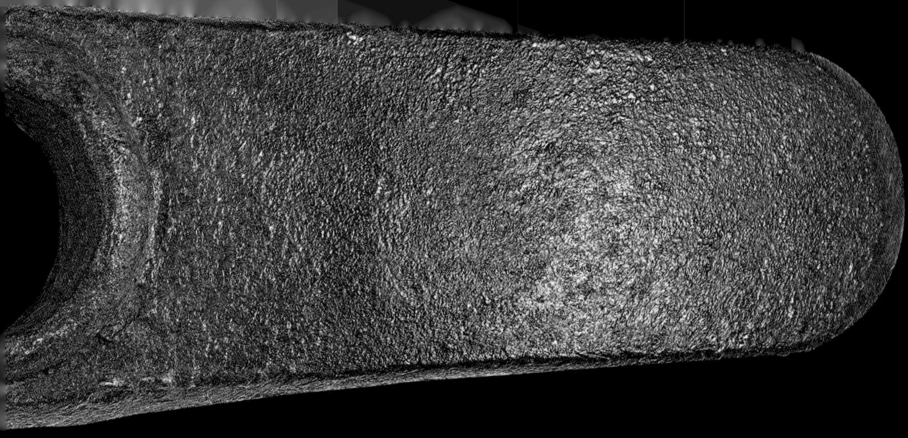

41

Double adze

Middle Minoan III – Late Minoan I (1700-1450 BCE)

Bronze

L. 25.7 cm, w. 4.7 cm

Knossos, palace, Northwest House

Archaeological Museum of Heraklion, X2080

Long, tongue-shaped blades of slightly different sizes set either side of a central circular shaft-hole, where the tool expands slightly into "shoulders". The shaft-hole is reinforced with a rim that protrudes-above and even more so below. The blade ends are rounded in a strongly convex line, showing a slightly bevelled cross-section. The edges show a slight folding (burring) deformation from use.

The rounded working edges just described have understandably provoked discussion about the dynamics and ergonomic range of the tool. Its identity is further affected by the context and interpretation given to the store of bronze tools found in the Northwest House at Knossos. If these rounded edges are blunted through use – an interpretation that contradicts the symmetry of the edge's curvature – the tool was probably being held for repair or even for recycling. If it is a functional feature, then the tool could be included in the kit of a carpenter, even a stonecutter. Its strong dynamics combined with its particular size make possible an alternative employment in chipping, quarrying and trenching in soft rock.

References

PM II, 627-29, fig. 392. Evely 1993, 62-63, 67.

(Dimitris Sfakianakis)

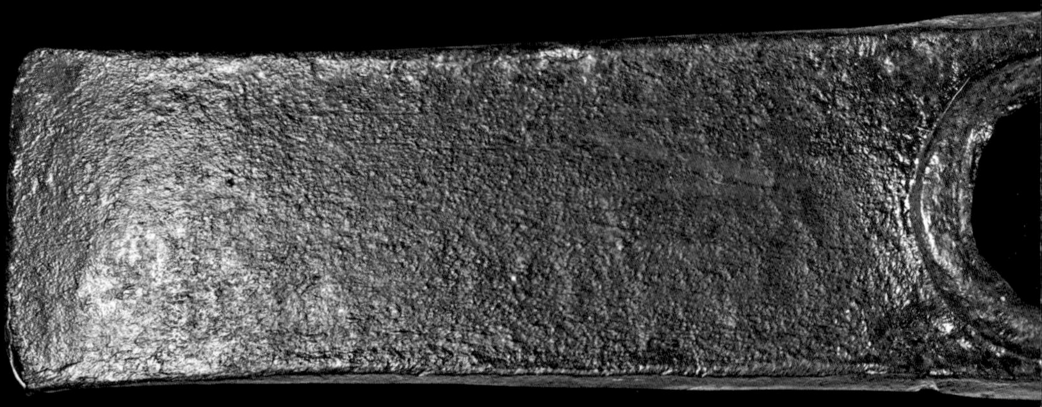

42

双刃扁斧

米诺斯中期Ⅲ至米诺斯晚期Ⅰ（公元前 1700 ~ 前 1450 年）

青铜

长 32 厘米，宽 5.2 厘米

发现于克里特岛克诺索斯王宫的西北厅

希腊伊拉克利翁考古博物馆藏，编号 X2079

双刃扁斧，两侧的长形刃边长度不等。刃部围绕着一个圆形斧眼呈对称分布，斧眼位于一个矩形凸起部分内，使得工具两侧形成明显的“肩部”。斧眼以管状边缘加固，上下方均明显凸出。工具的一侧刃边因使用而出现轻微的卷边变形。

这是从克诺索斯王宫西北厅青铜器窖藏中发现的一件独特工具，与其一同发现的还有几件同类型工具。工具的形状与“双刃斧”相似，但切削刃方向与斧柄所在轴线成直角。这种工具的功能一直是讨论的焦点，这也影响到其最终命名。若将其视为双刃扁斧，则该工具可能主要用于木材刨平和整形，而非简单的砍伐工作；此外，它也可能用于加工软石材料。由于缺乏该工具在其原始“使用寿命”期间的直接使用证据，我们只能根据它与现代农用扁斧或锄头的相似性进行命名。

（迪米特里斯·斯法基纳基斯）

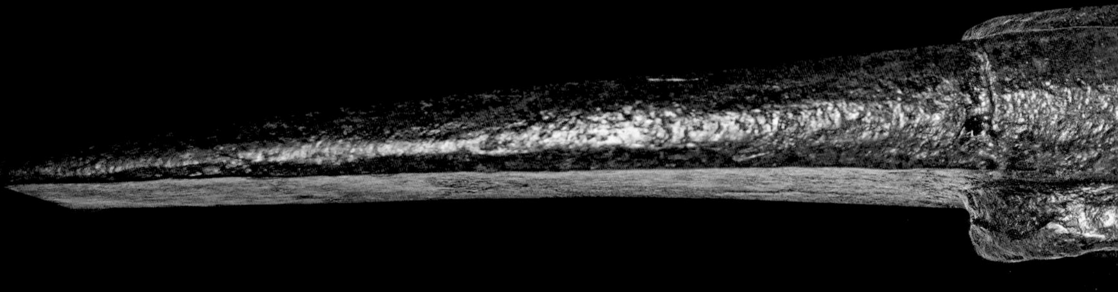

42

Double adze

Middle Minoan III – Late Minoan I (1700-1450 BCE)

Bronze

L. 32 cm, w. 5.2 cm

Knossos, palace, Northwest House

Archaeological Museum of Heraklion, X2079

Two long blades, squared off at the cutting edges, of unequal length. The blades are set on either side of a circular shaft-hole, itself placed within a rectangular swelling giving prominent "shoulders" to the centre of the tool's sides. The hole is reinforced with a tubular rim, protruding above and even more below. One of the edges shows a slight folding (burring) from use.

One of the distinctive tools in the hoard of bronze objects in the Northwest House of the Knossian palace, where others of the same type were also found. The form of the tool is comparable to that of the "double axe": the difference being in how the cutting edge here is at right angles in relation to the axis of the shaft. The functional dynamics of the tool is a subject of debate, which also affects the choice of its exact name: as a double adze, it is used not so much in chopping wood, as in planing and shaping it; but it may also work soft stones. In the absence of direct evidence of its use during its original "lifetime", substantial similarities to the modern agricultural adze or hoe are noted.

References

PM II, 627-29, fig.392. Evely 1993, 63.

(Dimitris Sfakianakis)

43

双刃斧

米诺斯中期Ⅲ至米诺斯晚期Ⅰ（公元前 1700 ~ 前 1450 年）
青铜
长 13 厘米，最大宽度 5.5 厘米，厚 2.5 厘米，斧眼直径 2 厘米
发现于克里特岛克诺索斯王宫的西北厅
希腊伊拉克利翁考古博物馆藏，编号 X2078

双刃斧，刃部压平且呈弧形。一侧刃部磨损严重，另一侧刃部卷边凸起，形成压平表面，表明其可能在石工作业中因严重撞击应力出现变形。两侧刃部保存状态不同，意味着两者用途可能不同。例如较重的刃部可能被用作锤子。

刃部表面也有磨损痕迹。斧眼两侧可以看到细长凹槽，可能是为了在此处嵌入垂直于木柄的楔子。此外，也有一种观点认为，经由纵向浇口倒入的熔融金属需要通过这些凹槽才能流入模具内部。

这件工具出土于克诺索斯王宫西北厅的地下室，一同发现的还有其他工具和青铜器（如双刃扁斧、双刃斧、匕首、三足碗形容器以及一把剑），它们共同构成了一个“窖藏”，被精心隐藏在石砌的壁龛中。

（斯特拉·曼达莱基）

43

Double axe

Middle Minoan Ⅲ– Late Minoan Ⅰ (1700-1450 BCE)
Bronze
L. 13 cm, max. w. 5.5 cm, th. 2.5 cm, diam. shaft-hole 2 cm
Knossos, palace, Northwest House
Archaeological Museum of Heraklion, X2078

Double axe with distinct flattened and curved ends. One is worn down to a pronounced thickness and the other has been folded back (burred) to create a flattened surface of convex profile; this is an obvious indication of having suffered severe impact stress, apparently due to the use of the tool in working stone. The two blades may have been put to different uses, given their different states of preservation. The heavier one could have been used as a hammer.

The surfaces of the blades are also worn. On either side of the shaft-hole, elongated grooves are seen – perhaps for accepting wooden wedges running perpendicular to the axis of the handle. Another view is that they indicate the points of entry of the molten metal into the interior of the mould, through vertical pouring gates.

The tool comes from the basement of the house, where it was deposited together with other tools and bronze objects (double adzes, double axes, daggers, a tripod lebes and a sword), which together constitute a “hoard”, carefully hidden in a stone-built alcove.

References

PM II, 627-29, fig.392. Evely 1993, 41-55, especially 47 no.119. Lowe-Fri 2011, especially 95 no.64.

(Stella Mandalaki)

44

双刃斧

米诺斯中期Ⅲ至米诺斯晚期Ⅰ（公元前 1700 ~ 前 1450 年）
青铜
长 22 厘米，最大宽度 5.5 厘米，厚 3.1 厘米，斧眼直径 1.8 厘米
发现于克里特岛克诺索斯王宫的西北厅
希腊伊拉克利翁考古博物馆藏，编号 X2076

双刃斧斧身和刃部轮廓浑然一体，呈近似矩形，刃部平直且锋利。斧眼两侧未设用于固定木柄的纵向凹槽，工具整体牢固性可能因此受到影响，对于这种斧身长、斧眼小的工具更是如此。一般而言，与椭圆形斧眼相比，采用圆形斧眼结构时，斧柄与斧头的结合不够稳固，容易导致斧头转动。因此，为确保稳定性，除了在轴孔两侧纵向凹槽中嵌入木楔外，还可能需要选用特殊形制的斧柄，确保其直径从斧眼处向上逐渐加大。此外，相较于短柄双刃斧，长柄双刃斧可能具有更好的操控性。

此工具刃部锋利，表明其主要用于木工作业。工具的主体表面已有磨损。

（斯特拉·曼达莱基）

44

Double axe

Middle Minoan Ⅲ – Late Minoan Ⅰ (1700-1450 BCE)
Bronze
L. 22 cm, max. w. 5.5 cm, th. 3.1 cm, diam. shaft-hole 1.8 cm
Knossos, palace, Northwest House
Archaeological Museum of Heraklion, X2076

Double axe with body and blade all of one profile (i.e. nigh rectangular) with straight and sharp cutting edges. It does not have the elongated depressions on either side of the shaft-hole to assist in locking the wooden handle to the metal head, a lack that would likely affect the solidity of the whole, especially so given the length of the tool and the small diameter of the shaft-hole. As a rule, the circular shaft-holes, in contrast to the elliptical ones, do not ensure such a safe fit of handle and head: the latter being able to turn around on the handle. For this reason, in addition to the wooden wedges that were placed in the elongated grooves on either side of the shaft-hole, it is assumed that the diameter of the shaft increased gradually between the shaft-hole to the handle's end above it. It is also possible that double axes with long wooden handles responded better in the hands of the user than those with short shafts.

The sharpness of the cutting edges of the tool indicates its use in carpentry. Body surfaces worn.

References

PM II, 627-29, fig.392. Evely 1993, 41-55, especially 42 no.4. Lowe-Fri 2011, especially 95 no.62.

(Stella Mandalaki)

45

双刃斧

米诺斯晚期 Ⅰ 至 Ⅱ（公元前 1600 ~ 前 1400 年）
青铜
长 15.8 厘米，最大宽度 5.4 厘米，厚 2.5 厘米，斧眼直径 1.9 厘米
发现于克里特岛罗塔西的阿斯普罗利瓦达遗址
希腊伊拉克利翁考古博物馆藏，编号 X2470

双刃斧的刃部具有清晰的切割边缘，弧形轮廓，因使用而变得圆润且有磨损痕迹。其中一侧刃部发现有数个较浅凹槽，可能是在使用过程中受损，而非开刃工艺特意制作。在闭合模具中铸造完成后，首先会用打击工具对刃部进行初步成型和削薄（形成斜面），然后使用磨石将其磨锐。开刃工艺决定了工具是用于木工还是石工，具体则取决于刃部的形状和锋利程度。此双刃斧刃部虽有磨损，但并未显示出过度使用痕迹，因此斧眼处的纵向裂纹可能是铸造过程中的失误所致。斧眼两侧有与刃部走向一致的较深凹槽，用于嵌入木楔，从而将斧头更好地固定到斧柄上。另一种观点认为，这些凹槽位于浇口末端，熔融金属在铸造过程中必须经由此处流入闭合模具。

（斯特拉・曼达莱基）

45

Double axe

Late Minoan Ⅰ–Ⅱ (1600-1400 BCE)
Bronze
L. 15.8 cm, max. w. 5.4 cm, th. 2.5 cm, diam. shaft-hole 1.9 cm
Rotasi, Asprolivada site
Archaeological Museum of Heraklion, X2470

Double axe with distinct cutting edges with a curved profile, which are rounded and worn from use. Additional shallow gouges are found on the side of one blade, probably related to work-damage suffered by the tool rather than shaping its edges. This last act, after the cast in a closed mould, was carried out first with a percussion tool to form and thin them (bevels), and then with grinding stones for putting on the actual edge. This final treatment determined the use of the tool for wood or stone-working, depending on the shape and sharpness of the striking edges. The strong crack across the width of the tool, at the point of the shaft-hole, may have been due to a failure during casting, since the edges of the blades, although worn, do not indicate heavy use of the blade. On either side of the shaft-hole, deep grooves running along the blades ensure a more effective securing of the metal head to the handle with wooden wedges, or according to another interpretation, they are the end of the pouring gates through which the molten metal was poured into the closed mould during casting.

References

Unpublished. Cf. Πλάτων 1957, 339; 1958, 480; Evely 1993, 41-55, especially 49 no.175-77; Lowe-Fri 2011, especially 110 no.157.

(Stella Mandalaki)

46

锯

米诺斯晚期 I 至 II（公元前 1600 ~ 前 1400 年）

青铜

残长 34.9 厘米，最大宽度 7.1 厘米

发现于克里特岛罗塔西的阿斯普罗利瓦达遗址

希腊伊拉克利翁考古博物馆藏，编号 X2484

长形、宽刃青铜锯，由一块金属薄片制成，上缘略微弯曲，锯齿边缘明显弯曲。锯片末端较窄且圆润，边缘有缺损，锯齿因磨损，大部分已缺失。柄部连接的矩形区域有三个贯穿孔，其中一个孔直径较小，可能是主孔的附加孔（该主孔与锯片末端的另一个孔位于同一水平轴线上，且直径相同）。

与此件青铜锯同批出土的青铜工具共计 18 件（包括凿器、刀具和双刃斧），另外还有一枚矛头。这些工具可能来自附近米诺斯聚落的一处工坊，也可能是为了躲避入侵者而藏匿起来的青铜物品。这是保存最好的古代锯子之一，可能用于木工，或用于切割软质石材。

（斯特拉・曼达莱基）

46

Saw

Late Minoan I – II (1600-1400 BCE)

Bronze

L. pres. 34.9 cm, max. w. 7.1 cm

Rotasi, Asprolivada site

Archaeological Museum of Heraklion, X2484

Long, broad-bladed saw, made from a sheet of metal, with a slightly curved upper edge and definitely curved serrated edge (teeth). The narrow rounded end to the blade is chipped at its edges, the teeth mostly worn away by abrasion. In the rectangular area of the handle attachment there are three through-holes, one of which, of a smaller diameter, seems to be an adjunct of the main one further in (on the same horizontal axis as another at the blade's end, and of the same diameter).

The single saw in the well-stocked set of 18 bronze tools and a spearhead (along with chisels, cutters and double axes) belongs either to a workshop located in an adjacent Minoan settlement, or more likely is from a hoard of bronzes, hidden to escape notice by unwelcome possibly invaders. This is one of the best surviving examples of a commonly encountered saw for carpentry, perhaps also soft stone cutting.

References

Unpublished. For the location see Πλάτων 1957, 339; 1958, 480.

(Stella Mandalaki)

47

双刃斧

米诺斯晚期Ⅰ至Ⅱ（公元前1600～前1400年）

青铜

长12厘米，最大宽度5.5厘米，厚2.5厘米，斧眼直径2厘米

发现于克里特岛古尔尼亚米诺斯居址的F18号房屋

希腊伊拉克利翁考古博物馆藏，编号X555

小型双刃斧，斧刃略高于工具主体。刃部略微弯曲且非常锋利，可能表明该工具使用频率不高或其刃部经过打磨，也可能表明其主要用于木工或日常家务中。斧眼两侧有两条非常明显的细长凹槽，这些凹槽是在工具铸造过程中形成的。它们可能是为了嵌入木楔，以增强斧头与木柄的连接稳定性，提高使用的安全性。另一种解释认为，这些凹槽是与纵向浇口相连的通道，熔融金属从陶坩埚中倒出后，通过这些凹槽流入闭合的双片模具。

与这件双刃斧一同出土的青铜工具还包括一把锯子、五柄凿具和一个鱼钩。

双刃斧不仅是木匠和伐木工的必要工具，也是满足日常家庭需求的基本工具。

（斯特拉·曼达莱基）

47

Double axe

Late Minoan Ⅰ–Ⅱ (1600-1400 BCE)

Bronze

L. 12 cm, max. w. 5.5 cm, th. 2.5 cm, diam. shaft-hole 2 cm

Gournia, Minoan settlement, House F18

Archaeological Museum of Heraklion, X555

Small double axe with cutting edges that scarcely protrude beyond the body of the tool. The cutting edges are only slightly curved and particularly sharp. This last indicates perhaps a limited use of the tool and/or the recent sharpening of its blades, or perhaps its employment in carpentry or everyday household work. On either side of the shaft-hole are two very distinct opposed and elongated grooves created during the casting of the tool. It has been suggested that they enabled the reinforcement of the wooden handle with wooden wedges to ensure the better stability of the tool and security of the attachment of the handle. According to another interpretation, these grooves were fue to the construction of the tool: they were connected to the vertical pouring gates through which the molten metal was poured from the clay melting crucible into the closed two-piece mould.

The axe is part of a "hoard" of bronze tools, which also includes a saw, five chisels and a fish-hook.

Double axes, in addition to being a necessary tool of the carpenter and woodcutter, are a basic tool in the context of the daily needs of the household.

References

Hawes et al. 1908, 34 pl.IV, no. 22. Evely 1993, 41-55, especially 42 no.13, Type 1. Lowe-Fri 2011, especially 93 no.50.

(Stella Mandalaki)

48

双刃斧锤

米诺斯晚期 I 至 II（公元前 1600 ~ 前 1400 年）

青铜

长 11.8 厘米，最大宽度 6.3 厘米，厚 2.5 厘米，斧眼直径 1.7 厘米

发现于克里特岛古尔尼亚的米诺斯居址

希腊伊拉克利翁考古博物馆藏，编号 X965

双刃斧，刃部略凸且被压平。由于工具过度使用和反复敲击，刃部受到了严重损坏。一侧刃部呈现出不规则的严重卷边（毛刺状），表明该工具可能原本作为双刃斧使用，但由于刃部磨损严重，后转而用作锤子。扎克罗斯也存在类似实例。工具变形可能是石工作业中反复敲击坚固凿器的末端所致。有一种观点认为，这是一把采矿工具，但由于其锡含量低，耐用性有限。

这件工具体现了双刃斧两侧刃部的实用性。首先，由于双刃设计，工具可以长时间连续使用，无需频繁打磨单侧刃部；其次，两侧刃部可以满足不同使用需求。

斧眼两侧有纵向短凹槽，用于向斧柄垂直方向嵌入楔子，斧眼直径也因此有所增大。

（斯特拉・曼达莱基）

48

Double axe-hammer

Late Minoan I–II (1600-1400 BCE)

Bronze

L.11.8 cm, max. w. 6.3 cm, th. 2.5 cm, diam. shaft-hole 1.7 cm

Gournia, Minoan settlement

Archaeological Museum of Heraklion, X965

Double axe with slightly protruding and flattened cutting edges, which have been severely damaged by excessive stress on the tool, from heavy use and repeated blows. On one of the two edges in particular, the edge of the blade has been folded back (burred) in an irregular and extensive manner, suggesting that the tool was used as a hammer, possibly after it had ceased to be used as a double axe due to the wear and damage done to the original cutting edges. A similar example comes from Zakros. The deformation of the tool could be due to continuous impacts on the butts of robust chisels in the context of stone-working. According to one interpretation, it is a mining tool, but one of limited durability due to a low tin content.

This tool highlights the practical importance of the two blades of the double axe. First, they allow the lengthy and uninterrupted use of the tool, since it has two cutting edges, with the result that frequent sharpening of a single edge is unnecessary; and second, the two blades can serve different needs.

Short longitudinal grooves on either side of the shaft-hole for fitting wedges perpendicular to the wooden handle have enlarged its diameter.

References

Shaw 1973, 45-47, 49 fig.35b (for a similar double axe from Zakros). Evely 1993, 49 no.200, 51, 101 no. 18. Lowe-Fri 2011, especially 93 no.51.

(Stella Mandalaki)

49

双刃斧

米诺斯晚期Ⅰ至Ⅱ（公元前1600～前1400年）

青铜

长13.3厘米，最大宽度6.4厘米，厚2.3厘米，斧眼直径1.8厘米

发现于克里特岛古尔尼亚宫殿建筑以北的G1号房间

希腊伊拉克利翁考古博物馆藏，编号X554

小型双刃斧，其切削刃略凸，呈扁平且弯曲的形状，边缘因过度使用而出现卷边。工具两侧不对称，表明其曾承受过强烈应力，导致两侧刃部长度有所差异。斧刃磨损严重，表明这件工具可能经常被用于劈砍坚硬的表面，例如树干或石材。

除了磨损痕迹外，此件双刃斧还存在铸造失误和成型不全的迹象。一侧刃部平坦，切削边缘存在小凹，可能是由于原料熔液温度不足，铸造过程中熔融金属未完全填充模具所致。另一侧刃部铸造后未得到完全修整，因此残留有金属小凸起。受模具未预热、熔融金属量不足、模具中气体留存等因素影响，双刃斧表面特别容易出现铸造缺陷。此外，铸造后刃部锻造不全、多余金属残留未清除等情况也较为常见。

（斯特拉·曼达莱基）

49

Double axe

Late Minoan Ⅰ–Ⅱ (1600-1400 BCE)

Bronze

L. 13.3 cm, max. w. 6.4 cm, th. 2.3 cm, diam. shaft-hole 1.8 cm

Gournia, north of the palatial building, Room G1

Archaeological Museum of Heraklion, X554

Small double axe with slightly protruding cutting edges that have a flattened, curved shape and a burred edge from heavy use. The strong stresses the tool was subject to are further evidenced by the alteration of the symmetry of the tool, with the two halves/blades differing in length. The heavy wear indicates the use of this tool in working hard surfaces, perhaps tree trunks or stones.

In addition to wear, manufacturing failures and incomplete formation in the casting are witnessed. The small hollow on the edge of the flattened cutting edge of one blade is due to the mould not being filled with sufficient molten metal in the cast, due to low temperature of the molten raw material. A small protruding portion of metal on the edge of the other blade was not chiselled off after the casting. Casting failures due to the non-preheating of the mould, an insufficient amount of metal, the entrapment of gases inside the mould and other factors are particularly often observed on the surface of double axes. Incomplete forging of the blades and negligence in removing excess metal during the last refining stage of the tools after casting are also detected.

References

Hawes et al. 1908, 34 pl.IV, no. 23. Shaw 1973, 45-47. Evely 1993, 41-55, especially 42 no.12, Type 1. Lowe-Fri 2011, especially 92-93 no.49.

(Stella Mandalaki)

50

钻杆（两件）

米诺斯晚期Ⅰ至Ⅱ（公元前1600～前1400年）

青铜

A) 长21厘米，直径0.7厘米

B) 长26厘米，宽0.65厘米

发现于克里特岛古尔尼亚的米诺斯居址

希腊伊拉克利翁考古博物馆藏，编号X567、X564

两件细长实心金属钻杆，保存完好。A呈圆柱形，两端均为平面；B呈方形棍状，一端有磨损，另一端略微扁平如抹刀状。它们细长的形状表明，这两件工具主要用于木工，特别是用于钻取较深的孔洞。旋转动作可以通过手动或机械方式实现。在古尔尼亚和扎克罗斯均发现了两件类似工具。不过，这些工具也可能在石雕工作中用作切割工具。

（斯特拉·曼达莱基）

50

Two drills

Late Minoan Ⅰ–Ⅱ (1600-1400 BCE)

Bronze

A) L. 21 cm, diam. 0.7 cm

B) L. 26 cm, w. 0.65 cm

Gournia, Minoan settlement

Archaeological Museum of Heraklion, X567, 564

Two long, slender drill shafts of solid metal, which are preserved intact. A is cylindrical with flat surfaces at both ends and B is rod-shaped, of a square section with one end worn and the other end slightly flattened, like a spatula. Their thin and elongated shape suggests uses in carpentry and in particular in drilling holes of considerable depth. The rotary motion was achieved by hand or mechanically. Two more similar instances also come from Gournia and another two from Zakros. However, it cannot be ruled out that these are cutting tools used in stone-carving.

References

Hawes et al. 1908, 34 pl.IV, no.12, 8. Shaw 1973, 69-70. Evely 1993, 76-85, especially 78 no.11, fig.35.

(Stella Mandalaki)

51

锯

米诺斯晚期ⅠB（公元前1500～前1450年）

青铜

现长53厘米，展开长约1.22米

发现于克里特岛卡托扎克罗斯王宫

希腊伊拉克利翁考古博物馆藏，编号X2600

长形青铜锯，锯片经过两次折叠。未钻孔一端明显较窄，宽度为7厘米，连接锯柄的钻孔一端的宽度则达到9.5厘米。宽端有至少6个直径不同的孔洞，以2—1—3的组合方式呈三角形排列，表明此处曾连接有一个特别坚固的木手柄，以确保切割过程中锯子不会弯曲变形。部分孔洞可能为后期钻制的，以便将手柄固定得更为牢固。

这件青铜锯发掘自宫殿西翼的工具堆中，是同类工具中保存最为完好的一件。此类工具的发现证实宫殿存在木工工坊。不过，锯齿的磨损程度也表明这些青铜锯可能用于切割多孔石材或其他石灰石。

扎克罗斯王宫出土了包含这些青铜锯在内的大量工具，证明宫殿工坊作业活动频繁，并且宫殿匠人普遍使用了先进、专业的工具套件。锯齿磨损严重、手柄可能进行过进一步加固，这些证据表明，该工具不仅是木工工具，还可能用作石工作业，并且使用频次极高，锯齿已完全钝化。锯片被折叠收纳起来，表明这件工具已不再使用，并准备进行金属回收。

（迪米特里斯·斯法基纳基斯）

51

Saw

Late Minoan I B (1500–1450 BCE)
Bronze
Current l. 53 cm – (unfolded) approx. 1.22 m
Kato Zakros, palace
Archaeological Museum of Heraklion, X2600

Long saw blade folded back on itself twice, the unpierced end being noticeably narrower (7 cm) than the pierced end to which the handle was attached (9.5 cm). The cluster of at least 6 holes of varying diameter in the wider end, in groups of 2 – 1 – 3 holes in a triangular arrangement, indicates that a particularly strong wooden handle was attached here, to ensure the safe use of the saw without it bending during the cutting action. Some of these groups of holes may have been pierced at a later date in order to attach the handle more securely.

This is the best-preserved saw from an assemblage of such tools found in the West Wing of the palace. They are evidence of the existence of carpentry workshops, although the wear on the teeth of the saws may indicate that they were also used to cut blocks of poros stone or other types of limestone.

The wealth of tools from the palace of Zakros, particularly the impressive saws, attest to the dynamic activity of the palatial masonry workshops and the intensive use of advanced and specialised toolkits by the palace craftsmen. The strong wear on the teeth of the saw, and the possibility that the handle may have been further reinforced, as the clusters of holes indicate, suggest that the tool was part of the equipment not only of a carpenter but perhaps also of a stonemason, and that it was intensively used until it was completely blunted. The way the long blade is folded up presumably puts the tool out of service and points to storage for metal recycling.

References

Shaw 1973, 56, 58, n.10, fig.43. Evely 1993, 30-1, fig.14.31.

(Dimitris Sfakianakis)

52

双刃斧

米诺斯中期 I 至 II（公元前 2100 ~ 前 1700 年）

青铜

长 17 厘米，宽（刃部中心）5 厘米

发现于克里特岛哈迈兹齐索乌洛托山的椭圆形房屋

希腊伊拉克利翁考古博物馆藏，编号 X1021

青铜双刃斧，带有弧形刃边，可能采用闭合式模具铸造。这件双刃斧发现于索乌洛托山椭圆形房屋屋外东侧，一同出土的其他青铜工具包括一把双刃斧、一把双刃镐、一件凿器和一件刀具。因此可以推断，这些物品属于一位米诺斯木匠。双刃斧至少从米诺斯早期 II 开始使用作木工工具，但现存的大多数双刃斧均晚于该时期。

这组青铜工具由一位村民发现，随后，斯特凡诺斯·赞图迪季斯（Stefanos Xanthoudides）对该遗址进行了发掘。由于这些工具并非通过正式发掘出土，尚不确定它们是出自椭圆形房屋，还是与其下方更早的建筑遗迹有关。

（伊万吉立亚·西克拉）

52

Double axe

Middle Minoan I – II (2100-1700 BCE)

Bronze

L. 17 cm, w. (at the centre of the blade) 5 cm

Chamaizi (Souvloto Mouri), Oval House

Archaeological Museum of Heraklion, X1021

Bronze double axe with curved cutting edges. It had been cast in a mould, perhaps of the closed type. It was found outside the east side of the oval house on the Souvloto Mouri hill along with other bronze tools: a second such axe, a double-bladed pickaxe, a chisel and a knife. The above items were the toolkit of a Minoan carpenter. Double axes were used as woodworking tools from at least the Early Minoan II period, although most surviving examples date to later periods.

The set of bronze tools was found by a villager and led to the excavation of the site by Stefanos Xanthoudides. As they were not revealed in a proper excavation, there is no certainty as to whether the tools are associated with the oval house or the earlier structures excavated below it.

References

Branigan 1974, 134, 164. Davaras 1972, 283-288. Ξανθουδίδης 1906, 117-156, pl.7:2.

(Evangelia Sikla)

53

矛头

米诺斯中期ⅠA（公元前2100～前1900年）

青铜

长19厘米

发现于克里特岛哈迈兹齐索乌洛托山的椭圆形房屋

希腊伊拉克利翁考古博物馆藏，编号X1019

带中脊的青铜矛头，现仅存部分，可能采用闭合式模具铸造。矛杆下部已经断裂缺失，无法复原，不过，从矛头中脊两侧保留的两个孔洞推测，这些孔洞可能用于将矛头固定在木矛杆上。

目前尚不清楚此矛头与索乌洛托山木工窖藏出土的其他金属工具是否存在关联。从技术角度看，克里特岛在米诺斯早期Ⅰ和米诺斯早期Ⅰ至Ⅱ过渡期便已掌握中脊铸造技术，具体实例包括哈吉亚-普蒂亚和波罗斯-卡桑巴斯出土的中脊匕首及其模具。与哈迈兹齐矛头最为相近的器物出自阿莫尔戈斯岛阿凯辛尼一座早期基克拉迪墓葬，这一发现表明此类矛头属于米诺斯中期初期。

（乔治娅·弗拉达）

53

Spearhead

Middle Minoan ⅠA (2100-1900 BCE)

Bronze

L. 19 cm

Chamaizi (Souvloto Mouri), Oval House

Archaeological Museum of Heraklion, X1019

Bronze mid-ribbed spearhead, fragmentary, most probably cast in a closed type mould. The lower part of the shaft has been broken off and cannot be reconstructed, but it seems that the two holes preserved on both sides of the mid-rib may have served for fitting the spearhead into the wooden pole of the spear.

The association of the spearhead with the rest of the metal objects constituting the carpenter's hoard recovered at Souvloto Mouri is not clear. From a technical perspective, the technology for casting mid-ribbed objects is now attested on Crete since the Early Minoan I and Early Minoan Ⅰ-Ⅱ transition by the cast mid-ribbed daggers and moulds from Haghia Photia and Poros-Katsambas. The nearest parallel to the spearhead from Chamaizi comes from an Early Cycladic tomb at Arkesine on Amorgos, a fact confirming that this type belongs to the start of the Middle Minoan period due to the relevant synchronisations.

References

Ξανθουδίδης 1906, 134-135, pl.7:5. Branigan 1968, 28-29, fig.7,2. Davaras 1972. Sherratt 2007, 249-250.

(Georgia Flouda)

54

祭祀用双刃斧

米诺斯中期Ⅲ至米诺斯晚期Ⅰ（约公元前 1700～前 1450 年）

青铜

长 15.2 厘米

发现于克里特岛中南部的阿尔卡洛科里洞穴

希腊伊拉克利翁考古博物馆藏，编号 X2415

大型祭祀用双刃斧，器形完整但部分腐蚀严重。器物由非功能性金属薄片制成，但带有一个实心圆形斧眼，表明其本应安装在斧杆上。

双刃斧于 20 世纪初在阿尔卡洛科里一处米诺斯圣窟中发现。与其一同发现的还有约 20 千克的青铜废料和许多金属制品，其中一些制品专门堆叠存放。这些金属制品包括青铜（或铜）饼锭、数十柄剑坯、细长三角形金箔小片，以及数百件刀刃和不同尺寸的祭祀用双刃斧。不过，这些器物中只有少部分存在使用痕迹，而多数则可能专门制作用于仪式祭典。因此，这批器物很可能是有意按照特定结构堆放，用作仪式展示或者充当祭祀供品。这批器物中有一件中心带有重要铭文的全尺寸双刃斧（“阿尔卡洛科里斧”），该器物具有很强的象征意义，很好地佐证了上述假设。

（乔治娅・弗拉达）

54

Votive double axe

Middle Minoan Ⅲ– Late Minoan Ⅰ (Ca. 1700-1450 BCE)

Bronze

L. 15.2 cm

Arkalochori Cave, south-central Crete

Archaeological Museum of Heraklion X2415

Large votive double axe, complete, with parts heavily corroded. It is made from non-functional sheet-metal but has a solid circular shaft-hole, which suggests that it was meant to be fitted on a rod.

The double axe was part of a homogeneous assemblage recovered from the sacred Minoan cave at Arkalochori in the early twentieth century. This assemblage consists of about 20 kg of scrap bronze and of numerous metal artifacts, some of which were found carefully stacked. It included bronze (or copper?) bun ingots, dozens of sword blanks, tiny foils of gold in elongated triangular shape; also, hundreds of knife blades and votive double axes in different sizes. Nonetheless, only some of the objects show signs of use, but many may have been made for ritual use. Consequently, it is plausible that this hoard resulted from intentional and structured deposition, possibly connected with rituals of ceremonial display and votive offerings. The symbolic power of a full-size double axe bearing an important inscription on its central part ("Arkalochori Axe") also substantiates this assumption.

References

Marinatos 1962. Evely 1999. Michailidou 2003. Rethemiotakis 2008a, 79-88. Flouda 2015.

(Georgia Flouda)

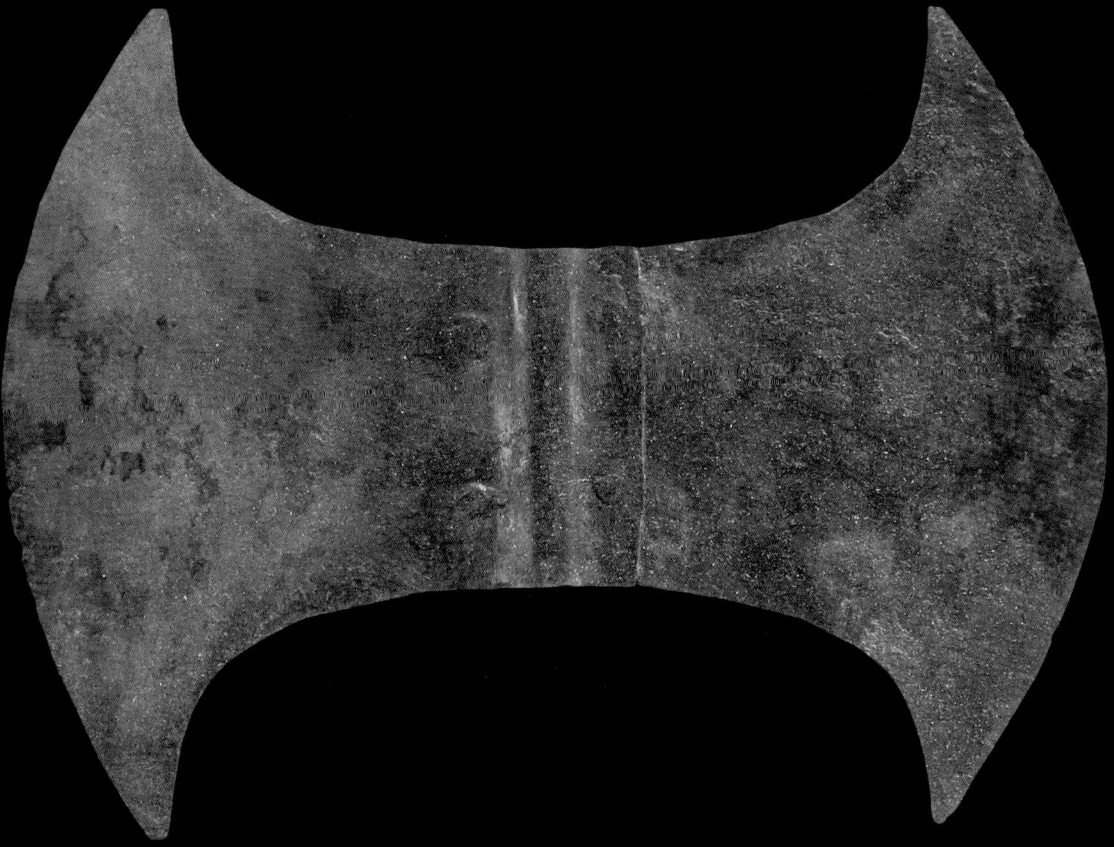

55

大型祭祀用双刃斧

米诺斯中期Ⅲ至米诺斯晚期Ⅰ（公元前1700～前1450年）

青铜

长50厘米

发现于克里特岛阿尔卡洛科里洞穴（1912～1935年发掘）

希腊伊拉克利翁考古博物馆藏，编号X2418

完整双刃斧，刃部向弯曲的切削边缘逐渐加宽，边缘有缺口。斧身装饰有双重凸起线条和带连续新月形图案的斜纹带。

此物品与其他同类文物一同发现于阿尔卡洛科里洞穴内。洞穴最北端堆放了数百件不同尺寸和用途的青铜斧（如薄型祭祀斧和实用斧）、大量祭祀用剑和匕首、圆柱形木制物品的残片、小型铜锭以及铜渣。洞穴中央还发现有若干小型金银双刃斧。大部分斧上有雕刻装饰，少数还带有铭文。

斯派里登·马里纳托斯（Spyridon Marinatos）是该洞穴的发掘者，他认为，在米诺斯中期Ⅲ至米诺斯文明晚期Ⅰ，人们会在该洞穴祭祀某位战神，向其供奉剑和双刃斧。不过，他后来提出，该洞穴也可能曾是一个冶金工坊。

在新王宫期，洞穴祭祀在克里特岛上非常普遍。一些洞穴发现了双刃斧，这种斧是米诺斯宗教的象征性标志。在普西克罗洞穴中，还发现了一个阶梯式滑石底座，用于固定大型双刃斧的斧柄。不过，阿尔卡洛科里洞穴的特殊性在于，这里虽然发现了大量双刃斧和祭祀用武器，但没有发现其他类型的祭祀或供奉物品。

（杜卡利翁·马尼达基斯）

55

Large votive double axe

Middle Minoan Ⅲ – Late Minoan Ⅰ (Ca. 1700–1450 BCE)

Bronze

L. 50 cm

Arkalochori Cave, 1912–1935

Archaeological Museum of Heraklion, X2418

Complete double axe with blades widening towards the curved cutting edges and chipped edges. It is decorated with double relief lines and oblique bands with consecutive crescent-shaped motifs.

The object was found together with other similar artifacts inside the Arkalochori Cave. Hundreds of bronze axes of different sizes and uses (e.g. thin votive axes, utilitarian axes), as well as a large number of votive swords and daggers, remains of cylindrical wooden objects, small copper ingots, and copper slags, had been deposited at the cave's northernmost end. Moreover, several small gold and silver double axes were found at the centre of the cave. Most of the axes have traced or incised decoration, whereas a few of them are also inscribed.

The excavator, Spyridon Marinatos argued that during the Middle Minoan Ⅲ–Late Minoan Ⅰ period the cave was dedicated to some war-deity, to whom the swords and double axes were offered. He later suggested that the cave served as a metallurgical workshop.

Worship in caves was widespread in Crete in the Neopalatial era. Some caves have yielded examples of the double axe, the emblematic symbol of the Minoan religion, and the Psychro Cave even contained a steatite stepped base to hold the pole of a large double axe. However, the Arkalochori Cave presents a unique case, because of the great number of double axes and votive weapons and the absence of any other type of ritual or votive object.

References

Buchholz 1959, 8-9, 33, pl.1. Hazzidakis 1912-1913. Μαρινάτος 1935. Marinatos 1935. Moss 2005, 115-19. Rethemiotakis 2002, 64-65. Rutkowski-Nowicki 1996, 24-26. Tyree 1975, 28-30, 306-11. Tyree 2001, 41.

(Deukalion Manidakis)

56

宽口壶

米诺斯晚期 I（公元前 1600 ~ 前 1450 年）
青铜
高 17.5 厘米，最宽 20 厘米
发现于克里特岛马利亚
希腊伊拉克利翁考古博物馆藏，编号 X2192

小型浇注容器，宽口边缘形成了一个明显的壶嘴，与位于对侧的纵向带状把手相呼应。此容器由单片锤打的青铜板制成，手柄通过铆钉固定。青铜时期的金属器物能够保存至今，实属难得，因为贵重金属通常会被回收再利用。通过此件器物，我们能够了解其制作技术，并且能够得知此类器物主要在宴会上用作展示。在新王宫期，金属加工在专业程度和创造力方面都达到了巅峰，这一点从住宅和墓葬中出土的实用性及装饰性器物中可见一斑。

（艾琳·尼古拉科普卢）

56

Wide-mouthed jug

Late Minoan I (1600-1450 BCE)
Bronze
H. 17.5 cm, max. w. 20 cm
Malia
Archaeological Museum of Heraklion, X2192

A small pouring vessel with a wide mouth forming a prominent spout on the rim, opposite the vertical strap handle. It is made of a single sheet of beaten bronze, while the handle is attached by rivets. The preservation of metal vessels of the Minoan period is a fortunate coincidence, as the valuable metal was often recycled. It gives us information on the manufacturing techniques and the use of the utensils, which were mainly intended for display at banquets. During the Neopalatial era in particular, metalworking reached the peak of technical specialisation and creativity, as is evidenced by the utilitarian and decorative artifacts that survive from residential and burial assemblages.

References

Matthäus 1980, 200 (no.302), pl.36: no.302.

(Irene Nikolakopoulou)

57

压扁状提水罐

米诺斯晚期ⅢA（公元前 1400 ~ 前 1375 年）

青铜

高 50 厘米，最大直径 35 厘米

发现于克里特岛克诺索斯扎法帕普拉的 36 号竖穴墓

希腊伊拉克利翁考古博物馆藏，编号 X1089

青铜提水罐，罐身配有一个位于肩部的纵向手柄和一个位于下部的水平手柄，底座为高盘状。此器物由三片锤制青铜板通过铆钉连接而成，这些铆钉在罐颈底端和罐身中部清晰可见。金属板压扁后，与原始位置相比稍有偏移，但底部仍保持原位。手柄末端装饰有两个凸起的贝壳图案。

提水罐出自 36 号竖穴墓（又称“酋长之墓”），墓内葬有一具遗骸。这件器物是 14 件宴会用青铜器物之一，其他器物包括一个大型三足锅、一个小型锅具、一个青铜盆、三盏灯以及各种用于盛装液体的器皿。同一墓地中的“三足炉墓”（14 号墓）以及迈锡尼的Ⅳ号竖穴墓中也发现了类似的提水罐。此外，墓中还出土了两把珍贵的刀剑、两枚长矛头、一面铜镜和一顶金头饰。这些器物彰显了墓主（可能是克诺索斯贵族或精英战士）的社会地位与显赫身份。

（乔治娅・弗拉达）

57

Hydria, compressed

Late Minoan ⅢA (1400-1375 BCE)

Bronze

H. 50 cm, max. diam. 35 cm

Knossos, Zafer Papoura, Shaft Grave 36

Archaeological Museum of Heraklion, X1089

Bronze hydria with a vertical handle on the shoulder, a horizontal handle on the lower body and a tall disc base. It is made of three hammered sheets joined together by rivets which are visible at the base of the neck and in the middle of the body, where the sheets have been compressed and shifted from their original position. The sheet forming the base of the vessel remains in place. Two relief seashells adorn the ends of the handle.

The hydria comes from Shaft Grave 36 ("The Chieftain's Grave"), which contained one burial. It forms part of an assemblage of 14 bronze banqueting vessels including a large tripod cauldron, a small cauldron, a bronze basin, three lamps and various vessels for offering liquids. A similar hydria was found in the "Tomb of the Tripod Hearth" (Grave 14) of the same cemetery, and another in Shaft Grave IV of Mycenae. Two valuable swords, two spearheads, a mirror and a gold head ornament also accompanied the deceased in this grave, one of the richest in the Zafer Papoura cemetery. All these objects were intended to display the social status and prestige of their owners, who were probably members of the Knossian aristocracy or elite warriors.

References

Evans 1906, 51-55, figs.52, 54. Matthäus 1980, 172 (no.242), pl.30: no.242. Clarke 2012, 82 fig.1g. Driessen and Macdonald 1984, 67n.100. Steinmann 2012, 184, Taf.44p.

(Georgia Flouda)

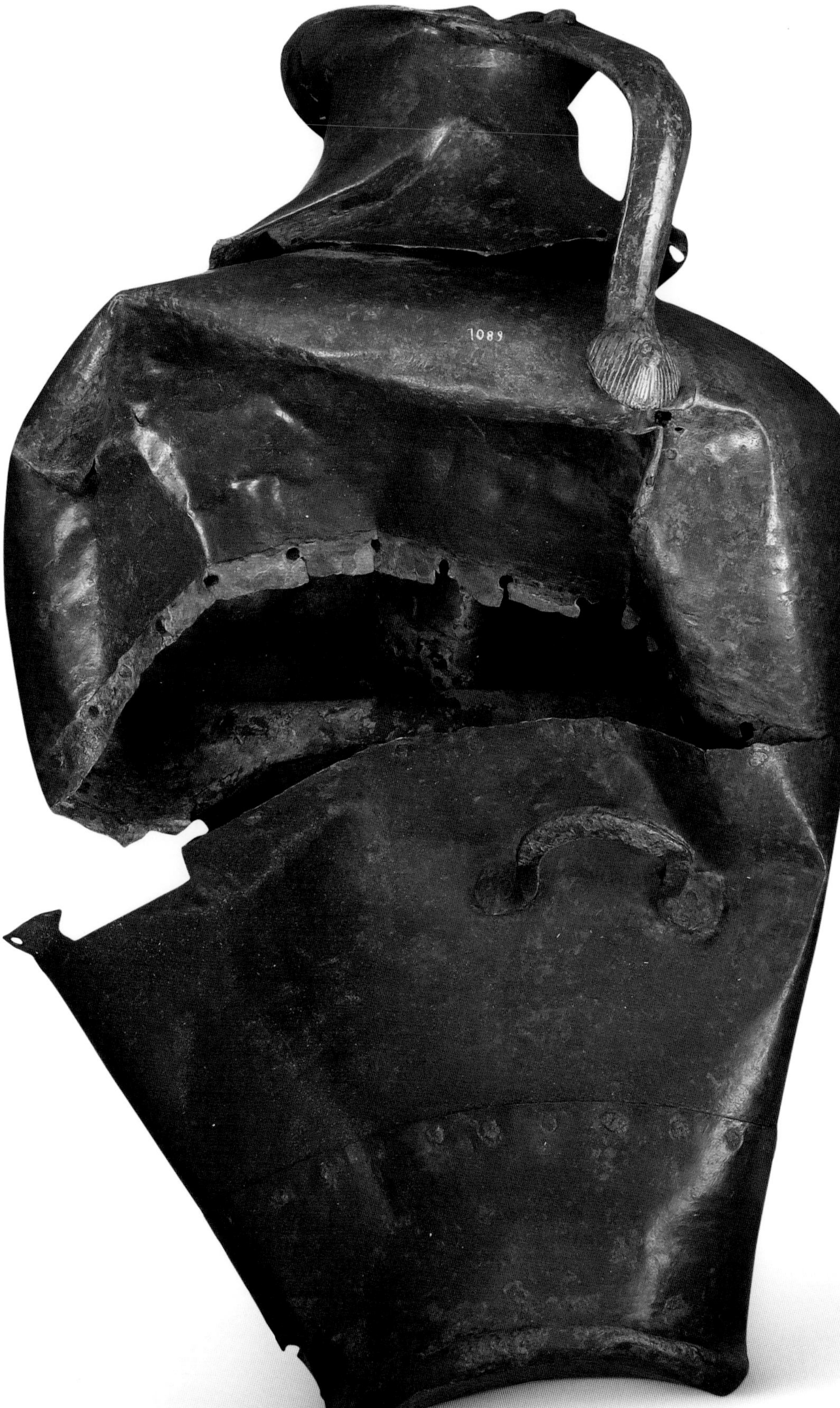
1089

58

浅盘

米诺斯晚期ⅢA（公元前 1400 ~ 前 1300 年）

青铜

高 2.5 厘米，边缘直径 11 厘米，把手高度 8.5 厘米

发现于克里特岛斐斯托斯的卡利维亚墓室

希腊伊拉克利翁考古博物馆藏，编号 X689

小型器物有一个浅圆形碗状盘，边缘近乎垂直，一端延伸出一个略微倾斜的实心杆状把手。其具体用途尚不明确，但很可能与火有关（如用作炭火炉、灯具或烹调少量食物的炊具），把手位置也证实了这一点。此器物出自卡利维亚公墓的一间墓室，是墓主的随葬品。公墓位于距法伊斯托斯宫东南约一千米的一座低矮山坡。墓地可能属于一个身份尚未明确的小型聚落。墓中出土的随葬品（如武器、工具、珠宝、青铜器和陶器）与米诺斯晚期ⅢA 的其他墓地类似，表明迈锡尼文化影响十分深远。从陪葬的武器、珠宝和金属器具不难看出，墓主是一位精英阶层人士或赫赫有名的战士，拥有尊贵的社会身份和地位。

（艾琳·尼古拉科普卢）

58

Shallow pan

Late Minoan Ⅲ A (1400–1300 BCE)

Bronze

H. 2.5 cm, rim diam. 11 cm, h. of handle 8.5 cm

Phaistos, Kalyvia, Chamber Tomb

Archaeological Museum of Heraklion, X689

This small vessel consists of a shallow circular bowl or pan with almost vertical walls and a rod-shaped solid handle extending, at a slightly oblique angle, up from the rim. Its use is not definitely understood, but it seems likely that it had to do with fire (a brazier, a lamp, or some vessel for preparing food or other substances in small quantities), as is indicated by the ergonomic position of the handle. It was placed with a burial in a tomb of the Kalyvia cemetery, which is located on the slopes of a low hill, one kilometre southeast of the palace of Phaistos. The cemetery probably belonged to a small settlement that has not yet been identified. The grave goods (weapons, tools, jewellery, bronze and clay vessels), like those of other contemporary cemeteries of the Late Minoan ⅢA period, testify to a strong Mycenaean influence. The weapons, jewellery and metal utensils in particular were intended to project the social identity and high prestige of their owners, probably members of an elite class or illustrious warriors.

References

Savignoni 1904, no. 17, 544, fig.29.

(Irene Nikolakopoulou)

59

D 型剑

米诺斯晚期ⅢA（公元前 1400 ~ 前 1300 年）

青铜

长 60.7 厘米，龙骨最宽处 9.42 厘米

发现于克里特岛克诺索斯扎法帕普拉的 98 号墓室

希腊伊拉克利翁考古博物馆藏，编号 X1100

根据基利安–迪尔迈尔（Kilian–Dirlmeier，1993 年）提出的分类，这柄青铜剑被归类为 D1 型，其特征是剑刃上部呈十字形。该剑的锻造年代大约为公元前 15 世纪至前 14 世纪初。与克里特岛早期刀剑相比，此型剑的主要结构优势在于其龙骨和剑刃的一体铸造，这增强了武器的耐用性。

这柄剑出土于第 98 号墓室，该墓室由岩石凿成，葬有两具遗骸。这柄剑出土于墓室南侧，属于其中稍年轻者，随葬品还包括一把青铜剃刀、一个炭火盆和一个石容器。墓中随葬武器的做法表明逝者拥有贵族战士身份，这一社会阶层高度重视武器的获取，死后也采取英雄化的埋葬方式。

（乔治娅·弗拉达）

59

Sword of Type D

Late Minoan ⅢA (1400-1300 BCE)

Bronze

L. 60.7 cm, widest point of tang 9.42 cm

Knossos, Zafer Papoura, Chamber Tomb 98

Archaeological Museum of Heraklion, X1100

The sword is classified as Kilian-Dirlmeier's (1993) type D1 thanks to the cruciform upper part of the blade. It dates from the 15th to the first quarter of the 14th century BCE. The comparative constructional advantage of this type over earlier Cretan swords is the tang, which is integral with the blade, ensuring the greater durability of the weapon.

The sword comes from the rock-cut Chamber Tomb 98, which contained two burials. It accompanied the earlier burial, on the south side of the tomb, together with a bronze razor, a brazier and a stone vessel. Weapons placed in graves were marks of rank and status of members of an aristocratic warrior class that was ideologically invested in their acquisition and had adopted a heroic mode of burial.

References

Evans 1906, 86-87. Steinmann 2012, 31, 186, Taf.44p. Kilian-Dirlmeier 1993, 59 no.114. Molloy 2010.

(Georgia Flouda)

60

匕首

米诺斯晚期Ⅱ至米诺斯晚期ⅢA1（公元前1450～前1375年）
青铜
长29.4厘米，宽5.9厘米
发现于克里特岛克诺索斯圣伊奥尼斯的“金杯墓”
希腊伊拉克利翁考古博物馆藏，编号X2499

青铜匕首，完整未破损。匕刃肩部有凸缘，一直延续到龙骨末端，龙骨基部设有一个铆钉孔，用于固定匕首柄头（遗失，可能为木质）。这把匕首发现于伊拉克利翁至克诺索斯要道旁的一座“战士墓”。该墓为单墓室，包含一个长方形主墓室和通往墓室的下沉墓道。墓中木棺埋葬着一位战士，随葬物品包括青铜时代克里特岛常见的多种武器，如剑、箭头和长矛。

在青铜时代，匕首是克里特岛生产最多的金属制品。因为克里特岛本身缺乏青铜资源，其制造需要通过海上贸易路线进口原材料，这件匕首由当地工坊制造，展现出高超的青铜锻打和铸造工艺。将匕首和其他武器与战士的遗体一同埋葬，表明这些武器除了实际用途外，还具有象征意义，可能代表着战士崇高的社会地位。墓中发现的其他珍贵物品（包括一只金杯和两枚用于行政事务和经济交易的印章石）也印证了这一猜想。

（帕拉斯克维·斯塔马塔基）

60

Dagger

Late Minoan Ⅱ – Late Minoan ⅢA1 (1450-1375 BCE)
Bronze
L. 29.4 cm, w. 5.9 cm
Knossos, Agios Ioannis, "Gold Cup Tomb"
Archaeological Museum of Heraklion, X2499

Bronze dagger, complete and unbroken. The shoulders of the blade bear flanges that continue along the tang, at the base of which there is one rivet-hole for affixing the pommel (missing, possibly wooden). The dagger was found in a "warrior grave" situated just off the road leading to Knossos from Heraklion. This was a chamber tomb that had a main, rectangular room with a sunken passage ("dromos") leading to it. The bronze objects that accompany the single warrior who was buried in a wooden coffin in this tomb consist of a wide array of weapons used in Bronze Age Crete, including a sword, arrowheads and spears.

Bronze daggers were the most widely produced metal objects during this period on the island. Their manufacture required access to the raw material that had to be imported via the maritime trade routes, since it was not available on Crete. This dagger was produced by a local workshop using technological expertise in bronze hammering and casting. Burying daggers and other weapons with their warrior owner suggests that, apart from their practical function, they also had a symbolic meaning, probably indicating the warrior's high social status. This is borne out by the discovery of other prestige objects in the same tomb, a unique golden cup and two sealstones used by high-ranking administrators and for economic transactions.

References

Dimopoulou 2015, 172-173. Hood 1956, fig.3.7, plate 15a. Steinmann 2012, 155, 408 (no 244).

(Paraskevi Stamataki)

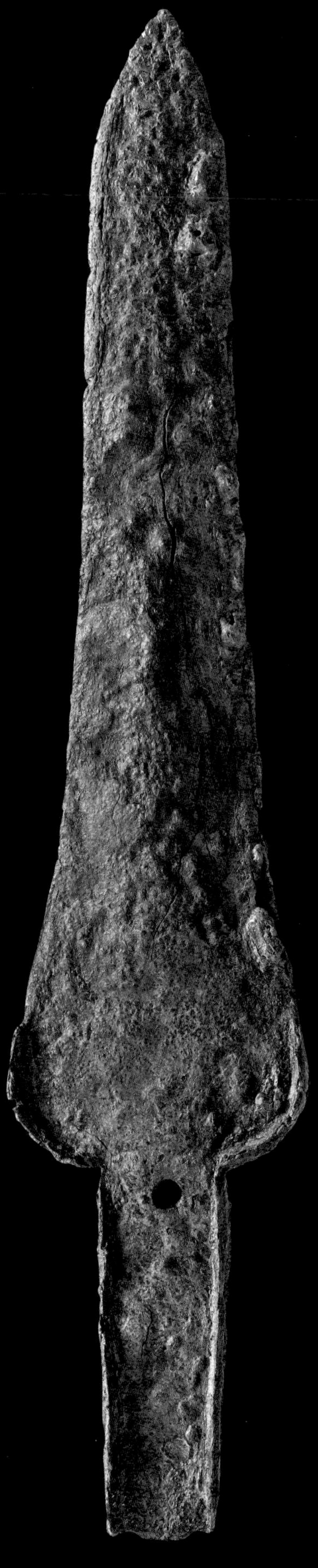

IV

第四单元　巧匠

Unit 4 Craftsman

代达罗斯为国王米诺斯设计迷宫，为公主阿里阿德涅建造舞池。他是绝无仅有的天才，是智慧机敏的匠师，是发明创造的能手。

不管代达罗斯是否确有其人，考古发现的众多精美之器证明克里特岛米诺斯时代果真拥有丰富的物产、高超的技术、出色的审美。陶瓶朴拙，彩色纹饰勾勒奇趣之美；金光灿灿，项饰耳坠闪烁贵人华彩；石皿莹润，天然纹理包罗浩渺苍穹；印章玲珑，微雕细刻凝缩大千世界。

杰出工艺让人看到米诺斯文化强劲的生产力和旺盛的消费需求，数千年前爱琴海青铜时代的岛民们已经享受了品质卓越的劳动成果。精巧的生产技术当归功于孜孜不倦的勤劳实践，代达罗斯神话恰是克里特史前经济的文学投射。更有可能，并非代达罗斯造就了工艺，而是百工千艺塑造了大师。

巧匠，何止代达罗斯一人。巧匠，是千千万万隐匿于历史烟尘的劳动者。

Daedalus designed the labyrinth for King Minos and built the dance floor for Princess Ariadne. He was a unique genius, an ingenious craftsman and an inventor.

Whether Daedalus was historical or legendary, archaeological evidence, particularly the exquisite artifacts unearthed, attests to Minoan Crete's prosperity, advanced craftsmanship, and remarkable artistic sophistication. The pottery, with its rustic charm, is adorned with colorful patterns that outline a whimsical beauty. The golden jewelry, necklaces and earrings, glimmers with the splendor of nobility. The stone vessels, smooth and lustrous, feature natural textures that evoke the vast expanse of the heavens. The seals, delicate and intricate, encapsulate the boundless universe through meticulous carving of the Minoan civilization.

Outstanding craftsmanship reflects its advanced productivity and vibrant consumer demand. Thousands of years ago, islanders of the Aegean Bronze Age already enjoyed the fruits of high-quality labor. The myth of Daedalus is a literary projection of the prehistoric Cretan economy, with sophisticated production techniques attributed to thousands of years of hard work. More likely, it was not the legendary Daedalus who invented these techniques, but rather generations of craftsmen who refined them over time.

Daedalus was not the sole master craftsman of his age; he stood among countless unnamed artisans now lost to history's dust.

彩陶绘奇趣

新石器时代和青铜时代早期，克里特陶器受小亚细亚、黎凡特（古地名，主要包括今叙利亚、黎巴嫩、巴勒斯坦、以色列）与基克拉泽斯群岛同类产品影响，造型与装饰相对简单。随着经济与贸易日趋繁荣，出现了职业化的陶工群体。他们促进了陶器量产与技术进步，陶轮的使用亦带来品质提升与风格创新。到青铜时代中期，一种名为“卡马雷斯”的陶器兴盛起来，至青铜时代晚期又出现了所谓的“王宫风格”陶器。这些陶器身上绘有抽象或具象的纹饰，画风奇巧，意趣盎然，表现出鲜明的自然主义和装饰意识，拉开了古希腊彩绘陶器艺术的序幕。

Painted Pottery: A World of Fantasy

During the Neolithic and early Bronze Age, Cretan pottery, influenced by styles from Anatolia, the Levant, and the Cyclades, featured relatively simple shapes and decorations. As the economy and trade flourished, a professional class of potters emerged, driving advancements in production techniques and quality. The introduction of the potter's wheel further enhanced craftsmanship and spurred stylistic innovation. By the middle Bronze Age, a distinctive style known as Kamares pottery became prominent, followed by the so-called Palace Style pottery in the late Bronze Age. These ceramics were adorned with abstract or figurative designs, showcasing a playful and imaginative aesthetic marked by naturalism and decorative flair. This artistic tradition laid the foundation for the later development of painted pottery in ancient Greece.

61

陶轮

米诺斯中期Ⅲ至米诺斯晚期Ⅰ（公元前 1700 ~ 前 1450 年）

陶土

直径 33.4 厘米，最大厚度 6.2 厘米

发现于克里特岛古尔尼亚

希腊伊拉克利翁考古博物馆藏，编号 Π3165

可自由旋转的陶轮，保存较为完好，仅缺少部分边缘。材质为红色陶土，含杂质。由单块陶土手工制成，可能采用了轮制工艺。表面覆盖一层红色光滑涂层，上表面等区域有磨损痕迹。受制作工艺影响，陶轮上表面向中心略微凹陷，边缘稍凸起。轮边部分带有斜面和阶梯状边缘，并刻有两道水平凹槽。底部有一个宽大的凸出领圈，其中央设有一个锥形阶梯状插口，用于连接垂直旋转轴。领圈底部平面有多道切割痕迹，这些痕迹确保连接材料（陶土）黏接更加牢固，从而将陶轮固定在垂直旋转轴上。

（帕拉斯克维·斯塔马塔基）

61

Potter’s wheelhead

Middle Minoan Ⅲ – Late Minoan Ⅰ (1700-1450 BCE)

Clay

Diam. 33.4 cm, max. th. 6.2 cm

Gournia

Archaeological Museum of Heraklion, Π3165

Clay wheelhead from a freely-rotating potter’s wheel. Preserved almost intact (part of the rim is missing). Red clay with inclusions. Handmade from a single body of clay and probably finished on the wheel. Covered by a red, glossy coating, worn in places, especially on the upper surface. The upper surface is slightly concave towards the centre and slightly raised at the edge due to the manner of construction. Around the edge runs the bevelled and stepped rim, which bears two horizontal grooves. The underside of the disc has a wide projecting collar with a central tapered and stepped socket for the vertical axle on which it pivoted. On the lower flat surface of the collar are multiple incisions which ensured the more effective adherence of the connecting material, clay, with which the potter’s wheelhead was fixed on the vertical rotating axle.

References

Hawes et al. 1908, 42 no.32, pl.VIII no.32. Xanthoudides 1927, 113-14, pl.XVIII.a-b. Evely 1988, 89 Type 3B, no.35, 99 fig.4 no.35, pl.13 no.35.

(Paraskevi Stamataki)

62

陶轮

米诺斯中期Ⅲ至米诺斯晚期Ⅰ（公元前 1700 ~ 前 1450 年）

陶土

直径 29.9 厘米，最大厚度 5 厘米

发现于克里特岛古尔尼亚

希腊伊拉克利翁考古博物馆藏，编号 Π6738

可自由旋转的陶轮，保存完好，仅边缘处有部分剥落。材质为棕黄色陶土，含杂质。由单块陶土手工制成，可能采用了轮制工艺。受制作工艺影响，陶轮上表面向中心略微凹陷，表面可能曾经过打磨（现已严重磨损）。边缘设计简洁，略微凸起，侧边垂直，转角圆润。陶轮底部有一个锥形浅凹槽，用于与垂直旋转轴相连。在锥形插槽和边缘之间，有七道同心圆凹槽。这些凹槽确保连接材料——陶土（其残余部分仍保留在中央插槽及其周围）黏接更加牢固，从而使陶轮固定于垂直旋转轴上。

（帕拉斯克维・斯塔马塔基）

62

Potter's wheelhead

Middle Minoan Ⅲ– Late Minoan Ⅰ (1700-1450 BCE)

Clay

Diam. 29.9 cm, max. th. 5 cm

Gournia

Archaeological Museum of Heraklion, Π6738

Clay wheelhead from a freely-rotating potter's wheel. Preserved intact, with some flaking on the rim. Clay brownish-yellow with inclusions. Handmade from a single body of clay and probably finished on a wheel. The upper surface is slightly concave towards the centre from the method of construction and was probably smoothed (now quite worn). The edge is simple, slightly raised and so accentuated, vertical at the side and with rounded corners. The underside has a shallow conical hollow by which to attach the wheelhead to the vertical rotating axle. Between the conical socket and the rim are seven concentric circular grooves. These ensured the more effective adherence of the connecting material – clay (whose remains are preserved in and around the central socket) – with which the potter's wheelhead was fixed on the vertical rotating axle.

References

Xanthoudides 1927, 112, pl.XVIII.a-b. Evely 1988, 89 Type 3A, no.33, 99 fig.4 no. 33, pl.13 no.33.

(Paraskevi Stamataki)

63

陶轮

米诺斯中期Ⅲ至米诺斯晚期Ⅰ（公元前1700～前1450年）

陶土

直径45.5厘米，最大厚度6.7厘米

发现于克里特岛瓦塞佩特罗别墅

希腊伊拉克利翁考古博物馆藏，编号Π25821

可以自由旋转的陶轮，已经修复与补全。材质为黄色陶土，含杂质。由单块陶土手工制成，可能采用了轮制工艺。本件陶轮设计精密，边缘凸出且厚实，增加了旋转时的稳定性。受制作工艺影响，圆盘上表面略微凸起，边缘附近有三道同心圆凹槽。圆盘底部向中心凹陷，中央有一个凸出领圈，内有一个锥形插槽，用于连接垂直旋转轴。领圈的平面带有斜刻痕迹，其垂直外侧有一圈水平排列的小浅孔。中心部分则带有水平凹槽、棱状装饰以及斜刻痕迹。这些设计可能用于确保连接材料（陶土）黏接牢固，从而帮助转盘与垂直旋转轴相连。转盘边缘凸起部分有多条近乎垂直的凹槽，便于手动转动轮盘。边缘对称地分布着两对孔洞，以对角线方向从边缘延伸至转盘底部。

（帕拉斯克维·斯塔马塔基）

63

Potter's wheelhead

Middle Minoan III – Late Minoan I (1700-1450 BCE)

Clay

Diam. 45.5 cm, max. th. 6.7 cm

Villa of Vathypetro

Archaeological Museum of Heraklion, Π25821

Clay wheelhead from a freely-rotating potter's wheel. Repaired and completed. Yellowish clay with inclusions. Handmade from a single body of clay and probably finished on a wheel. It belongs to the most sophisticated type of clay wheelhead, with a pronounced, heavy rim which intensified and maintained the rotary motion. The upper surface of the disc is slightly convex in profile due to its manner of construction and bears three circular grooves near the rim. The underside of the disc is concave towards the centre, where there is a protruding collar with a central conical socket for the vertical axle on which the wheelhead pivoted. The collar has oblique incisions on its flat surface, and on the vertical external sides runs a horizontal series of small shallow holes. The central portion bears horizontal grooves and ridges, as well as oblique incisions. These components may have served to effect a more secure adherence of the connecting material, clay, with which the ceramic wheelhead was fixed on the vertical rotating axle. The convex sides of the rim carry near vertical grooves that facilitated turning the wheel by hand. Two pairs of holes are placed diametrically opposite: these run diagonally from the rim to emerge in the underside of the wheelhead.

References

Μαρινάτος 1952, 270. Evely 1988, 91 Type 3C, no.52, 104 fig.7 no.52, pl.17 no.52.

(Paraskevi Stamataki)

64

折腹碗

石器时代，新石器时代晚期Ⅱ（公元前 4900 ~ 前 4500 年）

陶土

高 12 厘米，口径 17.7 厘米，最大宽度 23 厘米

发现于克里特岛克诺索斯王宫

希腊伊拉克利翁考古博物馆藏，编号 Π19027

敞口陶碗，带把手，表面为深色且经过抛光，饰成组刻线。新石器时期的陶器普遍采用敞口及折腹设计。虽然新石器陶器的器形总体较为保守，但技术上有一定的发展，例如烧制工艺逐渐改进。陶器数量的增加以及制作工艺的进步，也反映出克诺索斯新石器定居点的发展壮大。克诺索斯是克里特岛上首个永久性定居点，建立于公元前七千纪初期。在新石器时代末期以及青铜时代，这里一直是岛上最大的居住地。

（伊万吉立亚・西克拉）

64

Carinated bowl

Stone Age, late Neolithic Ⅱ (4900-4500 BCE)

Clay

H. 12 cm, rim diam. 17.7 cm, max w. 23 cm

Knossos, palace

Archaeological Museum of Heraklion, Π19027

Open bowl with handle. The dark surface of the bowl is burnished and decorated with groups of incised lines. Open shapes with angled walls dominate the pottery of the Neolithic period. Although generally conservative in the variety of vessel types, this pottery reveals some technological development: for example, the firing technique gradually improves. The number of vessels and the improvement of the potter's craft also reflects the development of the Neolithic settlement of Knossos. This was the first permanent settlement established in Crete at the beginning of the 7th millennium BCE and remained the largest occupation site on the island up to the end of the Neolithic period and during the Bronze Age.

References

Dimopoulou-Rethemiotaki 2005, 26, 30. Μανδαλάκη 2015a, 17. Tomkins 2007, 30-32.

(Evangelia Sikla)

65

圣奥诺夫里奥斯型壶

米诺斯早期 I（约公元前 3000 年）

陶土

高 18.8 厘米

1951 年出土于克里特岛基帕里西的墓葬洞穴

希腊伊拉克利翁考古博物馆藏，编号 Π10853

陶壶精美完整，口径小于罐身最宽处，上半部呈锥形，圜底。壶颈短而窄，连接着一个上翘的壶嘴。壶身烧制均匀，呈黄褐色，表面饰有几组纵向红线，这些线条在壶底交会，形成网状图案。

此陶壶出自克里特岛中部基帕里西村附近的一处墓葬洞穴，是一件典型的圣奥诺夫里奥斯陶器。从这一遗址中发掘出人类骨骼、大量陶器以及其他陪葬品，如金属武器、珠宝、黑曜石工具和石项链珠。

彩绘陶器工艺是米诺斯器物文化早期的一大进步，标志着克里特岛进入青铜时代初期。这表明在岛上第一座宫殿建立前近千年，克里特岛就已具备了较高的技术水平、独特的制造品分配系统以及相对复杂的陶器生产组织形式。

“圣奥诺夫里奥斯陶器”以克里特岛梅萨拉平原的一处考古遗址命名，其特点为以浅色背景作底，用橙红色或棕红色绘制装饰图案。红色是通过在受控的烧制条件下创造氧化氛围得到的，这也是使用封闭窑炉的最早证据之一。在早期陶器中，线性图案与陶器器形有机结合，通常以交叉的线条形成网格状图案，令人联想到篮编装饰。

陶壶是圣奥诺夫里奥斯陶器中最为流行的器形，是主要的液体盛具，常见于家居和葬礼场景。这种特定器形在爱琴海东北部和小亚细亚西部非常流行，其设计可能受到葫芦形容器的启发，因为后者直至公元前 20 世纪初一直被用作液体容器。

（艾琳·加利）

65

Haghios Onouphrios Ware jug

Early Minoan I (Ca. 3000 BCE)

Clay

Max. h. 18.8 cm

Kyparissi, burial cave, 1951

Archaeological Museum of Heraklion, Π10853

Finely made jug, complete. The conical upper body angles abruptly into a rounded bottom, which is smaller than the maximum diameter. The short, narrow neck ends in a raised spout. The evenly fired yellowish surface is decorated with groups of vertical red lines that converge under the base to form a net pattern.

This jug, which comes from a burial cave near the village of Kyparissi in central Crete, is a typical sample of Haghios Onouphrios Ware. The excavated deposit included human bones, a large number of vases, and other types of grave gifts, such as metal weapons and jewellery, obsidian tools and stone necklace beads.

The production of pottery with painted decoration is one of the earliest developments of Minoan material culture and a significant marker of the beginning of the Early Bronze Age period in Crete. It also shows a relatively high degree of technical knowledge, a distribution system for manufactured goods, and the organisation of pottery manufacture, which appears to have been fairly complex even before the establishment of the first palaces, almost a thousand years later.

Haghios Onouphrios Ware, named after an archaeological site in the Mesara Plain of Crete, is characterised by painted decoration of orange-red to brownish-red motifs on a light background. The red colour is achieved by creating an oxidizing atmosphere within controlled firing conditions and is among the earliest pieces of evidence of the use of a closed kiln. In the earliest examples, the linear motifs are organically related to the shape of the vase. They consist of groups of lines that often criss-cross to create grids reminiscent of basket-weaving.

The jug, the main serving vessel for liquids, is the most popular shape in Haghios Onouphrios Ware and occurs in both domestic and funerary contexts. This particular shape, very popular in the northeast Aegean and western Asia Minor, may have been inspired by the flask-shaped gourd, which had been used as a liquid container until the beginning of the 20th c. BCE.

References

Αλεξίου 1951, 227, pl.13, fig.1.1. Alexiou-Warren 2004, 72, 125-126. Betancourt 2008, 16-23. Day-Wilson-Kyriatzi 1998. Todaro 2019.

(Irene Galli)

66

罐

米诺斯早期Ⅱ（公元前2700～前2200年）

陶土

高14.2厘米，罐身直径16.1厘米

发现于克里特岛伦达斯盖罗坎波斯的Ⅱ号墓

希腊伊拉克利翁考古博物馆藏，编号Π15472

球形容器，由红棕色陶土烧制而成。圆柱形罐颈长度较短，罐口狭窄，原配罐盖现已佚失，圈足，罐体肩部设有四个纵向小系，用于将盖子固定在容器上。器表光滑，并饰深刻水平槽纹。器身为泥条盘筑法制成，可能借助了简易手工轮盘塑形。这种容器通常用于存放香氛油或软膏，可能用于墓葬中熏香，也可能仅作象征用途，例如作为死者个人财产陪葬，供其在来世使用。

（帕拉斯克维·斯塔马塔基）

66

Pyxis

Early Minoan Ⅱ (2700-2200 BCE)

Clay

H. 14.2 cm, body diam. 16.1 cm

Lendas (Gerokampos, Tomb Ⅱ)

Archaeological Museum of Heraklion, Π15472

Globular vessel of reddish-brown fired clay, with low cylindrical collar, narrow opening with lid (missing), ring base and four small vertical perforated lugs on the shoulder, allowing the lid to be attached to the vessel. The exterior surface is smoothed and decorated with deep horizontal grooves. The main body was built up from successive coils that were subsequently formed into its final, globular shape, possibly on a simple rotating disc turned by hand. It contained scented oils or unguents either for perfuming the tomb or for purely symbolic reasons, such as accompanying the deceased as a personal possession in the afterlife.

References

Alexiou-Warren 2004, 18, 101 (no.404), 191, fig.29 (no.404), pl.88A. Betancourt 1985, 86-91. Rethemiotakis 2024, 22.

(Paraskevi Stamataki)

67

瓦西利基型“茶壶”

米诺斯早期ⅡB（公元前2400～前2300年）

陶土

高14.5厘米，最大宽度（含壶嘴）28.3厘米，底径7.5厘米

发现于克里特岛瓦西利基耶拉佩特拉

希腊伊拉克利翁考古博物馆藏，编号Π3729

带流陶“茶壶”，器表饰有瓦西利基陶器典型的斑驳装饰。这种特殊工艺在米拉贝洛湾地区的餐具制造中得到了广泛使用。这种斑驳装饰通过刻意调节窑炉温度形成，体现了米诺斯早期Ⅱ－Ⅲ克里特岛陶工的高超技艺。瓦西利基陶器的金属光泽和器形可能模仿了金属器物，因此属于早期“仿制器”。这种陶器通过有序的分配网络在克里特岛的东部和中部地区广泛流传。

（乔治娅·弗拉达）

67

Vasiliki Ware "Teapot"

Early Minoan ⅡB (2400-2300 BCE)

Clay

H. 14.5 cm, max. w. (with spout) 28.3 cm, diam. base 7.5 cm

Vasılıkı, Ierapetra

Archaeological Museum of Heraklion, Π3729

Clay "teapot" with eyed spout. It has the mottled decoration typical of the Vasiliki Ware, a special technique widely used in the Gulf of Mirabello area for the manufacture of tableware. The mottled decoration is the intentional result of controlled but variable kiln-firing, which demonstrates the advanced technical skills of the Cretan potters during the Early Minoan Ⅱ-Ⅲ period. The metallic sheen and the shapes of the Vasiliki Ware vessels probably imitate ones of metal, thus attesting to an early case of skeuomorhism. Vasiliki Ware was fairly widespread, via an organised distribution network, mainly in East and Central Crete.

References

Betancourt 1979, 59, pl. 4A. Betancourt 1985.

(Georgia Flouda)

68

卡马雷斯风格嵌贝彩绘三耳壶

米诺斯中期Ⅲ（公元前 1750 ~ 前 1700 年）

陶土

高 59 厘米

发现于克里特岛斐斯托斯王宫（LV 号房间）

希腊伊拉克利翁考古博物馆藏，编号 Π10577

用于盛装液体的大型陶壶，配三个把手，便于搬运和倾倒内容物。这件陶壶是典型的“卡马雷斯陶器”，以深色为背景，饰有多彩图案。其风格和功能与斐斯托斯王宫同一房间中发现的其他器物相符，可能用作宫殿宴会餐具。此陶壶上装饰有小型模制贝壳，排列对称，置于壶体的白色条带内。这种装饰反映了米诺斯文化与海洋的特殊联系，也开启了在陶器上运用海洋主题装饰的悠久传统。

（乔治娅・弗拉达）

68

Three-handled jug with relief shells and painted decoration

Middle Minoan Ⅲ (1750-1700 BCE)

Clay

H. 59 cm

Phaistos, palace (Room LV)

Archaeological Museum of Heraklion, Π10577

This large jug for serving liquids has three handles for carrying and to assist in pouring out the contents. A typical example of Kamares Ware, with polychrome decoration on a dark ground, its style and function match those of the other vessels found in the same room of the palace of Phaistos, constituting a "dinner service", probably for use at palace banquets. This vase features a decorative band of small mould-made shells, symmetrically placed in white bands on the body of the vessel. These demonstrate the special connection of Minoans with the sea and the beginning of a long tradition of marine motifs applied on pottery.

References

Levi 1976, 101, F1041, fig.128, tab.77a. Betancourt 1985.

(Georgia Flouda)

69

卡马雷斯风格有流罐

米诺斯中期 I B 至 II A（公元前 1900 ~ 前 1750 年）

陶土

高 17.5 厘米

发现于克里特岛斐斯托斯王宫（LXV 号房间）

希腊伊拉克利翁考古博物馆藏，编号 Π11194

陶罐呈卵形，配有短颈、喙形流和三个纵向把手，用于宫殿宴会期间盛装液体。罐身由逐层堆叠的陶土盘条制作，最后在陶轮上塑形完成。此器物饰有卡马雷斯陶器装饰，以白色、橙色和红色的多彩几何及抽象图案绘于深色背景上。壶身大部分表面还带有"巴尔波丁装饰"，通过添加细小黏土团块在壶身表面形成粗糙浮雕凸起。这种技艺在青铜文明中期初始阶段尤为流行，主要有两种式样，本罐采用的"颗粒状装饰"和模仿海洋生物壳表面的"藤壶状装饰"。

卡马雷斯陶器是青铜文明中期克里特岛中部的典型陶器，因最初发现于普斯洛里蒂斯山南坡的卡马雷斯洞穴而得名。在克诺索斯米诺斯王宫、希腊大陆和埃及也曾出土此类复杂陶器，表明米诺斯人在公元前二千纪上半叶与克里特岛外地区联系密切。

（帕拉斯克维・斯塔马塔基）

69

Beak-spouted jug

Middle Minoan I B–II A (1900-1750 BCE)

Clay

H. 17.5 cm

Phaistos, palace (Room LXV)

Archaeological Museum of Heraklion, Π11194

Clay vessel with ovoid body, low neck, beaked spout and three vertical handles, used for serving liquids during palace banquets. The main body was built up from successive coils that were subsequently thrown on the wheel to produce the final shape. It features Kamares Ware decoration, which consists of complex, polychrome, geometric and abstract designs painted in white, orange and red on a dark ground. It also bears relief "Barbotine" decoration on most of its body, consisting of rough relief protuberances on the surface created by adding fine lumps of clay. This technique was particularly popular in the early Middle Bronze Age in two versions, "Granular" (in this case) and "Barnacle Work" (which imitates the surface of shells of marine organisms).

Kamares Ware, characteristic of Middle Bronze Age Central Crete, is named after the Kamares Cave on the southern slopes of Mount Psiloritis, where it was first discovered. Examples of this elaborate prestige ware have also been found at the Minoan palace of Knossos, as well as in mainland Greece and in Egypt, evidence of the strong contacts of the Minoans outside Crete in the first half of the second millennium BCE.

References

Betancourt 1985, 83-85, 94-101. Levi 1976, 147-151, tab.23b, 23e, pl.XIIIb. Rethemiotakis 2024, 36-41. Walberg 1976.

(Paraskevi Stamataki)

70

折腹饮杯（带 11 个小号杯）

米诺斯中期Ⅱ（公元前 1800 ~ 前 1700 年）
陶土
高 8.5 厘米
发现于克里特岛米尔托斯-皮尔戈斯
希腊伊拉克利翁考古博物馆藏，编号 Π22066

陶饮杯内含 11 个相同形状的小号杯，器表涂有光亮的棕黑色釉料。它出土于米尔托斯-皮尔戈斯的一个聚落，与米诺斯文明中期该聚落最重要的建筑有关。这种套娃式陶饮杯可能是一件用于仪式供奉的祭器。折腹、花口且带两个带状把手的陶饮杯在旧王宫期的克里特岛便已出现。研究认为，这种陶器的原型来自安纳托利亚（现代土耳其内陆），为金属材质，古尔尼亚发现的一件银质饮杯便印证了这一点。米诺斯陶饮杯的深色器表可能是为了模仿原始银质器物氧化后变暗的颜色。

（伊万吉立亚・西克拉）

70

Carinated kantharos with 11 miniature cups

Middle Minoan II (1800-1700 BCE)
Clay
H. 8.5 cm
Myrtos Pyrgos
Archaeological Museum of Heraklion, Π22066

Clay kantharos containing eleven miniature cups of the same shape. It is painted a glossy brownish-black. It was found in the settlement of Myrtos Pyrgos and may be associated with the most important building of the Middle Minoan settlement. The kantharos containing miniature kantharoi would have been a cult vessel, perhaps for making offerings during a ceremony. This type of cup with strongly carinated body, crinkled rim and two strap handles appears in Crete in the Protopalatial era. It is believed to imitate metal prototypes from Anatolia (the interior of modern Turkey), as we see from the unique silver kantharos found at Gournia. The dark shade in which clay Minoan kantharoi were painted is thought to be an attempt to imitate the colour of the original precious vessels of tarnished silver.

References

Cadogan 1977-78. Dimopoulou-Rethemiotaki 2005, 224. Girella 2002.

(Evangelia Sikla)

71

卡马雷斯风格折腹杯

米诺斯中期ⅡB（约公元前 1700 年）

陶土

高 7.5 厘米，口径 10.7 厘米，底径 6.7 厘米

发现于克里特岛斐斯托斯

希腊伊拉克利翁考古博物馆藏，编号 Π10085

这是一件“卡马雷斯陶器”折腹杯的复原品，使用泥条盘筑法手工成型，在陶轮上完成加工。器表饰有多彩装饰，棕色背景上绘有带白色花形图案的双色圆形装饰。花形图案中心的棕色装饰尤为突出，在双色圆形装饰的两侧，点缀着由相对的白色半圆组成的带状图案。

（乔治娅·弗拉达）

71

Carinated cup

Middle Minoan ⅡB (Ca. 1700 BCE)

Clay

H. 7.5 cm, diam. rim 10.7 cm, diam. base 6.7 cm

Phaistos

Archaeological Museum of Heraklion, Π10085

Carinated cup in the Kamares Ware, a reconstructed example of a vase handmade from thin coils of clay and finished on the potter's wheel. It bears polychrome decoration. A two-tone medallion with a white rosette is painted onto a brown ground. The centre of the rosette is highlighted with added brown decoration, while the medallion is flanked by two bands with opposed white semicircles.

References

Levi 1976, 365, 368, pl.131n.

(Georgia Flouda)

72

卡马雷斯风格折腹杯

米诺斯中期ⅡB（约公元前 1700 年）

陶土

高度 5.5 厘米，口径 9 厘米

发现于克里特岛斐斯托斯王宫的 IL 号房间

希腊伊拉克利翁考古博物馆藏，编号 Π10180

这件彩绘折腹杯属于典型的“卡马雷斯陶器”，这种陶器类型于米诺斯中期Ⅱ在克里特岛中部，特别是梅萨拉平原地区发展起来。卡马雷斯陶器不仅用于制作餐具，还用于制作宴会用的大型容器。此器物使用泥条盘筑法手工成型，在陶轮上完成加工。器表装饰有自由展开的花形旋涡图案，这种图案在当时的印章雕刻中也非常流行。

（乔治娅·弗拉达）

72

Carinated cup

Middle Minoan ⅡB (Ca. 1700 BCE)

Clay

H. 5.5 cm, diam. rim 9 cm

Phaistos, palace, Room IL

Archaeological Museum of Heraklion, Π10180

Carinated cup, a typical polychrome example of the famed Kamares Ware that was developed during the Middle Minoan II period in Central Crete and especially in the area of the Mesara Plain. It was employed for the production of tableware, as well as for large vases for use at banquets. The shape of the vessel is a combination of handmade construction with thin clay coils and a final processing on the potter's wheel. The decorative rosette-whorl developed so freely on the surface of the cup was also a particularly popular motif in contemporary seal-carving.

References

Levi 1976, 48-49, pl.131h.

(Georgia Flouda)

73

卡马雷斯风格半球形杯

米诺斯中期ⅡB（公元前1750～前1700年）

陶土

高16厘米，直径16.5厘米

发现于克里特岛斐斯托斯王宫（XI号房间）

希腊伊拉克利翁考古博物馆藏，编号Π10091

大型陶半球形杯，配两个纵向把手，用于在宫殿宴会上搅拌和盛装液体。杯身以泥条盘筑法制成，随后利用陶轮塑形。装饰采用白色、橙色和红色多彩几何及抽象图案，绘于深色背景上。此杯的主要装饰主题为一个巨大的白、橙双色花形图案，呈现于深色背景上。

（帕拉斯克维·斯塔马塔基）

73

Semiglobular cup

Middle Minoan ⅡB (1750-1700 BCE)

Clay

H. 16 cm, diam. 16.5 cm

Phaistos, palace (Room XI)

Archaeological Museum of Heraklion, Π10091

Large clay semiglobular cup with two vertical handles, used for mixing and serving liquids during palace banquets. The main body was built up from successive coils that were subsequently thrown on the wheel to produce the final shape. Its decoration consists of polychrome geometric and abstract designs in white, orange and red on a dark ground. In this case, the main decorative theme is a very large rosette in white and orange on a dark ground.

References

Betancourt 1985, 83-85, 94-101, pl.9J. Levi 1976, pl.120e. Rethemiotakis 2024, 36-41. Walberg 1976.

(Paraskevi Stamataki)

74

卡马雷斯风格壶

米诺斯中期ⅡB（公元前1750～前1700年）

陶土

高23.3厘米，壶身直径12.7厘米

发现于克里特岛波罗斯的伊卡鲁街墓葬

希腊伊拉克利翁考古博物馆藏，编号Π29593

陶壶呈卵形，配有长颈、宽口以及垂直把手。壶身主要通过堆叠陶土盘条制作，随后在陶轮上完成塑形。长颈则以一小块陶土附于壶身，通过轮制成型。长颈底部形成凸环，用以确保接缝牢固，同时也作为装饰性设计。本件器物采用“卡马雷斯风格”装饰，饰有复杂的多彩几何及抽象图案，以白色、橙色和红色绘于深色背景上。主要装饰主题包括平行带状的旋涡图案、斜线或竖线，以及深色背景上的实心白色与橙色条纹。这种壶原本用于盛装液体，后被放置在墓中，作为象征性随葬品陪伴逝者进入来世。

（帕拉斯克维·斯塔马塔基）

74

Jug

Middle Minoan ⅡB (1750-1700 BCE)

Clay

H. 23.3 cm, body diam. 12.7 cm

Poros, Tomb on Ikarou Street

Archaeological Museum of Heraklion, Π29593

Clay vessel with ovoid body, long neck, wide mouth and vertical handle. The main body was manufactured by adding successive coils that were subsequently thrown on the wheel to produce the final shape. The long neck was joined to the main body as a small mass of clay and then wheel-thrown. A relief ring was formed at the base of the neck to ensure a secure join; this is also a decorative feature. The vessel is decorated in the Kamares Style, consisting of complex, polychrome, geometric and abstract designs painted in white, orange and red on a dark ground. In this case, the main decorative themes are parallel bands of running spirals, diagonal or vertical lines, and solid white and orange bands on a dark ground. This jug, originally used for serving liquids, was placed in the tomb to symbolically accompany the deceased as personal possession in the afterlife.

References

Dimopoulou-Rethemiotaki 2004. Dimopoulou-Krzyszkowska 2019, 41-96, especially 64-65.

(Paraskevi Stamataki)

75

特殊王宫风格带流壶

米诺斯晚期ⅠB（公元前 1500～前 1450 年）

陶土

高 28 厘米

发现于克里特岛圣特里亚达的莱贝特之家

希腊伊拉克利翁考古博物馆藏，Π3936

梨形壶，配有宽阔、倾斜的喙状流和纵向把手。装饰采用米诺斯晚期ⅠB 流行的特殊王宫风格。壶身饰有大面积双斧图案，并配有“祭祀结”和各类填充纹样，以及多组线条和形式化的岩石装饰图案。

一般认为双斧是牛祭的主要仪式工具，而牛祭正是米诺斯宗教崇拜的核心仪式。这种风格中双斧和“祭祀结”反复出现，表明这件壶可能是祭祀仪式中的奠酒器。

（艾琳·尼古拉科普卢）

75

Beaked jug of the Special Palatial Tradition

Late Minoan ⅠB (1500-1450 BCE)

Clay

H. 28 cm

Hagia Triada, Casa del Lebete

Archaeological Museum of Heraklion, Π3936

Piriform jug with wide, bevelled, beaked spout and vertical handle. The decoration follows the Special Palatial Tradition that dominates the vase-painting of the Late Minoan IB period. In a wide zone around the body runs a pattern of double axes combined with the "sacral knot" motif and filling motifs, groups of lines and stylised rocks.

The emblematic symbol of the double axe is believed to depict the main ritual instrument used for bull sacrifice, a ceremony central to Minoan worship. The repetition of these symbols, the double axe and the sacral knot, in the style of the period, indicates that this jug was used as a ritual libation vessel.

References

Halbherr-Stefani-Banti 1977, fig.175. Puglisi 2014, Tav.XII, X.7.

(Irene Nikolakopoulou)

76

海洋风卵形来通杯

米诺斯晚期ⅠB（约公元前 1525/1500 ~ 前 1450 年）

陶土

高 33.2 厘米

发现于克里特岛扎克罗斯的 A 号房屋

希腊伊拉克利翁考古博物馆藏，编号 Π2085

卵形来通杯，瓶口折沿，口下有一个垂直小把手。瓶肩与瓶颈的过渡处有浮雕领圈。此器物已经修复完整。

这件来通杯出土于扎克罗斯西北山坡 A 号房屋内，其装饰风格采用海洋元素，主题灵感来自海洋生物。主要图案为海星，瓶身通体饰有布满珊瑚和海草的海底岩石。来通杯瓶身和瓶颈还绘有特里同螺图案。

这件来通杯可能曾用于宗教仪式和其他祭祀活动。此类来通杯出产于宫殿工坊，装饰风格通常采用海洋元素，有时也采用珍贵材料制作，例如石材以及金属。这种来通杯造型仅存在于克里特岛新王宫期的最后阶段（公元前 1525/1500 ~ 前 1450 年）。米诺斯是爱琴海地区重要的海上力量和商业强国，以海洋生物作为装饰主题反映出海洋对米诺斯人的重要性。来通杯上对海洋生物细节的精细表现以及高超的技术水平，证明这件器物出自专业工匠之手。

（克莱奥・察纳基）

76

Ovoid Rhyton (libation vessel) with Marine Style decoration

Late Minoan Ⅰ B (Ca. 1525/1500 - 1450 BCE)

Clay

H. 33.2 cm

Zakros, House A

Archaeological Museum of Heraklion, Π2085

Ovoid rhyton with flat everted rim and a small vertical handle under the rim. Relief collar ring at the transition from shoulder to neck. Mended and restored.

The vessel, which was found in House A on the NW hill at Zakros, is decorated in the Marine Style, whose themes were inspired by marine life. The central motifs are starfish, while seabed rocks with coral and seaweed adorn the whole surface of the rhyton. Tritons also decorate the main body and the neck of the vessel.

The rhyton would have been used for libation rituals and other religious activities. This type of rhyton was decorated in the Marine Style and produced by palace workshops. Rhyta were also manufactured in precious materials, such as different kinds of stones and probably, also, metal. This rhyton shape only appears in the last phase of the Neopalatial era on Crete (1525/1500 - 1450 BCE). The motifs inspired by marine life indicate the importance of the sea for the Minoans, a major maritime and commercial power in the Aegean. The exceptional rendering of the details of marine life, together with the highly skilled technical features, are evidence that this rhyton was manufactured by specialised artisans.

References

Hogarth 1902, 333-38. Betancourt 1985, 135, 144-45. Koehl 2006, 31-32, 108, 264 (fig.11).

(Kleio Tzanaki)

77

特殊王宫风格海洋生物纹壶

米诺斯晚期ⅠB（公元前1500~前1450年）

陶土

高29厘米，壶口直径17厘米

发现于克里特岛扎克罗斯王宫

希腊伊拉克利翁考古博物馆藏，编号Π32612

陶壶采用“海洋风格”装饰，壶口外翻，壶身以对角线交织形成一张鳞片状网格，将船蛸图案包裹其中。壶颈周围也装饰有一圈船蛸图案，鳞片状网格间还可见水草纹样。壶口饰有鳞状网格图案，边缘则环绕着一圈叶状纹带；壶口斜边饰有V形图案。壶颈与壶肩过渡处点缀有海绵图案。叶状纹带还出现在壶颈顶部、肩部、柄表面、柄背面及其与壶身的连接处，以及壶足。

这件陶壶来自扎克罗斯王宫，是米诺斯晚期ⅠB特殊王宫风格的代表作之一。在克里特岛出土的特殊王宫风格陶器中，有八件采用了海洋风格的装饰，但其中仅有三件保存较为完好，能够复原。在所有同类制品中，精美程度比肩扎克罗斯陶壶的共有两件，一件出自伊拉克利翁波罗斯墓室，一件可能来自埃及（现藏于马赛波雷利博物馆）。考古学家普拉东（N. Platon）最初认为扎克罗斯陶壶与马赛陶壶出自同一位工匠之手。然而，1986年波罗斯墓中发现的陶壶推翻了这一本就备受质疑的假设。不同于其他两件陶壶，波罗斯陶壶还带有模制装饰。但在装饰和制作工艺上，波罗斯陶壶与马赛陶壶确实存在相似之处（如相同的三叶形壶口设计），并且两者尺寸也十分接近（扎克罗斯陶壶比波罗斯和马赛的陶壶都高），研究者也由此推断这两件陶壶出自同一位陶工，甚至可能是同一位画匠之手。马赛陶壶可能是在19世纪中叶由走私者从克里特岛转移到埃及，后被马赛市政府购得。总的来说，这三件器物似乎都制作于米诺斯晚期ⅠB的克诺索斯陶器工坊，扎克罗斯王宫陶壶的陶土实物检测也证实了这一点。

人们推测这些陶器主要用于仪式活动。在波罗斯墓中，除此陶壶外，还发现了一枚黄金图章戒指，表明两者可能是某位祭司或社会显赫人物的随葬品。虽然尚无法确认海洋风格陶器是否为仪式专用，但可以肯定的是，海洋对米诺斯人具有特殊的宗教意义。许多印石和图章戒指上都描绘了仪式用奠酒器，其中最具代表性的便是带“S”形手柄的水壶，这种造型与海洋风陶壶完全一致。在梯林斯金戒上，神怪手持的正是此种水壶。此外，克诺索斯王宫西翼的“游行壁画”似乎也刻画了壶口外翻的陶壶形象。这些陶器的艺术价值从古至今始终无可争议。值得注意的是，在埃及底比斯的高官墓葬壁画中，这些陶器被描绘为克里特岛居民（Keftiu）献给法老的厚礼。

（莱夫特里斯·普拉东）

77

Ewer with Marine Style decoration of the Special Palatial Tradition

Late Minoan I B (1500-1450 BCE)

Clay

H. 29 cm, rim diam. 17 cm

Zakros, palace

Archaeological Museum of Heraklion, Π32612

Ewer with everted rim, decorated in the Marine Style with argonauts framed within a scale-like net of diagonal intersecting lines. Argonauts are also shown in a row around the neck along with seaweed in a scale-like net. On the upper surface of the rim are a scale-like net with dots, and a foliate band around the edge; on the bevelled lip of the rim is a row of chevrons. Sponge pattern imprints embellish the transition point from the neck to the shoulder. Rows of foliate bands are placed at the top of the neck, at the shoulder, and on the handle ridge itself, on its back and outlining it, where it joins the body, and at the foot.

The ewer from the palace of Zakros numbers among the exceptional pieces of ceramics executed in the so-called Special Palace Tradition of the Late Minoan IB period. Eight examples of this group in Crete are decorated in the Marine Style. However, only three have survived in such a state that it has been possible to restore them to completeness. In addition to the Zakros ewer, excellent examples of the type are the one from a chamber tomb in Poros Heraklion and another housed in the Borély Museum in Marseilles, probably coming from Egypt. N. Platon considered that the latter and the Zakros piece were works by the same artist. However, the discovery of the one from Poros, in 1986, overthrew this hypothesis, which had in any case already been disputed. The Poros example is unique, as it is additionally embellished with applied moulded decoration. Other decorative and constructional features (such as the identically formed trefoil-shaped mouth), as well as its size, which is almost equal to the Marseilles vase (the Zakros ewer is taller than both), constitute criteria for the identification, at least, of one potter, if not painter, as the sole creator of these two pieces. It is also a likely hypothesis that the Marseilles ewer was transferred from Crete to Egypt by antiquity-smugglers in the mid-19th century, to be purchased later by the Municipality of Marseilles. Broadly speaking, though, all three vessels seem to have been crafted in a specialised Knossian workshop of the mature Late Minoan IB phase. This is also supported by the macroscopic examination of the clay of the ewer from the palace of Zakros.

As for the use of these vessels, it is reasonable to assume that it was primarily ceremonial. It is worth noting the discovery in the tomb of Poros, along with the ewer, of a gold signet ring, which suggests that the two objects were burial offerings for some priestly or other socially prominent figure. Although it has never been confirmed that the vases with Marine Style decoration were made to be used in rituals, it is nevertheless certain that the sea had a special religious significance for the Minoans. Moreover, there are many depictions of ritual libation jugs on sealstones and signet rings. The most characteristic are the jugs with S-shaped handles, exactly like those of the Marine Style ewers, held by the genii in procession depicted on the gold ring of Tiryns. A depiction of an actual ewer with everted rim seems to be included in the Procession Fresco, in the West Wing of the palace of Knossos. The enormous artistic value of these vases seems to have been – even in their time – unquestionable. Suffice it to note that they are depicted, among other objects brought as gifts to the Pharaoh by those considered to be residents of Crete (Keftiu), in the frescoes of the tombs of Egyptian officials in Thebes.

References

Πλάτων 1974, 92. Dimopoulou-Rethemiotaki 1999, 217-226. Betancourt, 1985, 136, fig.101. Mountjoy 1985, 231-242. Wachsmann 1987, pls.LIV-LVIII.

(Lefteris Platon)

78

芦苇纹来通杯

米诺斯晚期Ⅰ（公元前 1600～前 1450 年）

陶土

高 17.7 厘米，口径 15 厘米，底径 4.7 厘米

发现于克里特岛阿尔哈内斯的宫殿建筑

希腊伊拉克利翁考古博物馆藏，编号 Π19267

大型半球形杯，配纵向带状把手和圆盘形底座，杯口外翻，杯足较短。杯底在烧制前已打好倾倒孔，表明此物设计用于倒出液体或在特殊的奠酒仪式中进行液体供奉。细带状把手及其与壶口交接处的装饰钮突表明这类陶器与类似的金属器物有所关联。

新王宫期，来通杯的形状和尺寸千差万别。本件器物采用典型的花卉风格陶器绘画技艺，杯身绘有彼时非常流行的红棕色芦苇图案。此来通杯杯壁细腻，陶土经过精心烧制变得坚硬，表面经过抛光，彩绘鲜亮，充分展示出青铜文明晚期初始阶段，克里特岛核心区域陶工们卓越的技术成就。

（艾琳·尼古拉科普卢）

78

Cup-rhyton with reed pattern decoration

Late Minoan Ⅰ (1600-1450 BCE)

Clay

H. 17.7 cm, diam. rim 15 cm, diam. base 4.7 cm

Archanes, palatial building

Archaeological Museum of Heraklion, Π19267

Large hemispherical cup with everted rim, vertical strap handle, short foot and disc base. The pouring hole in the bottom was made before the pot was fired, indicating that it was intended to be used for decanting liquids or in special libation ceremonies for making liquid offerings. The thin strap handle and the applied knob at the juncture of handle and rim indicate the relationship of this pottery type to similar metal vessels.

Cup-rhyta are found in various shapes and sizes during the Neopalatial era. This vase is a typical example of the Floral Style of vase-painting. The body is decorated with reddish-brown reeds, a particularly popular theme in this period. The fine walls, the well-fired hard clay fabric, the polished surface and the glossy paint all bear witness to the technological achievements of the potters active in the major centres of Minoan Crete at the beginning of the Late Bronze Age.

References

Σακελλαράκης – Σακελλαράκη, fig.408β.

(Irene Nikolakopoulou)

79

王宫风格罐

米诺斯晚期Ⅱ至ⅢA（公元前 1450 ~ 前 1300 年）
陶土
高 85 厘米，最大直径 30.5 厘米
发现于克里特岛克诺索斯王宫
希腊伊拉克利翁考古博物馆藏，编号 Π7705

王宫风格陶罐，壶身呈梨形，带有折沿、圆柱形窄罐颈以及三个纵向罐柄。罐柄模仿金属器物设计，中部有棱状凸起。此罐用于储存液体，如酒类或橄榄油。罐身通过泥条盘筑法制成，随后在慢速陶轮上完成塑形。器物表面装饰为典型的王宫风格，深棕色的各种图案在浅白色背景上水平排列，形成不同的区域，覆盖整个器表。罐肩中央的条带内重复出现装饰性的百合图案，而在其上方和下方的带状区域则饰有波浪纹。这件陶器是典型的王宫风格器物，该风格延续了前一时期花卉风格和海洋风格的主题，但呈现出更为明显的形式化倾向。这类器物主要出现在宫殿和精英阶层宅邸，是极致奢华的体现。

（帕拉斯克维・斯塔马塔基）

79

Palace Style pithoid jar

Late Minoan Ⅱ–ⅢA (1450-1300 BCE)
Clay
H. 85 cm, max. body diam. 30.5 cm
Knossos, palace
Archaeological Museum of Heraklion, Π7705

Clay three-handled Palace Style pithoid jar with piriform body, narrow cylindrical neck, everted rim and three vertical handles with a central relief spine (imitating metal prototypes) on its pronounced shoulder. It was used for storing liquids (such as alcoholic beverages or olive oil). The body was built up from successive coils that were subsequently thrown on a slow potter's wheel. It bears Palace Style decoration in dark brown on a whitish ground, arranged in horizontal zones covering the entire surface of the vessel. In the central band on the shoulder is a repeated ornamental derivative of the waz-lily motif, with wavy striations in the bands above and below. The vessel is a representative example of the Palace Style, which depicted motifs of the Floral and Marine Styles of the previous period with a tendency towards stylisation. These vessels were intended for use as luxury display vessels in palatial and elite buildings.

References

Betancourt 1985, 155-158. PM III, 385-387, fig.258. Mountjoy 1993, 41, fig.50. Mountjoy 1986. Rethemiotakis 2024, 94.

(Paraskevi Stamataki)

80

带盖棺椁

米诺斯晚期ⅢB（公元前 1300～前 1200 年）

陶土

高 94 厘米，长 102 厘米，宽 43 厘米

发现于克里特岛普雷韦利亚纳的安尼摩米里洛斯

希腊伊拉克利翁考古博物馆藏，编号 Π18858

陶棺椁，带有短支腿和高耸的山墙形盖子，用于以蜷缩姿势（“胎儿式”）埋葬死者。器物以矩形陶土板拼接制作，并通过手工塑形。棺盖上端有两个对角孔及两个便于掀盖的凸出把手。棺盖两长边的下部末端附近有两对较小的孔，棺椁长边下侧也有两对位置对应的孔洞，可能是用于套绳固定棺盖。棺椁饰有红棕色图案，绘于米色背景上。装饰主题以海洋生物为主，两长侧绘有风格独特的章鱼和船蛸，窄侧则描绘米诺斯圣树“生命之树”，其中一窄侧还绘有弯曲的祭坛图案。棺椁主体的竖直面和棺盖窄侧均绘有螺旋图案，棺椁边缘下方则饰以水平波浪线条。

如其他米诺斯晚期Ⅲ棺椁一样，此器物的海洋生物图案以简化方式表现。棺椁的装饰主题可能暗示了对来世的宗教信仰，即在神灵护佑下，生灵死后，其生命会在大海彼岸延续。此外，米诺斯艺术中的棕榈树图案象征着重生，通常与米诺斯神祇祭坛并置。

（帕拉斯克维·斯塔马塔基）

80

Chest larnax with gabled lid

Late Minoan IIIB (1300-1200 BCE)

Clay

H. 94 cm, l. 102 cm, w. 43 cm

Preveliana, Anemomilos

Archaeological Museum of Heraklion, Π18858

Ceramic chest larnax or sarcophagus with short legs and high gabled lid, used as a coffin for the dead, buried in a contracted, "foetal" position. It was made by putting together wet, rectangular slabs of clay and hand finishing them into their final shape. On the upper end of the lid are two holes opened diagonally and two projecting handles for lifting the lid. Two pairs of smaller holes are found towards the end of the lower part of each of the long sides of the lid. There are also two matching pairs of holes in roughly the same position below the rim on the long sides of the larnax, probably used to tie on the lid with a rope. The chest larnax is decorated in reddish-brown paint on a buff ground, depicting marine creatures: on the two long sides are stylised octopuses and argonauts, while on the narrow sides of the larnax is painted the sacred Minoan "palm tree of life", with an incurved altar on one narrow side. The vertical sides of the main body of the larnax are decorated with spirals, as are the narrow sides of the lid, with horizontal wavy lines under the rim of the larnax.

As on other Late Minoan III larnakes, Minoan marine life is represented in a schematic manner. The decorative themes of the larnax probably imply a religious belief in the afterlife, namely that life after death continues somewhere beyond the sea, under the protection of the divine. Besides, the palm motif symbolising the regeneration of life in Minoan art appears next to the sacred altar devoted to the Minoan gods.

References

Αλεξίου 1971. Betancourt 1985, 161-163. Marinatos 1993, 54, 239. Marinatos 1984. Rethemiotakis 2024, 114-119. Watrous 1991.

(Paraskevi Stamataki)

金饰竞辉光

跨入青铜时代的克里特上层人士钟爱各种材质的珠宝首饰。早期金饰造型简单，用捶打、切割和压花等工艺制成头冠、发簪、手镯、项链及挂坠等物品。至旧王宫期，工匠们可能受到巴比伦人启发，用造粒技术生产戒指、耳环等金饰，让它们看上去十分细腻精致。在新王宫期及米诺斯文化后期，金饰品种类丰富多样，尤其挂坠的珠子被塑造成谷粒、宝石、瓜果、莲花、纸莎草、石榴等形状。有些单体挂坠则以狮子、山羊、公牛等动物为造型。随着宫殿的毁灭，用于制作首饰的贵金属变得稀有，逐渐被廉价材料代替。米诺斯金饰品似乎对后世古希腊珠宝的设计和工艺产生了一定影响。

The Radiance of Gold Ornaments

As Crete entered the Bronze Age, its elite developed a fondness for jewelry made from various materials. Early gold ornaments were simple in design, crafted through hammering, cutting, and embossing to create diadems, hairpins, bracelets, necklaces, and pendants. By the Protopalatial era, artisans had adopted granulation techniques, possibly inspired by the Babylonian, to produce intricate rings and earrings. During the Neopalatial era and the later stages of Minoan civilization, gold ornaments became even more diverse, with pendants shaped like grains, gemstones, fruits, lotuses, papyrus, and pomegranates. Some standalone pendants featured animal forms such as lions, goats, and bulls. However, with the destruction of the palaces, precious metals became scarce, gradually replaced by cheaper materials. The gold ornaments of Minoan civilization appear to have influenced later Greek jewelry design.

81

叶形饰

米诺斯早期Ⅱ至Ⅲ（公元前 2700 ~ 前 2000 年）
黄金
最大长度（叶片与茎部）7 厘米
发现于莫克洛斯Ⅰ/Ⅱ/Ⅲ号墓葬群的Ⅱ号墓
希腊伊拉克利翁考古博物馆藏，编号 X–A319

金质装饰品呈四叶形，近似橄榄叶。每片叶子独立制作，并带有细金属茎。叶片由锤制的金箔制成，边缘装饰有精细的浮雕点状纹路，展现出工匠的娴熟技艺。叶片茎部拧成一股金属线，可能用于连接复合头饰。

这件金橄榄叶与大量其他金饰一起出土于莫克洛斯墓地Ⅱ号墓，这也是墓群中随葬器物最为丰富的一座墓葬。由于当时的葬俗，遗骸和随葬品会不定期迁移，因此无法确定这些金饰的归属。不过，这些随葬品显然属于莫克洛斯当地特别显赫的群体，他们可能长期从事商业活动，或至少享受到了海上贸易的成果。

（艾琳·加利）

81

Leaf-shaped ornament

Early Minoan Ⅱ-Ⅲ(2700-2000 BCE)
Gold
Max. length of leaf and stem: 7 cm
Mochlos Cemetery, Tomb Ⅱ (from Tomb Complex Ⅰ/Ⅱ/Ⅲ)
Archaeological Museum of Heraklion, X-A319

Gold ornament in the shape of a spray of four leaves resembling olive leaves. Each leaf is individually made with its wire stem. The hammered foil leaves have a border of carefully applied repoussé dots, the work of a skilled and experienced artisan. The stems are twisted together into a single wire which may have been attached to a composite diadem.

The gold olive leaves were found with a plethora of gold ornaments in Tomb Ⅱ, the richest tomb in the Mochlos cemetery. Due to the burial practices of the period, which involved moving the remains and the accompanying grave goods, the gold ornaments cannot be associated with specific individuals. However, the latter belonged to a particularly powerful group of the Mochlos community, a group which engaged in intensive and systematic commercial activity or at least enjoyed the fruits of this maritime trade.

References

Seager 1912. Soles 1992. Legarra Herrero 2018.

(Irene Galli)

82

带状头饰（一对）

米诺斯早期Ⅲ至米诺斯中期Ⅰ（公元前 2300 ~ 前 1800 年）
铜、黄金
总长 13.8 厘米（X–A491：7 厘米，X–A492：6.8 厘米），
最大宽度 0.9 厘米
发现于克里特岛普拉塔诺斯的 A 号圆顶墓
希腊伊拉克利翁考古博物馆藏，编号 X–A491 和 X–A492

带状金饰由金箔制成，可能是头饰的一部分，制作时采用了最古老、最基础的金工技艺。金匠首先在硬表面上捶打原材料，将其制成薄片，在捶打过程中可能采用了软布或皮革来保护金箔表面。随后，金匠利用金属刀或黑曜石刀将金箔切割成所需的形状，并用工具（如锥子或圆头针）通过多次敲击制作出点状装饰，同时开孔以便固定和组装各部件。

制作过程中出现了一些小失误，例如 X–A491 存在切割位置错误，并且点状装饰呈非对称排布，因此可能是学徒工匠制作的。

这件头饰出土于普拉塔诺斯墓地中最古老且最大的墓葬，墓地中的所有金饰均出土于此。该头饰可能是一件传家宝，虽然其发现地点位于墓葬上层年代较晚的填土层，但它与较深地层出土的时期更早（早约 400 年）的金饰在颜色上非常相似，可能使用了类似的合金。

（艾琳·加利）

82

Band-shaped diadem (two matching pieces)

Early Minoan Ⅲ– Middle Minoan Ⅰ (2300-1800 BCE)
Copper, gold
Total l. 13.8 cm (X-A491: 7 cm, X-A492: 6.8 cm), max. w. 0.9 cm
Platanos, Tholos Tomb A
Archaeological Museum of Heraklion, X-A491 and X-A492

Two associated pieces of jewellery in the form of bands, possibly part of a diadem, made of thin gold leaf. For its construction, the craftsman used the oldest and simplest techniques of goldsmithing. Beating the raw material on a hard surface, he made the sheet first, possibly using a soft cloth or leather cover to protect the surface of the gold from the impacts. Then he cut it to the desired shape, with a metal knife or obsidian blade. He worked the pointillé decoration with repeated sharp blows from a tool, such as an awl or a pin with a rounded end, and opened holes for fixing and assembling the parts.

Small failures in this construction, such as a misplaced cut in X-A 491 and the asymmetry in the placing of the dots, have been put down to the piece being made by an apprentice craftsman.

The diadem was found in the cemetery of Platanos, in the oldest and largest tomb, which contained all the gold jewellery of the cemetery. It may be an heirloom, i.e. an item that its owner had inherited from his/her ancestors. This possibility has been suggested because, although the diadem was found in the higher, more recent fill of the tomb, it was similar in colour, possibly due to a similar alloy being used, to the jewellery found in deeper fills and dating from about 400 years earlier.

References

Xanthoudides 1924, 111. Evely 2000, 405. Hickman 2008, 30.

(Irene Galli)

83

线形头饰

米诺斯早期Ⅱ（公元前 2600 ~ 前 2300 年）

黄金

长 23 厘米，直径 6.7 厘米

发现于克里特岛伦达斯泽尔沃斯地区的 III 号圆顶墓

希腊伊拉克利翁考古博物馆藏，编号 X–A751

这条细长的金带是采用简单的锤制工艺制作而成的，在金属尚温热时拧成条状，以达到类似丝带的独特效果，同时增强黄金的反射光泽。金带可能是一种头饰配件，固定于头部；也可能是单独佩戴的发饰。这条金带出自圆顶墓最深、最早的填土层，发现时紧邻一个头骨，可能曾戴于其上。

（艾琳・加利）

83

Wire of a head ornament

Early Minoan Ⅱ (2600-2300 BCE)

Gold

L. 23 cm, diam. 6.7 cm

Lendas, Tholos Tomb III at Zervos

Archaeological Museum of Heraklion, X-A751

The thin strip, manufactured by the basic technique of hammer-work, was twisted when the metal was still warm, to achieve the special effects of making it look like a ribbon and enhancing the reflected lustre of the gold. It was probably a diadem accessory, fixed to the head; or it could have been worn by itself as an ornament for the hair. The band was found in the deepest and earliest fill of the tholos tomb, next to a human skull, to which it was probably once fixed.

References

Alexiou-Warren 2004, 188. Hickman 2008, 137.

(Irene Galli)

84

饰片

米诺斯早期Ⅱ至Ⅲ（公元前 2600 ~ 前 2100 年）

黄金

直径 1.1 厘米

发现于莫克洛斯Ⅳ/Ⅴ/Ⅵ号墓葬群的Ⅳ号墓

希腊伊拉克利翁考古博物馆藏，编号 X-A364

金质小圆片，其上有孔，便于缝制在布料或皮革等柔软材质上。制作时，将温热的金属置于模具上敲打，形成中间略微弯曲的表面和平坦的边缘。这枚金质圆片出土于莫克洛斯岛的IV/V/VI 号墓葬群，一同发现还有其他一些小型金饰。现今的莫克洛斯是一座小岛，但在米诺斯时期曾与大陆相连，形成了一个天然的双港口，这里也因此发展成为青铜时代早期克里特岛上最富有、活跃的定居点之一。这片墓地出土的黄金首饰可能是当地工坊专为墓葬中的显赫家庭打造，其时间可追溯到公元前三千纪，在数量上是爱琴海地区出土之最。

（艾琳·加利）

84

Appliqué disc

Early Minoan Ⅱ-Ⅲ (2600-2100 BCE)

Gold

Diam. 1.1 cm

Mochlos, Tomb Complex Ⅳ/Ⅴ/Ⅵ, Tomb Ⅳ

Archaeological Museum of Heraklion, X-A364

A small disc with holes for sewing to a soft material, perhaps cloth or leather. It was made by beating the warmed metal around a form, creating a curved surface with a flat surrounding edge. It was found with a number of small gold ornaments in Tomb Complex IV/V/VI on the islet of Mochlos. This present island is believed to have been united with the mainland in the Minoan period, creating a natural double harbour, and facilitating the emergence of one of the richest and most active settlements of Crete during the Early Bronze Age. The gold jewellery of this cemetery, constituting one of the largest collections of Aegean gold of the 3rd millennium BCE, is considered the product of local workshops that covered the needs of the prominent families buried there.

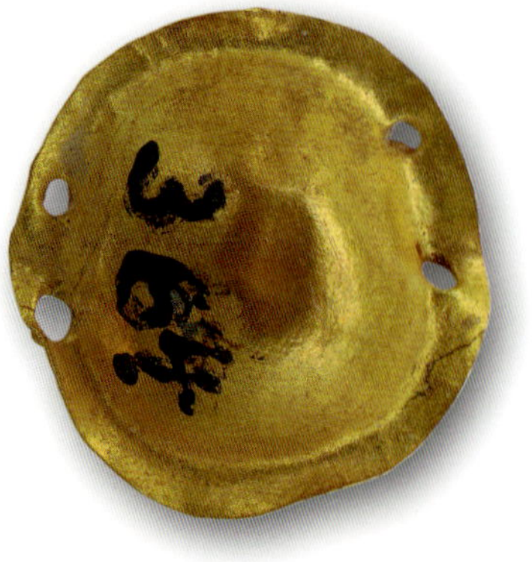

References

Seager 1912, 48, fig.20.IV.8. Βασιλάκης 1996, pl.56a. Hickman 2008, 146.

(Irene Galli)

85

带颗粒装饰的珠子

米诺斯早期Ⅲ至米诺斯中期Ⅰ（公元前 2300 ~ 前 1800 年）

黄金

直径 1.2 厘米

发现于克里特岛库马萨的 B 号圆顶墓

希腊伊拉克利翁考古博物馆藏，编号 X–A388

这是一枚部分保存的金珠，是克里特岛上最早采用造粒装饰工艺的制品之一。这些细小的金粒直径约 1 毫米，虽然并非已知最小的金粒，但其形状规则且圆润，只有部分表面略平，可能是在金属熔化成球时与平坦表面接触形成的。珠子间的连接点非常小，几乎不可见，可能通过使用铜盐和黏合剂实现。铜盐和黏合剂加热后会与黄金形成合金，最终将各组件焊接在一起。这种焊接技术在公元前三千纪下半叶的特洛伊和叙利亚等有着悠久金工传统的地区已有应用。从公元前二千纪开始，造粒装饰在整个地中海东部地区得到广泛传播。而克里特岛的工匠则以其独特的美学和技术偏好，将这一工艺发展到了新的高度。

这颗金珠出土于库马萨墓地的一座圆顶墓中，这里是梅萨拉地区的一个大型墓地。墓地中还发现了其他精美的随葬品，其中最为著名的便是带造粒装饰的米诺斯“青蛙护身符”，以及使用象牙和青金石等外来原料制成的物品。

（艾琳・加利）

85

Bead with granulation

Early Minoan Ⅲ– Middle Minoan Ⅰ (2300-1800 BCE)

Gold

Diam. 1.2 cm

Koumasa, Tholos Tomb B

Archaeological Museum of Heraklion, X-A388

Part of a gold bead, one of the oldest Cretan examples of the granulation technique. The tiny gold balls have a diameter of about 1 mm, and are not among the smallest known. They have a regular spherical shape with just tiny flat spots perhaps acquired when, in the process of melting the metal to a ball, it sat on a flat surface. The points at which the beads stick together are particularly thin, almost invisible. This was probably achieved by using copper salts and glue: on being heated all together, they alloy with the gold and eventually cause the pieces to weld together. This soldering technique was known from the second half of the 3rd millennium BCE in Troy and Syria, areas with a long tradition of gold-working. From the 2nd millennium BCE, granulated decoration spread throughout the East Mediterranean. However, the Cretan craftsmen developed their own distinct aesthetic and technical preferences.

The bead was found in a tholos tomb in the cemetery of Koumasa, a large burial ground in the Mesara. One of the best-known Minoan gold-granulated pieces was also recovered from the cemetery, the frog amulet, among other objects made from "exotic", imported raw materials, such as ivory tusks and lapis lazuli.

References

Xanthoudides 1924, 29. Hickman 2008, 46. Morero-Prévalet 2015, 63, fig.3.

(Irene Galli)

86

项链

米诺斯早期 II 至米诺斯中期 III（公元前 2700 ~ 前 1600 年）
半宝石、费昂斯、黄金
长约 10 厘米
发现于莫克洛斯的 XX/XXI 号墓
希腊伊拉克利翁考古博物馆藏，编号 Σ-K789

项链由15颗珠子组成，包括两颗扁圆形紫水晶珠、一颗带浮雕装饰的圆柱形滑石珠、两颗金珠及多颗费昂斯珠，排列方式颇具现代风格。这条美丽珍贵的项链作为随葬品陪伴墓主一同长眠。除滑石产自克里特岛本土，其他所有原材料及费昂斯工艺均源自东地中海的其他地区。

米诺斯工匠运用了先进的半宝石制作技术，并打造了精致的金器和费昂斯饰品，充分展示出他们的高超技艺。自公元前三千纪末期起，随着海上交流日益频繁，克里特岛的外向型群体积极参与了贵重原材料的贸易和交换。这条项链及其他类似发现表明，自公元前二千纪初起，莫克洛斯这个小社区在米诺斯克里特岛的技术和文化发展方面一直扮演着重要角色。

（艾琳·尼古拉科普卢）

86

Necklace

Early Minoan II – Middle Minoan III (2700-1600 BCE)
Semiprecious stones, faience, gold
L. approx. 10 cm
Mochlos, Tomb XX/XXI
Archaeological Museum of Heraklion, Σ-K789

Necklace of 15 beads (in a modern arrangement) including two lentoid amethyst beads, a cylindrical steatite bead with relief decoration, two gold beads and a few faience beads. Found as a burial offering in a tomb in Mochlos, this beautiful and precious piece of jewellery accompanied its wearer even in death. With the exception of the steatite, a mineral found in Crete, all the raw materials used, as well as the faience-working technique, were imported from other regions of the East Mediterranean.

The advanced techniques used to work the semiprecious stones and the elaborate creations in gold and faience attest to the great skill of the Minoan artisans. With the development of maritime communications from the end of the 3rd millennium BCE onwards, the outward-looking communities of Crete actively participated in the trade in valuable raw materials and the exchange networks of the period. This necklace and other similar finds bear eloquent witness to the active part played by the small community of Mochlos in shaping the technological and cultural landscape of Minoan Crete from the dawn of the 2nd millennium BCE.

References

Soles 1992.

(Irene Nikolakopoulou)

87

圆环链

米诺斯早期Ⅱ至米诺斯中期Ⅱ（公元前 2600 ~ 前 1700 年）
黄金
长 5.7 厘米，圆环直径 0.8 厘米
发现于克里特岛圣特里亚达的圆顶墓
希腊伊拉克利翁考古博物馆藏，编号 X–A221

金链由简单的金线环连接而成，是克里特岛迄今发现采用此技术制作的最大金链。每个金环单独制作，先将金线弯成圆形，然后迅速焊接两端以闭合，焊接点清晰可见。这是最简单、最古老的链条制作技术之一。尽管工艺简单，但制作时间长，成品呈现出一种特殊的美感。这条金链是用作颈饰还是头饰目前尚无定论。此金链出土于圣特里亚达 A 号圆顶墓，距法伊斯托斯王宫较近。

（艾琳・加利）

87

Link chain

Early Minoan II – Middle Minoan II (2600-1700 BCE)
Gold
L. 5.7 cm, diam. of link 0.8 cm
Hagia Triada, Tholos Tomb
Archaeological Museum of Heraklion, X-A221

Gold chain consisting of simple wire links, the largest surviving in Crete fashioned in this particular technique. The rings are made individually, from wire bent into a circular shape and with the ends welded shut by a quick firing immediately after connecting it to its neighbouring link. The points of juncture on the rings are visible. This is one of the simplest and oldest chain-making techniques. However, despite its simplicity, it is a time-consuming technique producing a special aesthetic effect. It is not absolutely certain whether the chain was worn around the neck or the head. Found in Tholos Tomb A in the cemetery of Hagia Triada, near the palace of Phaistos.

References

Banti 1933, 194 fig.63. Branigan 1974, 190, no.2908-14. Effinger 1996, 180.

(Irene Galli)

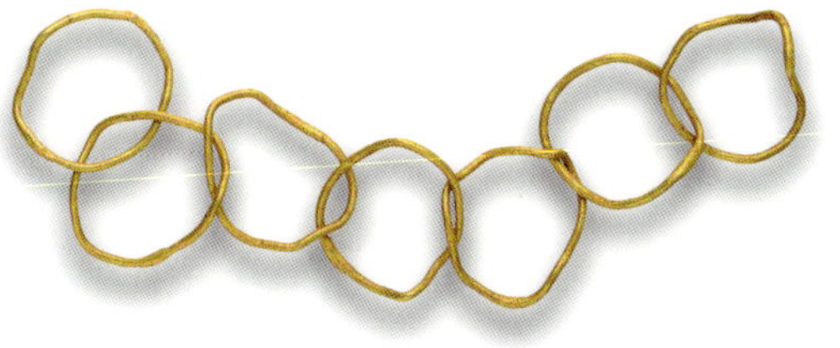

88

带链叶形吊坠

米诺斯早期Ⅱ至米诺斯中期Ⅱ（公元前 2600 ~ 前 1700 年）

黄金

高 2.7 厘米

发现于克里特岛帕莱卡斯特罗

希腊伊拉克利翁考古博物馆藏，编号 X–A85

水滴状吊坠由较厚的金片制成，通过一条截面为矩形的弯曲金线与金链相连。链条使用椭圆环套接技术，每个椭圆环单独焊接后对折相连，工艺精细且耗时。该技术于公元前 3 千纪传入克里特岛，在此地的流行程度与埃及和东地中海繁荣地区不相上下。带叶形吊坠的链条通常用作头饰或发饰。

（艾琳・加利）

88

Leaf-shaped pendant with chain

Early Minoan Ⅱ – Middle Minoan Ⅱ (2600-1700 BCE)

Gold

H. 2.7 cm

Palaikastro

Archaeological Museum of Heraklion, X-A85

Drop-shaped item, of relatively thick sheet, hanging by a bent piece of rectangular-sectioned wire from the last link in a chain. The chain is fashioned using the technique of connecting ellipsoid loops (loop-in-loop). It is a dainty and time-consuming work, as the ellipsoid links were soldered individually and then bent double and threaded together into the chain. This particular technique, appearing in Crete in the 3rd millennium BCE, became widespread there, as popular as it was in Egypt and the prosperous regions of the East Mediterranean. Chains with a leaf-shaped pendant were usually hung from diadems or other ornaments for the head and the hair.

References

Ogden 1992, 47. Hickman 2008, 149. Morero-Prévalet 2015, 61.

(Irene Galli)

89

微型双刃斧

米诺斯中期Ⅲ（公元前 1700 ~ 前 1600 年）
黄金
高 3.97 厘米，最大宽度 4.4 厘米
发现于克里特岛阿尔卡洛科里洞穴
希腊伊拉克利翁考古博物馆藏，编号 HM X-A596

微型祭祀用双刃斧，由非功能性金质薄片制成，带有线形装饰。斧柄有孔，表明该器物可能倒置摆放。

此双刃斧与一批其他金属物品专门存放在洞穴中。如此大量且贵重的金属物品摆放于此却并未被米诺斯人取回，可能表明这批物品与某种仪式性展示和祭祀活动有关。从阿尔卡洛科里洞穴发掘的金属藏品可以看出，当时社会偏爱微型器物。该洞穴共发现 7 件银质和 35 件金质双斧，均以微缩形式呈现双刃斧这一米诺斯象征符号。伊拉克利翁考古博物馆收藏着一件带线形文字 A 铭文的微型双刃银斧，波士顿美术馆收藏的一件微型双刃金斧也可能来自此洞穴。

双刃斧是重要的米诺斯标志，曾用多种材料和形式反复塑造表现。它可能曾用作圣地标志、地母女神的象征、从宇宙山升起的太阳标志，或者一个社会阶层的徽章。

（乔治娅・弗拉达）

89

Miniature double axe

Middle Minoan Ⅲ (1700-1600 BCE)
Gold
H. 3.97 cm, max. w. 4.4 cm
Arkalochori Cave
Archaeological Museum of Heraklion, HM X-A596

Miniature votive double axe, made from non-functional sheet-metal with linear decoration. The hole in the shaft suggests that it was meant to hang upside down.

The axe was part of a hoard of metal objects intentionally deposited in the cave, which represents a significant capital in metal that was not recovered by the Minoans. It is plausible that this hoard resulted from intentional and structured deposition, possibly connected with rituals of ceremonial display and votive offerings. Typical of a culture that favoured miniaturism, the seven silver and 35 gold double axes, like the one seen here, are the miniature version of this diachronic Minoan symbol. A miniature silver double axe at the Archaeological Museum of Heraklion bears an inscription in Linear A, whereas an inscribed miniature gold double axe in the Boston Museum of Fine Arts may also come from the cave.

The double axe was an important Minoan emblem, reproduced in all materials and forms. It may have served as the landmark of sacred places, as the attribute of a chthonic goddess, as a symbol of the sun that rises from the cosmic mountain or even as the badge of a social class.

References

Rethemiotakis 2008a. Flouda 2015. Marinatos 2010.

(Georgia Flouda)

90

耳环

米诺斯晚期ⅠA（公元前 1600～前 1500 年）

黄金

高 2 厘米

发现于克里特岛瓦塞佩特罗柱厅的 1 号储物罐

希腊伊拉克利翁考古博物馆藏，编号 X–A707

金耳环呈开放式环状，坠饰采用形似葡萄或浆果的金粒簇造型。虽然乍看之下金球部分似乎采用了复杂且耗时的造粒装饰工艺，但实际上，此件珠宝是通过模具铸造而成的。此类耳环在公元前 17 至前 16 世纪的东地中海地区（尤其是叙利亚和塞浦路斯）十分流行。在克里特岛，已经发现了至少两件用于制作此类耳环的石模具。

（艾琳·加利）

91

锥形耳环

米诺斯晚期ⅠB（公元前 1450 年）

黄金

高 3 厘米

发现于克里特岛鲁索拉科斯的帕莱卡斯特罗

希腊伊拉克利翁考古博物馆藏，编号 X–A196

环形金耳环由一根截面为圆形的金线制成，金线两端逐渐变细；耳环中心装饰有一个密布着大量金球的锥形金片，顶部还镶嵌一颗直径较大的金球。通常认为此类耳环象征牛头骨，在青铜时代晚期的叙利亚和塞浦路斯发现了许多类似物品。

这件耳环并非出土于墓葬，而是来自帕莱卡斯特罗一座毁坏的房屋，它也是克里特岛上唯一一对非墓葬中出土的此类耳环。

（艾琳·加利）

90

Hoop earring with hanging granulated cluster

Late Minoan ⅠA (1600-1500 BCE)

Gold

H. 2 cm

Vathypetro, Pillar Magazine, pithos 1

Archaeological Museum of Heraklion, X-A707

Gold earring of a characteristic open hoop shape with pendant granules resembling a bunch of grapes or a berry. Although the gold spheres recall the complex and time-consuming technique of granulation, this specific piece of jewellery is manufactured by casting in a mould. Earrings of this type were popular in the East Mediterranean and especially in Syria and Cyprus during the 17th and 16th centuries BCE. In Crete, at least two stone moulds for making such earrings have been recovered.

References

Μαρινάτος 1952, 606. Levi 1963, pl.IV. Laffineur 1980, 281-96.

(Irene Galli)

91

Hoop earring with conical granulated cluster

Late Minoan ⅠB (1450 BCE)

Gold

H. 3 cm

Roussolakkos, Palaikastro

Archaeological Museum of Heraklion, X-A196

Gold ring of wire of circular cross-section, tapering to its ends; at its midpoint it bears a cone of gold sheet thickly covered in gold spheres. One of a larger diameter tips the cone. This is a type of earring – which is considered to schematically represent a bucranium – that has numerous comparanda of the Late Bronze Age in Syria and Cyprus.

This particular example is from the only pair of earrings of this type in Crete that does not come from a tomb, but from a destroyed house in Palaikastro.

References

Bosanquet 1902-03, 280, 292. Higgins 1980, 62. Laffineur 1980, 283.

(Irene Galli)

92

耳环铸造模具

米诺斯中期Ⅲ至米诺斯晚期Ⅰ（约公元前 1600 年）
绿色片岩
长 4 厘米，宽 3.3 厘米，厚 3.4 ~ 3.5 厘米
发现于莫克洛斯Ⅰ/Ⅱ/Ⅲ号墓葬群的Ⅱ号墓
希腊伊拉克利翁考古博物馆藏，编号 Λ1305

这是一件长方形两片式模具的一半，该模具曾用于铸造带有类似葡萄串状坠饰的环状耳环。模具保存完好，仅有少量碎裂痕迹。

模具外表面略微凸起，带有粗略抛光痕迹。内表面平整且经过仔细打磨，确保与另一半模具安全合拢。模具内部凹槽呈浮雕状雕刻，铸造腔体呈开口圆环形，内侧刻有密集线条，以及九个球体组成的锥形类葡萄串图案。腔体中心的圆形穿孔既用作绘制环形的参考，也用作固定两部分模具的附加孔。一端的小漏斗形槽口用于倒入熔融金属。

带球体串吊饰的金耳环在公元前 17 至前 16 世纪的叙利亚–巴勒斯坦和塞浦路斯地区十分常见，在克里特岛也有类似器物发现。

根据莫克洛斯模具以及另外两件相似模具（一件为梅塔克萨斯的个人收藏，另一件可能来自克里特岛，现藏于牛津阿什莫尔博物馆），可以推测此类耳环可能是在克里特岛本地生产。模具所用片岩是一种典型的克里特材料，由此进一步验证了克里特岛本地能够完成从模具制造到器物铸造及成品加工全工艺流程的猜想。

（卡特琳娜·阿塔纳萨基）

92

Mould for casting earring

Middle Minoan Ⅲ – Late Minoan Ⅰ (Ca. 1600 BCE)
Green schistoid stone
L. 4 cm, w. 3.3 cm, th. 3.4-3.5 cm
Mochlos, Tomb Complex Ⅰ/Ⅱ/Ⅲ Tomb Ⅱ
Archaeological Museum of Heraklion, Λ1305

Half of a two-piece mould, rectangular in shape, for the casting of hoop earrings with a pendant like a bunch of grapes. Complete with only minor flakings.

The external surface is slightly convex, with some rough smoothing traces. The inner surface is flat, smoothed with special care for its secure fitting with the second part. In this is cut the casting hollow for the earring in intaglio: it has the shape of an open-ended ring with dense packed lines cut within and a conical attachment of nine spheres, in a grape-like cluster. A circular through-hole in the centre was used here both as a guide for drawing the ring and to serve as an additional hole to secure the two parts of the mould. At one narrow end is a small but neatly cut funnel-shaped groove for pouring in the molten metal.

Gold hoop earrings with an added bunch of spheres are examples of a type widespread in Syro-Palestine and Cyprus during the 17th and 16th centuries BCE, with examples also known from Crete.

The Mochlos mould, together with another similar one from the Metaxas Collection and a third, probably originating from Crete, now in the Ashmolean Museum in Oxford, is particularly interesting because it indicates the possible local manufacture of this type of earring. The material used for the construction of the mould, a typical Cretan schistoid mineral, strengthens the case for the production process being conducted on the spot: from making the mould to casting and producing the final object.

References

Πλάτων-Δαβάρας 1963, 283, pl.348. Boardman 1961, 127, no.546, pl.XLVI. Laffineur 1980, 285. Effinger 1996, 20-21. Σακελλαράκης-Σαπουνά-Σακελλαράκη 1997, 642. Evely 2000, 411.

(Katerina Athanasaki)

93

戒指

米诺斯晚期 I（公元前 1600 ~ 前 1450 年）
黄金、蓝色玻璃釉
戒面直径 1.3 厘米，戒圈直径 1.45 厘米
发现于克里特岛波罗斯 Π 1967 号墓
希腊伊拉克利翁考古博物馆藏，编号 HM X-A1022

黄金戒指带有环形戒圈，是波罗斯米诺斯墓地一座洞穴状墓室中的随葬品。这是一件米诺斯金匠大师打造的艺术杰作，戒面由金条分为多个小隔层，形成几何图案，并采用掐丝珐琅技法镶嵌白色和蓝色玻璃釉。

米诺斯人从埃及人那里学会了掐丝珐琅技法，并加以改进。这种技法将黄金条或金丝弯曲或锤制成所需形状，从而形成小隔层，随后再将彩色玻璃釉填入其中。波罗斯出土的戒指表明，带嵌入式戒面的戒指制作工艺至少在公元前 15 世纪早期的克诺索斯地区就已出现。在晚期迈锡尼墓中，这种戒指形式已十分常见。

波罗斯可能曾是克诺索斯的一大港口。在对此地的米诺斯聚落开展考古发掘时，发现了利用模具铸造珠宝的专业工坊遗址，以及制造过程中使用的工具和废料。

（乔治娅・弗拉达）

93

Ring

Late Minoan I (1600-1450 BCE)
Gold, blue glass paste
Bezel diam. 1.3 cm, ring diam. 1.45 cm
Poros, Chamber Tomb Π 1967
Archaeological Museum of Heraklion, HM X-A1022

Gold ring with a circular bezel, deposited as a burial gift in a cave-like chamber tomb in the Minoan cemetery of Poros. A masterpiece of the Minoan goldsmith's art, it has a bezel consisting of compartments made of gold strips which form geometric patterns and are inlaid with white and blue glass paste in the cloisonné technique.

The Minoans adopted the cloisonné technique from the Egyptians and perfected it. In cloisonné, intricate designs are created with coloured glass paste placed within enclosures (cloisons) of gold strips or wire bent or hammered into the desired pattern. The ring from Poros demonstrates that the production of rings with an inlaid bezel, known primarily from later Mycenaean tombs, had already started in the Knossos area at least by the early 15th century BCE.

The excavations in the Minoan settlement at Poros, which probably served as the harbour of Knossos, have revealed the remains of specialised workshops for the production of mould-cast jewellery as well as tools and scraps from the manufacturing process.

References

Dimopoulou 2015, 178-179, Muhly 1992, 123-124, 188, Pl.26 no.240.

(Georgia Flouda)

94

项链

米诺斯晚期ⅢA1（约公元前 1400 ~ 前 1375 年）

黄金

长 39 厘米

发现于克里特岛塞洛普洛的 4 号墓

希腊伊拉克利翁考古博物馆藏，编号 X–A1037

项链由27颗呈纸莎草花形状的浮雕金珠组成。这些串珠由两片独立的金叶制成，通过金叶边缘连接，并在轴线上打孔。制作过程中使用了三种不同的模具。

纸莎草花作为埃及的标志性植物，在米诺斯晚期的克里特岛上也成为了珠宝制作中的热门主题。这些串珠出土于塞洛普洛 4 号墓，与采用费昂斯和玻璃等其他材质制作的纸莎草形串珠形制类似，彰显出金匠的高超技艺。这种带有浮雕图案的串珠常被用于制作项链、手镯、臂环及衣饰装饰。纸莎草串珠常见于米诺斯晚期Ⅲ的墓葬中，表明逝者社会地位较高。

（克莱奥・察纳基）

94

Necklace

Late Minoan ⅢA1 (Ca. 1400-1375 BCE)

Gold

L. 39 cm

Sellopoulo, Tomb 4

Archaeological Museum of Heraklion, X-A1037

A necklace comprised of 27 relief gold beads in the shape of papyrus flowers. The beads are made of two separate leaves of gold joined at their edges with a single piercing along the axis and manufactured in three different moulds.

The papyrus flower was the characteristic Egyptian plant and became a popular subject in jewellery-making in Late Minoan Crete. The beads, which were found in Tomb 4 at Sellopoulo, recall papyrus beads in other materials, such as faience and glass, and attest to the goldsmiths' high degree of specialisation. Beads with the same motif were often used in necklaces, bracelets, armlets and clothing ornaments. Relief papyrus beads are often found in Late Minoan Ⅲ grave contexts, evidence of the high social status of the deceased.

References

Evans 1906, 76. Popham-Catling 1974, 202, 210-213. Effinger 1996, 34-35, 219.

(Kleio Tzanaki)

95

项链

米诺斯晚期Ⅱ至ⅢA2（约公元前 1450 ~ 前 1350/1300 年）
黄金
长 31 厘米
发现于克里特岛克诺索斯扎菲尔帕普拉墓地的 66 号墓
希腊伊拉克利翁考古博物馆藏，编号 X–A204

项链由 46 颗中空浮雕金珠组成，每颗金珠都呈现出花形图案，这是米诺斯晚期Ⅲ珠宝设计中最流行的图案之一。这些金珠由两片单独制作的金片连接而成，底片平坦，而顶片则压印有八瓣花形图案，侧边轮廓圆润。

这种金珠的制作方法是将黄金置于模具上捶打成型，这种技术不仅能够实现标准化制作，还能有效提高生产效率。以自然元素（如花形）为灵感的各式金珠也常被用作装饰品缝制在衣物上。

这条项链出土于扎菲尔帕普拉墓地一个有着丰富随葬品的墓穴，说明墓主社会地位较高。该墓地位于克诺索斯王宫的东北部。

（卡特琳娜·阿塔纳萨基）

95

Necklace

Late Minoan Ⅱ–ⅢA2 (Ca. 1450–1350/1300 BCE)
Gold
L. 31 cm
Knossos, Zapher Papoura cemetery, Tomb 66
Archaeological Museum of Heraklion, X-A204

Necklace composed of forty-six hollow relief gold beads in the shape of rosettes, one of the most popular motifs in Late Minoan III jewellery design. They are crafted from two separate sheets of gold joined at the edges. The bottom sheet is flat, while the top is embossed with a stylised eight-petaled rosette with a rounded outline.

This type of bead was produced by hammering gold over a mould, a technique that enabled standardisation and increased production. Gold beads crafted in various shapes inspired by nature, such as rosettes, were also commonly used as ornaments sewn onto clothing.

The necklace was discovered in a tomb rich in offerings in the cemetery of Zapher Papoura, indicating the high social status of the deceased, northeast of the palace at Knossos.

References

Alberti 2004, 83-90. Effinger 1996, 37, 225. Evans 1906, 129-30, fig.119.

(Katerina Athanasaki)

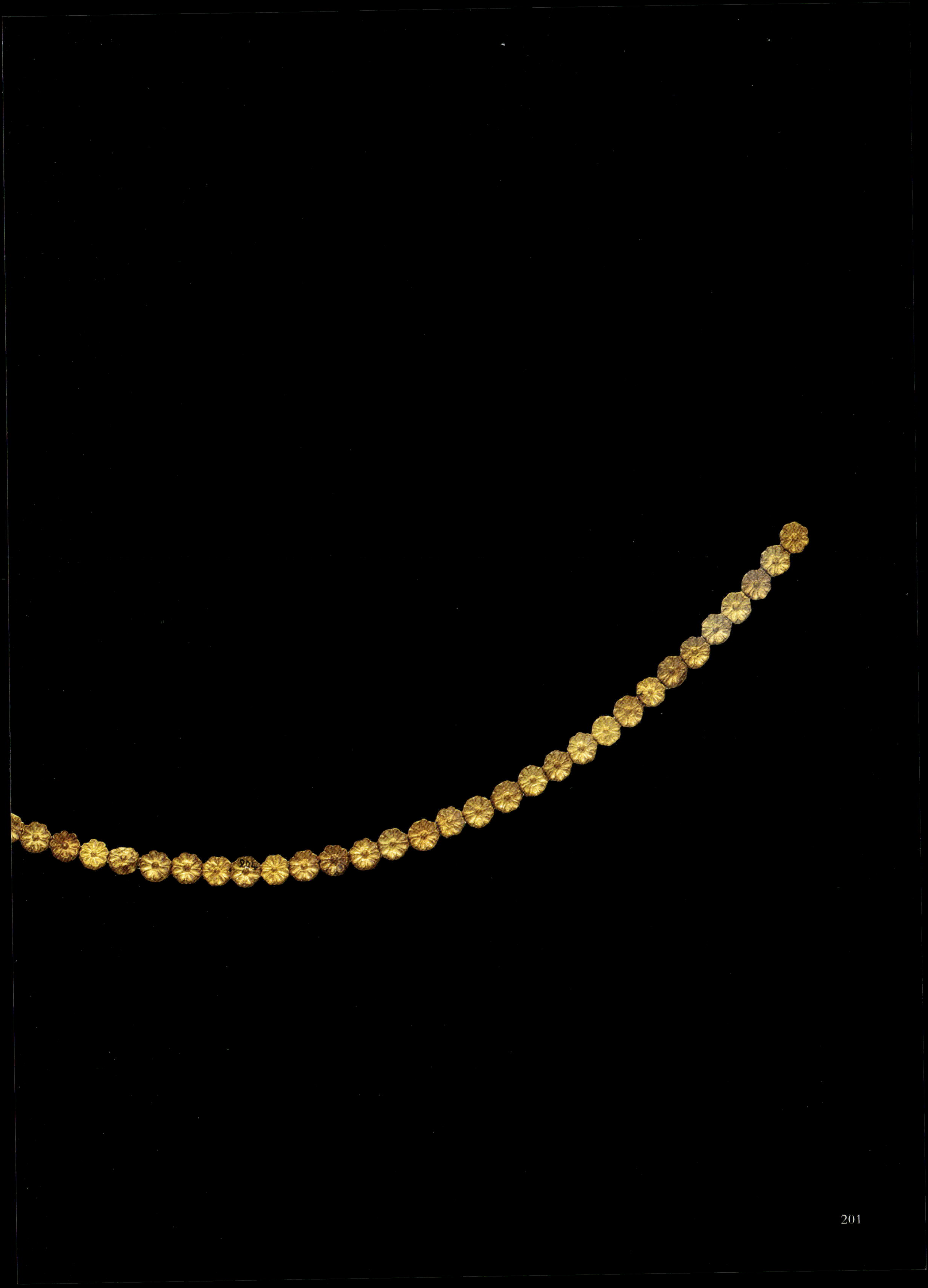

96

带颗粒装饰的戒指

米诺斯晚期ⅢC（公元前 1200 ~ 前 1070 年）

黄金

戒面长 3.1 厘米，戒面宽 2 厘米，戒圈直径 1.9 厘米

发现于克里特岛普莱索斯的福图拉遗址

希腊伊拉克利翁考古博物馆藏，编号 X–A765

装饰有细金丝和金粒的精美黄金戒指。戒圈带凹槽，饰以扭曲金丝制成的细条。椭圆形戒面的装饰图案在水平和垂直面均对称，戒面附有细金丝制成的对称螺旋图案以及细小金球。戒面边缘环绕一圈金丝，两侧排列着金粒。

这枚戒指出自普莱索斯福图拉遗址的一座圆顶墓，发现时位于一名埋葬在陶棺中的男子左手旁。陪葬物品均较为贵重，表明该男子很可能出身于贵族家庭。

（伊万吉立亚・西克拉）

96

Ring with granulation

Late Minoan ⅢC (1200-1070 BCE)

Gold

Bezel l. 3.1 cm, bezel w. 2 cm, hoop diam. 1.9 cm

Praisos, Photoula site

Archaeological Museum of Heraklion, X-A765

Ornate gold ring with filigree and granulated decoration. The hoop of the ring is grooved and adorned with rows of twisted wire. The decoration of the oval bezel is very symmetrical on the horizontal and vertical axis, with antithetical spiral motifs in filigree and microscopic gold spheres attached to the surface. The edge of the bezel is surrounded by a wire with a row of granules on either side.

This exquisite ring from Photoula in Praisos comes from a tholos tomb. It was found next to the left hand of a man inhumed in a clay larnax, who appears to have been of noble family, as he was accompanied by other valuable objects.

References

Effinger 1996, 291-292. Πλάτων 1960, 294-307, pl.244β, γ. Rethemiotakis 2008b, 181.

(Evangelia Sikla)

97

盾形饰片

几何时期（公元前 800 ~ 前 700 年）

黄金

长 9.3 厘米

发现于克里特岛普里尼亚斯墓地（G. 里扎于 1970 年发掘）

希腊伊拉克利翁考古博物馆藏，编号 X–A 1057

盾形金饰由一片椭圆形金属片通过锻造工艺制成。金片表面雕刻有希腊数字 8 字形盾牌，其轮廓以双层浮雕线勾勒，并饰有一系列点状装饰。盾牌上装饰有两个凸起的圆形浮雕，其外侧围有相应的环形浮雕线。金片外圈装饰着一排点状花纹，内侧饰锯齿形点状花纹。金片的上下边缘各有一个直径 2 毫米的孔洞，用于固定金片。

从孔洞可以看出，这块金片可能是某种附在布料或其他材料上的装饰品。其制作工艺较为粗糙，金片整体形状并不规整。一些金点也存在制作失误，工匠在锻打时用力过猛，导致金属工具打穿了金片。这块金片上的“皮奥夏盾”纹饰可与伊迪亚洞穴的“猎人盾”纹饰以及科莫斯发现的小型青铜盾牌的纹饰相比较，这些物品的用途可能与普里尼亚斯的这件金片相似。

（迪米特里斯・米洛纳斯）

97

Plate with figure-of-eight shield motif

Geometric period (800-700 BCE)

Gold

L. 9.3 cm

Prinias, Cemetery (G. Rizza excavation, 1970)

Archaeological Museum of Heraklion, X-A1057

The piece of gold jewellery in the shape of a shield consists of an oval piece of sheet-metal, formed by forging. A figure-of-eight shield is depicted on this, its outline indicated by a double embossed line and a series of dots. The shield is decorated with two raised bosses, enclosed by a corresponding circular and embossed line. The frame of the overall plate is decorated with an external row of dots and inside a zig-zag of dots. Two holes, with a diameter of 2 mm, are pierced through the upper and lower edge of the plate, opposite each other: they indicate how it was attached.

This plate was probably part of a decoration attached to some kind of cloth or other material, as can be seen from the holes. Its construction is not particularly precise, as the overall sheet was cut out in a rather irregular manner. In addition, some dots, created with a metal object, have gone all the way through, an error in its manufacture. The motif of the “Boeotian” shield that adorns the plate has parallels in the decoration of the “hunters” shield from the Idaean Cave and in the miniature bronze shields from Kommos, which were probably used in the same way as this gold plate from Prinias.

References

Rizza – Rizzo 1984, 166-167, fig.301. Gigli Patanè 2020, 295, fig.7. Rethemiotakis 2024, 154 fig.259.

(Dimitris Mylonas)

98

带爱神厄洛斯装饰的戒指

古典时期（公元前 4 世纪）

黄金

重 8 克

发现于克里特岛埃皮斯科皮－佩迪亚达的卡夫西遗址（1905 年购得）

希腊伊拉克利翁考古博物馆藏，编号 X–A210

这枚来自卡夫西遗址的黄金戒指造型简约，但令人印象深刻。戒指制于希腊化时期，戒面呈圆形，由薄金片制成，戒圈采用闭合式设计，较为纤细。戒面上刻有一幅微笑的爱神厄洛斯（丘比特）形象，其脚下是一条水平的浮雕线，表示地面。厄洛斯以裸身少年形象出现，身体呈侧立姿态，脚尖轻点地面，双翼张开（翅膀的细节以浮雕线表现），头部微微向上抬起，似乎正要飞向天空。厄洛斯右手持花冠，左手握火炬。

厄洛斯的形象在希腊化和罗马化时期的艺术中十分常见，尤其适合用作珠宝和其他器物上的微型图案。厄洛斯是阿芙洛狄忒之子，是爱情的化身，常在古代艺术中以手持花朵、七弦琴、花冠、丝带或弓的带翼少年或孩童形象出现。

这枚金戒指充分展现了希腊化时期艺术的美学与表现力。虽然尚不清楚确切的发现地点，但可以合理推测，这枚戒指可能是某位富裕女性的随葬品。

（迪米特里斯・米洛纳斯）

98

Ring depicting Eros

Classical period. 4th c. BCE

Gold

Weight 8 g

Episkopi Pediada, Kavousi site (purchased in 1905)

Archaeological Museum of Heraklion, X-A210

The gold ring from the Kavousi site at Episkopi Pediada is a simple but impressive piece of jewellery. Made during the Hellenistic period, it has a circular bezel made of thin gold sheet and a closed hoop, not particularly thick. The bezel bears an incised representation of a smiling Eros (Cupid) set on a horizontal embossed line denoting the ground. Eros is shown naked, in the form of a young boy and in a standing three-quarters pose. He is on tiptoes on the ground, his wings spread (the details of which are rendered in embossed lines), and his head turned upwards: he is about to take off in flight towards the heavens. He holds a wreath in his right hand and a torch in his left.

Representations of Erotes are common in the art of the Hellenistic and Roman periods and are an appropriate choice for miniature depictions in jewellery and other artifacts. Eros, son of Aphrodite, is the personification of love and is depicted in ancient art as a winged youth or child, holding in his hands a flower, lyre, wreath, ribbon or bow.

The gold ring is an excellent demonstration of the aesthetic and expressive power that characterises the refined works of the Hellenistic period. Although the exact findspot is not known, it can be reasonably assumed that the ring was a burial offering, perhaps that of a wealthy woman.

References

Rethemiotakis 2024, 174 fig.291. For parallels cf. Boardman 1994, 421, pl.754; Ζαφειροπούλου 1997, 132 no.127.

(Dimitris Mylonas)

99

鸽子形耳环（一对）

希腊化时期（公元前 2 世纪下半叶）

黄金

高 6.15 厘米，最大宽度 3.84 厘米，最大厚度 1.18 厘米

发现于克里特岛伊尼－佩迪亚达（1983 年，梅塔克萨斯收藏）

希腊伊拉克利翁考古博物馆藏，编号 ΣM1619

黄金耳环由圆盘形上部和鸟形下部组成。上部装饰有一朵九瓣花，花瓣呈矛尖形，用造粒工艺勾勒出轮廓。花心处有一个凹槽，可能曾镶嵌过宝石。圆盘部分的上方设有用金丝制成的双螺旋装饰，螺旋装饰上方延伸出耳环的挂钩。双螺旋的中心嵌有一颗红色石头（红玉髓）。圆盘下方连接着一只鸟，鸟身以造粒金丝勾勒出简约的轮廓。鸟尾呈扇形，爪部位于薄盒状底座上。鸟喙修长，鸟身为椭圆形，尾部逐渐收尖。尽管风格十分独特，但可以清楚地辨认出这是一只鸽子。

在希腊化时期出产的许多不同类型耳环中，鸟形耳环似乎格外受欢迎。鸽子象征着爱情，同时也是美神阿芙洛狄忒的圣鸟。

这对耳环中，一只耳环圆盘存在部分变形，另一只耳环缺失了装饰性的螺旋部分，鸟形部分与圆盘脱离并且一侧被压扁。

（迪米特里斯・米洛纳斯）

99

Pair of earrings in the form of doves

Hellenistic period, 2nd half of 2nd c. BCE

Gold

H. 6.15 cm, max. w. 3.84 cm, max. th. 1.18 cm

Ini Pediada (1983, Metaxas Collection)

Archaeological Museum of Heraklion, ΣM1619

A pair of gold earrings consisting of a disc-shaped upper part and a lower part in the form of a bird. The upper part is decorated with a nine-petalled flower with lanceolate petals, outlined in the granulation technique. In the centre is a cavity, where once an inset stone was probably placed. Double spirals formed with wire are set above the disc-like section, from which the suspension hook for the ear emerges. A red stone (carnelian) has been placed in the centre of the double spirals. A bird is attached below the disc-shaped part, the details of which are schematically rendered in granulated wire. The bird's tail is fan-shaped and its feet rest on a thin box-shaped base. The birds are given an elongated beak and an oval body with its sharp end at the tail area. The rendering is quite plastic and strongly stylised but it is quite clearly meant to be a dove.

Many different types of earring were made in the Hellenistic period, and those in the shape of birds seem to have been particularly popular. Of the birds, doves are considered the most amorous birds and the most frequent attributes of the goddess Aphrodite.

Some distortions are observed in the disc portion of one earring. The other one is missing the decorated spiral part, while the bird has come adrift from the disc and is squashed on one side.

References

Unpublished. For parallels cf. Oliver Jr., 1966, 276, fig.14; Δεσποίνη 1996, 125, fig.105

(Dimitris Mylonas)

100

带胜利女神尼姬装饰的耳环（一对）

希腊化时期（公元前 200 ~ 前 100 年）

黄金

长 7 厘米，重 6.2 克

发现于卡洛－霍里奥的米拉贝洛（1936 年 1 月上交）

希腊伊拉克利翁考古博物馆藏，编号 X－A592 和 X－A634

金耳环由上下两部分组成。上部为一片十二瓣花形金片，花瓣周围环绕着波浪形边纹，背面附有耳环的悬挂环。下部则由金丝制成，悬挂着一对背对背的展翅胜利女神（尼姬）。每位胜利女神背部均有条纹装饰。双翼展开并向上延伸，同时分别高举左手或右手，另一只手则微微向下倾斜。胜利女神身着束腰长袍，衣袍上的褶皱随风飘扬，展现出飞行时的动感。这种带坠饰（胜利女神、海妖、爱神等）的耳环在公元前 3 世纪末至 2 世纪期间的希腊化地区非常流行。耳环的装饰主题大多为带翼生物。

这对耳环工艺精湛、细节丰富，无论是花形金片还是悬挂的胜利女神，都体现出高超的工艺水平。

（迪米特里斯・米洛纳斯）

100

Pair of earrings depicting the goddess Nike

Hellenistic period, 200-100 BCE

Gold

L. 7 cm, weight 6.2 g

Kalo Chorio, Mirabello (handed in January 1936)

Archaeological Museum of Heraklion, X-A592 & X-A634

The gold earrings consist of two parts. The upper is a cut-out sheet in the form of a twelve-petalled rosette surrounded by a "wave". The suspension loop for the ear is attached to the reverse. Below, from gold wire, hang winged Nikes (Victories), facing in opposite directions. The back part of each Nike is ribbed. The Nikes have their wings open and spread upwards, with their left and right hand (respectively) raised. The two other hands are slightly inclined downwards. The Nikes wear a belted peplos, with strong folds formed by the wind of their flight. Similar earrings with pendant figures (Nikes, Sirens, Erotes, etc.) are known throughout the Hellenistic world during the late 3rd and 2nd centuries BCE. The decorative motifs are almost always winged creatures.

This is a particularly fine and high-quality piece of work, with much detail in the rendering of both the rosettes and the winged Nikes.

References

Rethemiotakis 2024, 174-175, fig.293. For parallels cf. Oliver Jr. 1966, 278, fig.17; Δεσποίνη 1996, 121, fig.100.

(Dimitris Mylonas)

101

“列斯波斯海浪”式珠链

希腊化时期（公元前 1 世纪）

黄金

长 35 厘米，重 27 克

发现于克里特岛阿诺–阿西特斯的希腊化时期墓地（1930 年上交）

希腊伊拉克利翁考古博物馆藏，编号 X–A569

项链由 25 颗形状相仿的金珠串联而成，金珠通过一条长金链相连。项链两端装饰有两片叶形金饰，一端配有环状扣，另一端则装有钩状闭合装置。每颗金珠均呈现出叶形，表面装饰有“列斯波斯海浪”纹路，底部有两道莨苕装饰线条。其中一颗金珠在发掘时受工具撞击出现了变形。所有部件均由极薄的金片制成，展现出精湛的锻造工艺。在同一墓葬中还发现了一对金耳环和一枚金别针。在希腊化时期（尤其是公元前 2 至 1 世纪）的珠宝纹饰中，变体植物造型尤为盛行，这反映了当时奢华的流行趋势。

（迪米特里斯・米洛纳斯）

101

Necklace with beads in the form of a “Lesbian wave”

Hellenistic period, 1st c. BCE

Gold

L. 35 cm, weight 27 g

Ano Asites, Hellenistic tomb (handed in 1930)

Archaeological Museum of Heraklion, X-A569

The necklace consists of 25 gold beads of similar shape, held together by a chain of elongated wire links passing through them. The ends of the necklace terminate in two gold leaf-shaped fittings. A loop at one end and a hook at the other served to fasten the necklace. Each bead features a leaf-shaped body, with a “Lesbian wave” decoration and two astragalus mouldings at the base. One bead was distorted by the impact of the excavator’s tool. All the parts are made from very thin sheet metal, suggesting a meticulous forging technique. A pair of gold earrings and a gold fibula were also found in the same burial. In the motifs employed on jewellery of the Hellenistic period, especially of the 2nd and 1st c. BCE, various stylised floral themes are particularly popular, highlighting a trend towards luxury.

References

Rethemiotakis 2024, 174-175 fig.293.

(Dimitris Mylonas)

102

常春藤叶花冠

希腊化时期（公元前 2 至 1 世纪）
黄金
直径 25 厘米
发现于克里特岛哈尼亚的罗多瓦尼（吉亚马拉基斯收藏）
希腊伊拉克利翁考古博物馆藏，编号 ΣΓ489

黄金花冠由一条圆柱形金枝及大量金片制成。金枝上的开口中插有叶茎，42 片叶子以金箔制作而成。叶身修长，基部有尖锐的角形末端，上部形成三叉叶尖。叶片表面刻有直线，从基部沿轴向上延伸到顶端，象征叶脉。

黄金花冠通常发现于富裕阶层的墓葬中，是逝者的个人物品，可能曾用于宗教仪式或宴会。花冠以花朵和（或）树叶为主题，模仿希腊本土植物的特征，与神话联系密切。这顶花冠的叶子造型简约，叶脉以直线刻画，可能为月桂叶，与神话中的阿波罗和达芙妮息息相关。小奥利弗（Oliver Jr.）曾报道，1900 年在哈尼亚的罗多瓦尼地区（接近埃吕罗斯古城所在地）也发现过一对装饰爱神厄洛斯的黄金耳环，由此进一步展示出这座克里特城市的富庶。

（迪米特里斯・米洛纳斯）

102

Wreath with ivy leaves

Hellenistic period (2nd – 1st c. BCE)

Gold

D. 25 cm

Rodovani, Chania (Giamalakis Collection)

Archaeological Museum of Heraklion, ΣΓ489

The gold hoop of the wreath consists of a single cylindrical stem, made of sheet. In sockets opened in the cylindrical branch are set the stems of 42 leaves, which are made of thin gold foil. The main physical features of the leaves are their elongated shape with a sharp angular end at their base and the three also angular, sharp-pointed components of their upper part. The surface of the leaves has straight lines, representing the ribs of the leaf running along the axis from the base to the tops of the three ends.

Gold wreaths have been found in the graves of wealthy men and women. They were a personal item of the deceased and were probably worn in religious ceremonies and at banquets. The wreaths were floral and/or leafy and reproduced plants native to Greece according to their properties and characteristics, which were associated with mythology. The simple, stylised way of rendering the leaves of the wreath, with the ribs indicated by straight lines, probably identifies them as laurel leaves, which are connected through the myth of Daphne with the god Apollo. It is interesting to note that Oliver Jr. reports that a pair of gold earrings in the form of Erotes were also found in Rodovani, Chania around 1900, in the area where ancient Elyros is located, highlighting the wealth of this Cretan city.

References

Rethemiotakis 2024, 180-1 fig.308. For gold wreaths cf. Δεσποίνη 1996, 47-55, figs.1-8; Ζαφειροπούλου 1997, 104-5 no.92; Oliver Jr. 1966, 278, fig.17.

(Dimitris Mylonas)

美石琢巧器

石质器皿是米诺斯文化极富特色的一类产品，可能在舶来的古埃及石器影响下发扬光大。最早的克里特自产石器可追溯至公元前 2600 年左右，不断尝试在各种软硬石材上做文章，把大自然的馈赠应用到极致。约公元前 1900 年始，随着宫殿兴起，匠人们青睐颜色迷人、纹理斑驳的石料，如角砾岩和橙色钟乳石，继而又开发黑曜石、水晶石、蛇纹石、雪花石膏，用沙子配合木钻或铜钻将它们雕琢打磨成精巧的日常用具。这些石器散发出奇异光彩，行云流水般的纹理美轮美奂，宛如从浩瀚苍穹中夺来的五彩星云。

Exquisite Stone Vessels

Minoan stone vessels, possibly influenced by Egyptian imports, became a distinctive hallmark of the civilization. The earliest locally produced Cretan stone artifacts date back to around 2600 BCE, showcasing the islanders' experimentation with both soft and hard stones to maximize nature's gifts. Beginning around 1900 BCE, with the rise of the palaces, artisans favored stones with captivating colours and intricate patterns, such as breccia and orange stalactite. They later expanded their materials to include obsidian, rock crystal, serpentine, and alabaster, using sand, wood or copper drills to carve and polish these stones into delicate everyday objects. These stone artifacts shimmer with an ethereal glow, their flowing patterns as sublime as nebulas drifting through the cosmos, each piece seemingly carved from celestial stardust.

103

带卧犬雕塑的首饰盒盖

米诺斯早期ⅡA（公元前2600～前2400年）
石料（绿泥石或绿泥片岩）
高6厘米，直径12.5厘米
发现于莫克洛斯墓地的Ⅰ号墓室
希腊伊拉克利翁考古博物馆藏，编号Λ1282

石质首饰盒圆盖是一处米诺斯早期Ⅱ墓葬的陪葬品。盖子表面装饰有轻刻的相邻三角形纹样，捉手则采用卧姿犬雕塑形式。扎克罗斯也出土了一件相同的盖子和配套容器，这两件器物被认为出自同一位艺术家之手或产自同一间工坊。盖子边缘有两对对称孔洞，用于将盖子固定到盒身。

扎克罗斯与莫克洛斯的这些首饰盒使用灰绿色的绿泥石材质，这种软质石材加工难度较低，在米诺斯早期Ⅱ前期广受石雕匠人喜爱，后期工匠则逐渐开始加工更硬的石材。从美学角度看，盖子上呈放松姿态的卧犬展现出米诺斯艺术自早期阶段起即盛行的自然主义特征。

（艾琳·尼古拉科普卢）

103

Pyxis lid with reclining dog

Early Minoan ⅡA (2600 - 2400 BCE)
Stone (chlorite or chloritic schist)
H. 6 cm, diam. 12.5 cm
Mochlos Cemetery, Tomb I
Archaeological Museum of Heraklion, Λ1282

Circular lid of a small cylindrical pyxis (jewellery box) found accompanying an Early Minoan Ⅱ burial. Decoration of lightly incised juxtaposed triangles covers the surface of the lid, while the handle is formed of a sculpted reclining dog. An identical lid, with the corresponding vessel, comes from Zakros, and the two vessels are believed to be the work of the same artist or workshop. Two pairs of holes placed diametrically opposite each other on the rim were used to secure the lid to the body of the pyxis.

The grey-green chlorite of which the Zakros and Mochlos pyxides are made is one of the soft stones preferred by stone-carvers in the first half of Early Minoan Ⅱ, as they were easier to carve, while artisans gradually began to work harder stones. In aesthetic terms, the skilfully rendered relaxed pose of the canine is yet another indicative feature of the prevailing naturalism that characterises Minoan art from its earliest stages.

References

Seager 1912, fig.4 I i and 5. Warren 1969, 82, P457.

(Irene Nikolakopoulou)

104

埃及风格微型双耳瓶

米诺斯早期Ⅱ（公元前 2600 ~ 前 2300 年）

蛇纹石

高 8.3 厘米，瓶口直径 3.2 厘米，瓶底直径 2.4 厘米

发现于莫克洛斯的居址

希腊伊拉克利翁考古博物馆藏，编号 Λ1234

微型双耳瓶近乎完好，仅底部、把手和瓶身周围有些许碎裂。瓶身呈梨形，肩部不对称，两个弯耳代替了传统把手。瓶口呈环形且外翻，瓶颈下部有塑形凸缘。

内部可见空心钻留下的加工痕迹，外表面经过了细致打磨和抛光，抛光过程中可能使用了研磨剂，并且还添加过润滑剂，可能是油。

此件器物可能是某种埃及流行罐型的仿制品，这种罐型在古埃及第五和第六王朝时期盛行，在第七和第八王朝时期也有生产。此器物的重要性在于其表明了埃及与克里特之间存在文化交流。

（卡特琳娜・阿塔纳萨基）

104

Miniature Egyptianising pithoid amphora

Early Minoan Ⅱ (2600-2300 BCE)

Serpentinite

H. 8.3 cm, diam. rim 3.2 cm, diam. base 2.4 cm

Mochlos, settlement

Archaeological Museum of Heraklion, Λ1234

Miniature pithoid amphora, almost intact. Chips around the base, on handles and body. Piriform body and asymmetrical shoulders with two curved lugs in place of the handles. Ring-shaped and everted rim with a plastic collar at the base of the neck.

On the inside are traces of a hollow drill. Highly worked outer surface with traces of smoothing and polishing. Abrasives were used for the grinding and polishing, with the addition of a lubricating agent, possibly oil.

The vase is considered a copy of an Egyptian type that was popular in the 5th and 6th Dynasties and still produced in the 7th and 8th. It is a particularly important indication of cultural contacts between Egypt and Crete.

References

Seager 1909, 288-89, pl.VIII 2. Karetsou et al. 2000/2001, catalogue, 31-32, no.10 (Serpetsidaki). Bevan 2007, 123-25.

(Katerina Athanasaki)

105

微型杯

米诺斯早期Ⅱ（公元前 2600 ~ 前 2300 年）

滑石

高 3.8 厘米，直径 3 厘米

发现于莫克洛斯（具体出土地不详）

希腊伊拉克利翁考古博物馆藏，编号 Λ1302

杯主体为圆柱形，束口，底部为圈足。底部经过修复，内部有修补痕迹。外表面经过细致的打磨和抛光，内部杯壁可见旋转实心钻留下的明显痕迹。这件器物可能产自当地工坊。

（卡特琳娜·阿塔纳萨基）

105

Miniature cup

Early Minoan Ⅱ (2600-2300 BCE)

Steatite

H. 3.8 cm, diam. 3 cm

Mochlos (unprovenanced)

Archaeological Museum of Heraklion, Λ1302

Cylindrical cup with torus foot, cylindrical body and marked off rim. Incomplete, restored at the base and mended internally. Very carefully smoothed and polished on the outside. Strong traces of rotating solid drill on the inner surface of its walls. It is probably the product of a local workshop.

References

Warren 1969, 73.

(Katerina Athanasaki)

106

碗

米诺斯早期Ⅱ至米诺斯中期Ⅰ（公元前 2600 ~ 前 1800 年）
大理石
高 3.8 厘米，直径 11.6 厘米
发现于莫克洛斯Ⅰ/Ⅱ/Ⅲ号墓葬群的Ⅱ号墓室
希腊伊拉克利翁考古博物馆藏，编号 Λ1180

薄壁浅碗，碗底平坦，整体轮廓略带棱角，口沿圆润且外翻。整件器物由三块碎片修复而成。

碗内外壁光滑且富有光泽，表明工匠在打磨和抛光工艺方面技艺高超，完全不见前期加工痕迹。

大理石碗出自莫克洛斯墓地最为宏伟、富有的Ⅰ/Ⅱ/Ⅲ号墓葬群，这一墓群似乎专用于埋葬社会上层阶级。这只碗很可能是当地工坊的作品。

（卡特琳娜·阿塔纳萨基）

106

Bowl

Early Minoan Ⅱ – Middle Minoan Ⅰ (2600-1800 BCE)
Marble
H. 3.8 cm, diam. 11.6 cm
Mochlos, Tomb Complex Ⅰ/Ⅱ/Ⅲ, Tomb Ⅱ
Archaeological Museum of Heraklion, Λ1180

Shallow bowl with thin walls. Flat base, slightly angular outline and rounded, everted rim. Restored from three pieces.

The smooth and shiny outer and inner surfaces indicate a high level of expertise in grinding and polishing, which, as in other cases, has eliminated all traces of previous processing.

The bowl comes from the most monumental and richest tomb complex of the Mochlos cemetery, Ⅰ/Ⅱ/Ⅲ, which seems to have been intended for high-status social groups. It is probably the product of a local workshop.

References

Seager 1912, 25, fig.7. Warren 1969, 23. Soles 1992, 43-51.

(Katerina Athanasaki)

107

无柄杯

米诺斯早期Ⅱ至米诺斯中期ⅠA（公元前2600~前1900年）

蛇纹石

高3.2厘米，直径6.4厘米

发现于克里特岛库马萨的E号墓

希腊伊拉克利翁考古博物馆藏，编号Λ696

半球形敞口杯，杯口圆润且稍微外翻。杯内可见明显的旋转研磨痕迹，杯底有一个旋钮状凸起，这是米诺斯早期至米诺斯中期Ⅰ器物的典型特征之一。

由于这件敞口杯内壁粗糙且外壁不规整，人们起初认为这是一件未完成的器物。结合其他完整石器和废弃品可以推断，当地可能存在一个工坊。不过，这也可能是一件成品。

（卡特琳娜·阿塔纳萨基）

107

Handleless cup

Early Minoan Ⅱ – Middle Minoan ⅠA (2600-1900 BCE)

Serpentinite

H. 3.2 cm, diam. 6.4 cm

Koumasa, Tomb E

Archaeological Museum of Heraklion, Λ696

Open hemispherical cup with a rounded, slightly everted rim. Strong traces of rotary grinding devices inside and a knob-shaped process at the bottom, which is a characteristic feature commonly seen in products of the Early Minoan-Middle Minoan Ⅰ period.

Initially, it was considered that the traces of the rough interior processing and the irregular surface on the outside were indications that this is an unfinished vessel, which, together with other complete stone vessels and wasters, is evidence of a local workshop. However, this may actually be a finished product.

References

Warren 1969, 161, 240. Branigan 1993, 114. Herrero 2014, 188.

(Katerina Athanasaki)

108

船形器

米诺斯早期Ⅱ至米诺斯中期Ⅰ（公元前 2600 ~ 前 1800 年）
蛇纹石或绿泥石
高 3.2 厘米，宽 5.8 厘米，长 10.5 厘米
发现于克里特岛普拉塔诺斯 A 号圆顶墓的长方形墓室，1957 年安装围栏时发现
希腊伊拉克利翁考古博物馆藏，编号 Λ2487

船形器皿，顶端"船头"处设流。

船身装饰有两条水平的交叉刻线带，在船头和船尾处以两条垂直线相连，垂直线同样饰有对角线刻纹。该器皿表面经过精细打磨和抛光，但流部末端有轻微缺损。

这件船形石器是已知的少数船形模型之一。其用途众说纷纭，可能是日常使用的容器，也可能与来世信仰有关，具有特殊的象征意义。

（卡特琳娜·阿塔纳萨基）

108

Boat-shaped vessel

Early Minoan II – Middle Minoan I (2600-1800 BCE)
Serpentinite or chlorite
H. 3.2 cm, w. 5.8 cm, l. 10.5 cm
Platanos, rectangular compartment of Tholos Tomb A. Found in 1957 during fencepost installation
Archaeological Museum of Heraklion, Λ2487

A boat-shaped vessel with an open spout at the highest end, considered its "prow".

Incised decoration of two horizontal hatched bands, joined at the "prow" and stern by two verticals also given diagonal hatching. Excellent quality smoothing and polishing. Chipped at the end of the spout.

This is one of the few known stone boat models. A variety of interpretations have been proffered regarding its use: as a vessel for everyday use, or as an object with a special symbolic dimension, related to afterlife beliefs.

References

Πλάτων 1955, 568. Gerontakou 2003, 312-313.

(Katerina Athanasaki)

109

微型鸟巢形碗

米诺斯早期Ⅱ至米诺斯中期Ⅰ（公元前 2600 ~ 前 1800 年）

角砾岩

高 3.3 厘米，直径 5.6 厘米

发现于克里特岛普拉塔诺斯的 A 号圆顶墓

希腊伊拉克利翁考古博物馆藏，编号 Λ1740

微型鸟巢形碗，敛口，内壁有密集的水平环纹。这些特征表明，在制作过程中使用了不同尺寸的旋转实心钻来完成内部的掏空工作。原材料中的角砾岩碎片呈现出天然的多彩色泽，极具装饰性效果。器物外部也经过了非常细致的抛光处理。

（卡特琳娜·阿塔纳萨基）

109

Miniature bird's-nest bowl

Early Minoan Ⅱ – Middle Minoan Ⅰ (2600-1800 BCE)

Breccia

H. 3.3 cm, diam. 5.6 cm

Platanos, Tholos Tomb A

Archaeological Museum of Heraklion, Λ1740

Miniature bird's-nest bowl. The dense-packed horizontal rings, as well as the inturned lip, are indications of the use of different-sized solid rotary drills used to shape the internal hollow. The natural polychromy of the brecciated fragments in their matrix produces a highly decorative result, while the polishing on the outside is also particularly meticulous.

References

Xanthoudides 1924, 99-100. Carter 2008. Herrero 2014, 44, 203.

(Katerina Athanasaki)

110

镶嵌红色物质的鸟巢形碗

米诺斯早期 II 至米诺斯中期 I（公元前 2600 ~ 前 1800 年）

绿色片岩

高 4.2 厘米，直径 11.3 厘米

发现于克里特岛普拉塔诺斯的 A 号圆顶墓

希腊伊拉克利翁考古博物馆藏，编号 Λ1827

鸟巢形碗，近乎平坦的肩部雕刻有开口三角形，饰以双重斜线纹的边框。三角形刻纹之间有四个用旋转工具凿出的圆形凹槽，其中嵌有红色物质（可能与编号 Λ1627 器物上镶嵌的物质相同，参见本书图版 111）。中央的凹槽由实心钻凿出，较小的规整凹槽上也可见使用实心钻留下的同心圆痕迹。碗的外部装饰很可能是用锋利的金属工具或非常坚硬的石头工具雕刻而成。

（卡特琳娜・阿塔纳萨基）

110

Bird's-nest bowl inlaid with red material

Early Minoan II – Middle Minoan I (2600-1800 BCE)

Green schistoid stone

H. 4.2 cm, diam. 11.3 cm

Platanos, Tholos Tomb A

Archaeological Museum of Heraklion, Λ1827

Bird's-nest bowl with incised decoration on the almost flat shoulder of open triangles, with a double, hatched border. Between them, four circular cavities were opened with a rotary device, and then inset with a reddish material (the same as that of the "kernos" HM Λ1627, cat. no. 111). The central cavity has been drilled out with a solid drill. The smaller, particularly regular-shaped cavities also appear to have been drilled with a rotary solid drill, as indicated by the concentric circles on their sides. The incised decoration on the outside was probably produced with a sharp metal or very hard stone tool.

References

Xanthoudides 1924, pl.11. Herrero 2014, 44, 203.

(Katerina Athanasaki)

111

双联“科诺斯”容器

米诺斯早期Ⅱ至米诺斯中期Ⅰ（公元前 2600 ~ 前 1800 年）
蛇纹石
高 3.5 厘米，长 9.1 厘米，宽 5.6 厘米
发现于克里特岛普拉塔诺斯的 A 号圆顶墓
希腊伊拉克利翁考古博物馆藏，编号 Λ1627

双联矩形容器近乎完好，器身带有两个圆柱形内腔，内壁留有明显的旋转工具使用痕迹。

器身雕刻有两条对置的斜线弧纹带。垂直壁面上分布着实心钻凿出的小直径圆孔，窄面各有一个，长面各有两个。这些圆孔中有一个仍嵌有红色物质（可能是石膏），另有两个圆孔则残留着相同物质的痕迹。每个长边中央靠近上表面处各有一对较小直径的孔洞（可能是用于固定其他物品）。

这种类型的“科诺斯”容器在梅萨拉地区尤其流行。这件器物与同一墓中编号 Λ1827（参见本书图版 110）的鸟巢形碗一样保留有红色镶嵌物质，这种实例极为罕见。

（卡特琳娜·阿塔纳萨基）

111

Composite vase, “kernos”

Early Minoan Ⅱ – Middle Minoan Ⅰ (2600-1800 BCE)
Serpentinite
H. 3.5 cm, l. 9.1 cm, w. 5.6 cm
Platanos, Tholos Tomb A
Archaeological Museum of Heraklion, Λ1627

A rectangular composite vessel, almost intact, with two cylindrical hollows carrying strong traces of a rotating drilling tool on their sides.

Incised decoration of two bands of opposed hatched arcs. The vertical walls each have circular cavities of small diameter, made with a solid drill: one on each narrow side and two on each long side. One of them is complete with its inlay of a reddish material (plaster?) and two others have remnants of the same material. Two pairs for suspension holes (or for fitting something to the vessel?), of smaller diameter, are also located in the middle of each long side, close to the angle with the upper surface.

This particular type of “kernos” is particularly popular in the Mesara. Along with the bird’s-nest bowl HM Λ1827 (cat. no. 110) from the same tomb, this is a rare case where the inlaid red material has survived.

References

Xanthoudides 1924, 99, pl.LII. Warren 1969, 11,12. Τσιποπούλου 1992,159 no.163.

(Katerina Athanasaki)

112

带盖罐

米诺斯早期Ⅲ至米诺斯中期Ⅰ（公元前 2300 ~ 前 1800 年）

方解石

高 7.3 厘米，直径 7.9 厘米

发现于莫克洛斯的Ⅵ号墓室

希腊伊拉克利翁考古博物馆藏，编号 Λ1228

圆柱形小罐，保存完好，顶部略微外扩，配有一个圆盘状凸面盖子，盖顶有一个纽扣状捉手。

此罐以较为罕见的白色半透明方解石制成，内腔使用圆柱形钻头钻空。

这件小罐出土自莫克洛斯墓地Ⅳ/Ⅴ/Ⅵ号墓葬群，是Ⅵ号墓室诸多陪葬品之一。

（卡特琳娜·阿塔纳萨基）

112

Pyxis with lid

Early Minoan Ⅲ– Middle Minoan Ⅰ (2300-1800 BCE)

Calcite

H. 7.3 cm, diam. 7.9 cm

Mochlos, Tomb Ⅵ

Archaeological Museum of Heraklion, Λ1228

Intact cylindrical pyxis, slightly flaring to top, with a disc-shaped plano-convex lid bearing a button-shaped handle.

It is made of whitish translucent calcite, the more rarely used variety in the manufacture of stone vessels; its interior has been removed with a cylindrical drill.

The pyxis comes from Tomb Ⅵ of Tomb Complex Ⅳ/Ⅴ/Ⅵ of the Mochlos cemetery, where it was deposited as a burial offering.

References

Seager 1912, fig.46, pl.VIIa. Soles 1992, 51-62.

(Katerina Athanasaki)

113

鸟巢形碗

米诺斯早期Ⅲ至米诺斯中期Ⅰ（公元前 2300 ~ 前 1800 年）
方解石
高 3.8 厘米，直径 7.4 厘米
发现于克里特岛普拉拉塔诺斯的 A 号圆顶墓
希腊伊拉克利翁考古博物馆藏，编号 Λ1752

鸟巢形容器，保存完好，轮廓呈曲线形。整体制作精细，外部经过高质量的打磨和抛光。内部可见使用旋转实心钻留下的痕迹。

这件器物出土于普拉塔诺斯的 A 号圆顶墓中，是该类型墓穴中最为常见的器物类型。与克里特岛同期其他墓地相比，该墓中的鸟巢形碗尤为多见。与墓中其他大多数器物一样，这件碗可能产自本地工坊。

（卡特琳娜·阿塔纳萨基）

113

Bird's-nest bowl

Early Minoan Ⅲ– Middle Minoan Ⅰ (2300-1800 BCE)
Calcite
H. 3.8 cm, diam. 7.4 cm
Platanos, Tholos Tomb A
Archaeological Museum of Heraklion, Λ1752

Intact bird's-nest-shaped vase with curved profile. Very carefully made with excellent quality smoothing and polishing on the outside. Traces of a rotating solid drill can be seen inside.

It comes from Tholos Tomb A of Platanos, where this bowl type is the most common vase encountered. It enjoys a particularly large representation compared to the cemeteries of the same period in the rest of Crete. It is, like the majority of the other vases in the tomb, the product of a local workshop.

References

Xanthoudides 1924, 99-100. Vargiolu et al. 2007. Herrero 2014, 44, 203.

(Katerina Athanasaki)

114

带流容器（半成品）

米诺斯早期Ⅲ至米诺斯中期Ⅰ（公元前 2300 ~ 前 1800 年）
玄武岩
高 3.3 厘米，直径 7.2 厘米
发现于克里特岛普拉塔诺斯 A 号圆顶墓的东北堆积层
希腊伊拉克利翁考古博物馆藏，编号 Λ1875

未完成的开放式容器（可能为灯具），边缘开口处刻有流部，两侧各有一个圆形凹槽。外部凿制而成，表面较为粗糙，仅进行了初步打磨处理。内部留有实心钻留下的细密纹路，底部带有旋钮状凸起。

由于外表面处理得较为粗糙，通常认为这件器物属于未完成品。结合其他完整的石器和废弃品可以推测，普拉塔诺斯地区可能存在一个本地石器工坊。

（卡特琳娜·阿塔纳萨基）

114

Unfinished open vase with spout

Early Minoan Ⅲ– Middle Minoan Ⅰ (2300-1800 BCE)
Basalt
H. 3.3 cm, diam. 7.2 cm
Platanos, Deposit NE of Tholos Tomb A
Archaeological Museum of Heraklion, Λ1875

Semi-finished open vase (lamp?) with a spout cut into the rim and two circular recesses on either side of the spout. Roughly chiselled on the outer surface, with traces of original smoothing. Internally there are dense-packed, fine grooves let by a solid drill, with a knob-shaped process at the base.

This vessel is considered unfinished due to the rough treatment of the outside. Together with other complete stone vessels and wasters, it constitutes an important indication for a local stone-vase production workshop in the area of Platanos.

References

Warren 1969, 210, 240. Branigan 1993, 114. Herrero 2014, 44, 203.

(Katerina Athanasaki)

115

三耳碗

米诺斯早期Ⅲ至米诺斯中期Ⅰ（公元前 2300 ~ 前 1800 年）
蛇纹岩或玄武岩
高 2.4 厘米，直径 7.3 厘米
发现于克里特岛普拉塔诺斯的 A 号圆顶墓
希腊伊拉克利翁考古博物馆藏，编号 Λ1864

完整的三耳小碗，带有双锥形碗身和三棍状耳柄。碗肩部分雕刻有平行的纵向凹槽作为纹饰。内部有明显的实心钻研磨痕迹，底部可见水平的同心圆环，中央有凸起。器物整体有抛光痕迹。

（卡特琳娜·阿塔纳萨基）

115

Three-handled bowl

Early Minoan Ⅲ– Middle Minoan Ⅰ (2300-1800 BCE)
Ophiolite (basalt?)
H. 2.4 cm, diam. 7.3 cm
Platanos, Tholos Tomb A
Archaeological Museum of Heraklion, Λ1864

Small three-handled bowl, intact though with some small chips, with a biconical body and three rod-shaped lug handles. Incised decoration of parallel vertical grooves on the shoulder. Strong traces of solid drill abrasion internally, leaving horizontal concentric rings and central protrusion at the base. Traces of polishing throughout the vessel.

References

Xanthoudides 1924, 99-100. Herrero 2014, 44, 203.

(Katerina Athanasaki)

116

圆柱形带盖盒

米诺斯中期Ⅱ至Ⅲ（公元前 1800 ~ 前 1600 年）
大理石
高 5.5 厘米，直径 4.5 厘米
发现于克里特岛普塞拉
希腊伊拉克利翁考古博物馆藏，编号 Λ1119

容器保存完好，盖子为圆盘状且带纽扣形捉手，盒身呈圆柱形，平底。容器内部有使用旋转钻留下的环形痕迹。外表面经过充分打磨和抛光，充分利用了天然石材的纹理来呈现强烈的装饰效果。普塞拉发现的石制器物主要出自定居点和墓地，岛外也有大量类似器物发现。

石制器物的材质多样，形态各异，且加工过程中表现出很高的专业化程度，表明此地可能曾有一个繁荣的石器工坊，弥补了普塞拉地区制陶水平低下的不足。

（卡特琳娜・阿塔纳萨基）

116

Cylindrical pyxis with lid

Middle Minoan Ⅱ–Ⅲ (1800-1600 BCE)
Marble
H. 5.5 cm, diam. 4.5 cm
Pseira
Archaeological Museum of Heraklion, Λ1119

The vase has a flat base, cylindrical body and disc-shaped lid with button handle. Intact. Internally, a few rings indicate the use of a rotary drill. The outer surface is highly smoothed and polished, while the exploitation of the natural banding of the stone has a strong decorative effect. Stone vessels on Pseira are known both from both the settlement and the cemetery, while their dispersion outside the island is extensive.

The variety of shapes and rocks used in the manufacture of stone vases and the high specialisation visible in their processing are evidence of the existence of a flourishing workshop, which helped to make up for the low level of pottery production at Pseira.

References

Seager 1910, 34-38. Betancourt 1990.Vargiolu et al. 2007.

(Katerina Athanasaki)

117

鸟巢形带盖容器

米诺斯中期Ⅲ至米诺斯晚期Ⅰ（公元前 1700 ~ 前 1450 年）

斑状石灰岩

高 6.3 厘米，直径 10.5 厘米

发现于克里特岛普塞拉

希腊伊拉克利翁考古博物馆藏，编号 Λ1138

鸟巢形带盖容器，完好无损。盖子呈圆盘状，中央有一个纽扣状捉手。外表面经过细致抛光，内部也同样经过打磨。由内部痕迹可知，制作时曾使用不同尺寸的钻头。

这件容器的鸟巢形设计和斑状石灰岩的色泽使其具有很高的装饰价值。

（卡特琳娜・阿塔纳萨基）

117

Bird's-nest vessel with lid

Middle Minoan Ⅲ – Late Minoan Ⅰ (1700-1450 BCE)

Brecciated limestone

H. 6.3 cm, diam. 10.5 cm

Pseira

Archaeological Museum of Heraklion, Λ1138

Bird's-nest vessel with lid. Intact. Traces of use of different-sized drills inside. The outer surface has a particularly careful polishing, while the interior is also smoothed. Disc-shaped lid with a central button handle.

The shapes and colour of the brecciated limestone of which the vessel is made are highly decorative.

References

Seager 1910, 34-38. Warren 1969, 10. Carter 2008.

(Katerina Athanasaki)

118

来通杯

米诺斯中期Ⅲ至米诺斯晚期Ⅰ（公元前 1700 ~ 前 1450 年）

带纹石灰岩

高 38.2 厘米

发现于克里特岛克诺索斯王宫中央宫殿神庙

希腊伊拉克利翁考古博物馆藏，编号 Λ42

石来通杯，主体为卵形，顶部（包括口部、颈部和环状浮雕领部）单独制作后拼接到主体上。主体有宽竖槽，领部饰有棱纹浮雕，这些设计元素可能受到了同时期金属器物的启发。这种石器是新王宫期的典型器具，造型与同类陶器相似，可能用于仪式祭酒，液体通过底部开口倒出。

石来通杯以其高超的技术工艺和无与伦比的美感著称，在神殿宝库、宫殿建筑和其他宅邸中皆有发现。这类器物制作难度极高，展现了米诺斯时期克里特岛工匠的高超技艺。这类器物（特别是以进口原材料制成的样式）不仅彰显着所有者的财力，还象征着他们在世俗和宗教仪式中享有的特权。

（艾琳·尼古拉科普卢）

118

Rhyton

Middle Minoan Ⅲ – Late Minoan Ⅰ (1700-1450 BCE)

Stone (veined limestone)

H. 38.2 cm

Knossos, palace, Central Palace Sanctuary

Archaeological Museum of Heraklion, Λ42

Stone rhyton with ovoid body and separately made upper part (mouth, neck and relief collar). Decorated with wide vertical grooves on the body, which, together with the relief ribbed collar, may reflect the influence of contemporary metal vessels. These stone vases are typical of the Neopalatial era, resembling their counterparts in clay, and were probably used for ritual libations, offerings of liquids poured out of the hole in the bottom.

Masterpieces of high technical skill and unsurpassed beauty, stone rhyta have been found in palaces, sometimes in rooms interpreted as shrine treasuries, as well as in palatial buildings and other residences. They are certainly among the most difficult vessels to make from a technical viewpoint and reveal the skill of the artisans of Minoan Crete. For their owners, they were means of displaying wealth, particularly when made of imported raw materials, and markers of privileged participation in secular and religious ceremonies.

References

PM II,2, 822 and fig.537b. Warren 1969, 86, P481.

(Irene Nikolakopoulou)

119

鸟巢形碗

米诺斯中期Ⅲ至米诺斯晚期Ⅰ（公元前1700～前1450年）

蛇纹石

高9厘米，最大直径13.8厘米

发现于克里特岛马菲兹-卡特罗斯的岩洞墓

希腊伊拉克利翁考古博物馆藏，编号Λ2176

鸟巢形碗，保存完好，底部狭窄，向上逐渐拓宽至碗肩。外表面经过抛光和打磨，碗肩有四道水平阶梯状凹槽/凸棱装饰，可能是通过车床工艺制作而成。内部可见实心钻留下的环形痕迹。

此碗出土于马菲兹-卡特罗斯岩洞墓4号石棺内，是诸多随葬品之一。

（卡特琳娜·阿塔纳萨基）

119

Bird's-nest bowl

Middle Minoan Ⅲ – Late Minoan Ⅰ (1700-1450 BCE)

Serpentinite

H. 9 cm, max. diam. 13.8 cm

Rock-cut tomb of Mafeze Karteros

Archaeological Museum of Heraklion, Λ2176

Bird's-nest bowl with narrow base and widening to upper portion of shoulder. Intact. Polished outer surface with traces of smoothing and a zone of four horizontal stepped grooves/ridges on the shoulder, probably made using a lathe. Solid drill rotary rings are distinguished internally.

It comes from sarcophagus 4 of the rock-cut cave tomb at Mafeze Karteros, where it was deposited as a burial offering.

References

Μαρινάτος 1927-28, 72, pl.1(12).

(Katerina Athanasaki)

120

石杯（半成品，两件）

A. 单柄半球形石杯（半成品）
米诺斯晚期Ⅰ（公元前 1600 ~ 前 1450 年）
红褐色蛇纹石
高 6.2 厘米，直径 8.5 厘米
发现于莫克洛斯
希腊伊拉克利翁考古博物馆藏，编号 Λ1171

B. 无柄石杯（半成品）
米诺斯晚期Ⅰ（公元前 1600 ~ 前 1450 年）
红褐色蛇纹石
高 4.7 厘米，直径 6.5 厘米
发现于莫克洛斯
希腊伊拉克利翁考古博物馆藏，编号 Λ1172

A）单柄半球形杯，壁厚，带有纵向拱形手柄，但未钻孔。

B）无柄杯，器身略外扩至平沿，杯口下有水平凹槽。

这两件器物表面处理粗糙，外部可见切割和粗磨痕迹，内部可见清晰的纵向和斜向凹槽。这些凹槽表明，在加工过程中使用了冲子和凿子，这些工具可能单独使用，也可能与钻头结合使用。外部仍可见刀片刻痕和介质研磨痕迹。

通常认为这些半成品器物、莫克洛斯定居点中发现的其他石材碎片以及墓地中的成品器物均产自聚落中的石器工坊。

（卡特琳娜·阿塔纳萨基）

120

Unfinished cups

A. Unfinished one-handled, hemispherical cup
Late Minoan Ⅰ (1600-1450 BCE)
Red-brown serpentinite
H. 6.2 cm, diam. 8.5 cm
Mochlos
Archaeological Museum of Heraklion, Λ1171

B. Unfinished handleless cup
Late Minoan Ⅰ (1600-1450 BCE)
Red-brown serpentinite
H. 4.7 cm, diam. 6.5 cm
Mochlos
Archaeological Museum of Heraklion, Λ1172

A) Single-handled hemispherical cup with thick walls and vertical arched handle, unperforated.

B) Cup, with a slightly expanding profile to a flat rim, with horizontal groove below the rim.

Roughly worked surfaces, with traces of cutting and rough grinding on the outside and distinct zones of vertical and oblique grooves on the inside. As can be seen from these grooves on both vessels, a punch and a chisel were used to remove the interior, either by themselves or in conjunction with a drill, while external traces of a blade and an abrasive medium are still visible.

As semi-finished products, in combination with other stone debris in the settlement of Mochlos as well as final products from the cemetery, these pieces are considered to be the products of a stone-vase worker's set-up in the settlement.

References

Seager 1909, 280, fig.4. Warren 1969, 207. Evely 2000, 77-96 and 171-94.

(Katerina Athanasaki)

121

"特里同"海螺形来通杯

米诺斯晚期 I（公元前 1600～前 1450 年）

蛇纹石

高 37 厘米（包括修复部分），最大宽度 14 厘米

发现于克里特岛帕莱卡斯特罗

希腊伊拉克利翁考古博物馆藏，编号 Λ505

蛇纹石"特里同"螺来通杯，很可能被用作宗教仪式中的器具。器物制作精良，以"特里同"螺壳为原型。仿制"特里同"螺壳的器物通常以陶土、石材或费昂斯制成，在米诺斯时期的克里特岛具有重要的宗教意义。这类器物在许多米诺斯遗址中都有发现，主要集中在宫殿和神庙。器物精准再现了"特里同"螺壳的特征，充分展示出米诺斯石雕工匠的高超技艺。

（克莱奥·察纳基）

121

Triton Rhyton

Late Minoan I (1600-1450 BCE)

Serpentine

Max. h. 37 cm (restoration included), max. w. 14 cm

Palaikastro

Archaeological Museum of Heraklion, Λ505

Triton shell model made of serpentine. The triton shell model found at Palaikastro probably served as a ritual vessel. Crafted with great skill, it imitates real triton shells. Imitations of triton shells, usually made of clay, stone or faience, must have been of special religious significance in Minoan Crete. They have been found at various Minoan sites, mainly palaces and sanctuaries. The features of the natural triton that have been perfectly copied in the model attest to the high technical proficiency of the Minoan stone-carvers.

References

Bosanquet-Dawkins 1923.

(Kleio Tzanaki)

122

天然“特里同”海螺壳

公元前 1650 ~ 前 1450 年

贝壳

高 22 厘米

发现于克里特岛西提亚佐乌的宫殿式住宅

希腊伊拉克利翁考古博物馆藏，编号 O–E810

小型特里同螺壳，完整，壳身呈乳白色，带有浅橙色斑点。可清晰分辨出至少七个螺旋生长环。螺尖可能为自然脱落。

特里同螺是水下世界最具辨识度的生物之一，这种典型的爱琴海海洋文化图像在米诺斯时期的克里特岛占有重要地位。人们不仅描绘其图案，还用石材、陶土和费昂斯大量制作立体模型。特里同螺壳是重要的仪式器物，可以充当祭酒器和发声装置。特里同螺壳能够自然发声，通过控制节奏和音调，可以在一定程度上进行演奏，不仅能够发出风声，也能模仿撼天震地的公牛咆哮之声。受其实际用途（发声、音乐、祭酒）影响，特里同螺壳也被赋予了多种象征意义，成为一类尊贵的器物。

（迪米特里斯·斯法基纳基斯）

122

Triton Shell

1650–1450 BCE

Shell

H. 22 cm

Zou Siteia, palatial house

Archaeological Museum of Heraklion, O-E810

Complete shell of a small, marine triton mollusc (Charonia tritonis), of a milky colour with light orange spots. At least seven spiral growth whorls can be distinguished. The small flake at the tip appears to have been lost naturally.

As a most recognisable denizen of the underwater world, the triton occupies a prominent place in the iconography of the Aegean maritime culture of Minoan Crete. The natural shell has inspired a multitude of representations and three-dimensional models in stone, clay and faience. It was a key piece of ritual equipment, both as a libation vessel and, above all, as a sound-generating object. The triton can produce natural noises, controlled both rhythmically and tonally, so that we can talk here about a sort of music: they may resemble the sighing of the wind but also the sounds of the roaring, world-shaking Bull. In its practical uses – sounds, music, libations – a multitude of symbolic meanings may be sought, making it a prestige object.

References

Binnberg 2013.

(Dimitris Sfakianakis)

123

带常春藤叶浮雕的高型灯

米诺斯晚期 I（公元前 1600 ~ 前 1450 年）
斑岩
高 46 厘米，口沿直径 23.2 厘米
发现于克里特岛帕莱卡斯特罗
希腊伊拉克利翁考古博物馆藏，编号 Λ616

这是一种新王宫期常见的石灯类型，但材质更为奢华。其顶部为浅盆状灯槽，灯槽边缘有两个相对的窄切口用于固定灯芯。灯身高耸，带圆盘状底座。灯具口沿垂下两个手柄，柱身中部有一圈装饰性凸起，方便提起这件沉重的灯具。

在青铜时代，照明装置是家庭中的必需品，通常采用多种材质（陶土、石材、青铜）和形式制作。而这件来自帕莱卡斯特罗的石灯尤其特别，它采用了一种产自伯罗奔尼撒半岛的深红色斑岩制成，这种材料在克里特岛极为罕见，主要用于制作此类灯具。石灯口沿和底座装饰有新王宫期典型的常春藤叶浮雕，表明这是一件奢侈品，可能出自服务于宫殿或精英阶层的工坊之手。

（艾琳・尼古拉科普卢）

123

Tall lamp with relief ivy leaves

Late Minoan I (1600–1450 BCE)
Stone (porphyry)
H. 46 cm, diam. rim 23.2 cm
Palaikastro
Archaeological Museum of Heraklion, Λ616

This is a luxury version of a common type of stone lamp of the Neopalatial era. It comprises a shallow basin at the top with two opposing narrow cuttings across the width of the basin's lip to hold a wick, and a high pedestal resting on a disc base. Two handles hanging down from the edge of the rim and a bulging decorative zone at mid-height of the pedestal were probably used to grasp and lift this heavy artifact.

Lighting fixtures, made in different materials (clay, stone, bronze), different sizes and many variants, were essential in Bronze Age households. However, this example from Palaikastro is quite exceptional: it was manufactured from a deep red stone from the Peloponnese called rosso antico, which was rarely worked on Crete and is mainly found in lamps of this kind. The imported material of which the lamp is made and the relief decoration of a scroll of ivy leaves, a characteristic motif of the Neopalatial era, at the rim and in the pedestal zone, classify it among luxury vessels, most probably produced in an organised workshop that operated in a palatial/elite context.

References

Bosanquet-Dawkins 1923, 139-140. Warren 1969, 58.

(Irene Nikolakopoulou)

124

高足杯

米诺斯晚期 I B（公元前 1500 ~ 前 1450 年）
辉长岩
高 9.5 厘米
发现于克里特岛扎克罗斯王宫
希腊伊拉克利翁考古博物馆藏，编号 Λ2711

这件容器由两个明显的部分组成：一个是高锥形杯身，另一个是与之相连的双凹形底座。其器形是石材制成的典型祭仪容器的终极体现；同时期的壁画、印章戒指等多种媒介都描绘过此类器物，表明其在“圣餐”祭仪过程中具有重要的功能性质。

这件祭仪容器发掘自岛上最东端的宫殿中心宝库，类似器物共有四件，均以金银容器为原型。这些器物在颜色和纹理上都令人印象深刻，所用石材不仅质地极为坚硬，而且有的十分稀有。因此，这些石器具有十分重要的意义和价值，证实了宫殿工坊在鼎盛时期所达到的极高的工艺水平和专业化程度。

（迪米特里斯・斯法基纳基斯）

124

Chalice

Late Minoan I B (1500–1450 BCE)
Stone-gabbro
H. 9.5 cm
Zakros, palace
Archaeological Museum of Heraklion, Λ2711

The vessel consists of two distinct parts, the high conical body, and the foot with biconcave profile to which the body is attached. Its shape is the ultimate manifestation in stone of the pre-eminent ritual vessel, one that is recognised in a myriad contemporary representations in many media (e.g. wall paintings, signet rings). Together they emphasise beyond doubt its functional character in the ritual process of "holy communion".

This particular ritual vessel is one of four similar ones found in the treasury of the easternmost palatial centre of the island. Their shape and details indicate that all four vessels are copies of metal prototypes in gold and silver. At the same time, the stones used to work these vessels are impressive in their colour and texture, very hard and, sometimes, rare. All these aspects give them a particular importance and value, confirming the highest level of skill and the specialisation in working stone the palace workshops achieved during their heyday.

References

Πλάτων 1974, 123-126. Warren 1969, 36-38.

(Dimitris Sfakianakis)

小印钤万方

在古代世界，印章并非中国所独有，埃及、美索不达米亚、南亚次大陆都曾使用过这种证物。大概受邻近文明的浸润，克里特人也钟爱印章，彰显出本土与外域的文化交融。它们个头不大，却在方寸之间微缩了广阔天地，可谓包罗万象、异彩纷呈。青铜文明早期阶段，克里特印章刻画的主要是抽象线条和几何图案，到旧王宫期开始以野羊、公牛、狮子、蜜蜂等动物形象作印面内容。在繁荣的新王宫期，印面图案更加复杂，构思设计和表现手法与壁画息息相关，能够描绘置身于风景当中的人和物，动感十足、复杂多样，来源于刻印工匠对日常生活的细微观察。

Small Seals, Big World

In the ancient world, seals were not unique to China, but were also used in Egypt, Mesopotamia and India. Presumably influenced by neighbouring cultures, the Cretans were also fond of seals, reflecting a blend of local and foreign traditions. These small objects captured the vastness of the world in miniature, showcasing a dazzling array of designs within a single square inch. During the early Bronze Age, Cretan seals primarily featured abstract lines and geometric patterns. By the Protopalatial era, motifs such as wild goats, bulls, lions, and bees began to appear. In the prosperous Neopalatial era, the seal designs were more complex, closely linked to mural art in both concept and execution. They depicted people and objects within landscapes, dynamic and diverse, reflecting the meticulous observation of daily life by the craftsmen who carved them.

125
梨形印章
米诺斯中期ⅠA至ⅠB（公元前2100～前1800年）
绿泥石
高1.5厘米，宽1.5厘米，厚2.5厘米
发现于克里特岛库马萨的E号圆顶墓
希腊伊拉克利翁考古博物馆藏，编号Σ-K540

梨形石印章，带有两个对称分布的凸耳，凸耳上有悬挂孔。它属于“瓶形”印章，主要由“软石印章工坊”制作。印章的下半部分镶嵌有四枚以珍珠母贝制成的花形饰物，这种装饰手法在早期印章中颇为常见。底部印面雕刻有旋转的S形螺旋、对称排列的点状图案以及其他无法辨认的填充纹样。

米诺斯印章主要出土于墓葬，属于个人随葬品。库马萨发现的此类印章证明阿斯泰鲁夏山脉地区也曾生产此类物品。

（乔治娅・弗拉达）

126
印章
米诺斯中期Ⅱ（公元前1800～前1700年）
银
直径1.2厘米，高1.6厘米
发现于莫克洛斯的XVII号墓
希腊伊拉克利翁考古博物馆藏，编号X－A378

银制印章，三个球形部件组成印钮，最上端有穿孔。底部圆形印面刻有八瓣花形纹样。此印章出土于一处墓葬群，是随葬品之一。

这种印章是旧王宫晚期流行的一种标记工具，常用于在未经烧制的陶土上压印标记，这些陶土通常附着在物品上，以确保其完整性。此外，印章也可用于办公管理，以陶土印记和标签等形式标记各项程序。

（乔治娅・弗拉达）

125
Piriform seal
Middle Minoan Ⅰ A–Ⅰ B (2100-1800 BCE)
Chlorite
H. 1.5 cm, w. 1.5 cm, th. 2.5 cm
Koumasa, Tholos E
Archaeological Museum of Heraklion, Σ-K540

Stone piriform seal with two symmetrically placed lugs bearing suspension holes. It belongs to the “bottle” type, mainly produced by the “Soft-stone Seals Complex”. The lower body of the seal bears four inlaid mother-of-pearl rosettes, following a practice that was common for early seals. The sealing surface at the base of the seal has been carved with an ornamental composition consisting of S-spirals in rotation, symmetrically placed dots and other undefinable filling motifs.

Minoan seals have mainly been recovered from tombs, where they were deposited as personal possessions. Examples such as this seal from Koumasa provide evidence for local production at this important site of the Asterousia mountain range.

References
CMS II.1, 156. Sbonias 1995, 61, 118-119, 121, 168.

(Georgia Flouda)

126
Stamp-seal
Middle Minoan Ⅱ (1800-1700 BCE)
Silver
Diam. 1.2 cm, h. 1.6 cm
Mochlos, Tomb XVII
Archaeological Museum of Heraklion, X-A378

Silver stamp-seal (Petschaft) with a handle formed of three spherical components, the uppermost one of which is perforated. The circular sealing surface forming its base bears an eight-petalled rosette. The seal was found in a funerary complex, where it had accompanied some burials as a grave good.

A popular type of the late Protopalatial era, the stamp-seal was a practical way of marking lumps of unbaked clay that were attached to objects as a means of ensuring their integrity or labelling them in the framework of bureaucratic administration (clay sealings and labels).

References
CMS II.2, 252.

(Georgia Flouda)

127

印章

米诺斯中期ⅡB（公元前 1750～前 1700 年）

青金石

长 1.7 厘米，宽 0.8 厘米

发现于克里特岛帕莱卡斯特罗

希腊伊拉克利翁考古博物馆藏，编号 Σ-K1678

矩形青金石印章，狭长且紧凑。两个印面的图案设计对称，图案位于两侧方形内，中间带有菱形网格。一个印面上是四瓣花饰与十字纹样的组合，另一个印面上则是结合了末端卷曲的 S 形曲线和百合花图案。

公元前 18 世纪，宝石车床技术引入克里特岛，这一技术彻底改变了印章的制作方式，使工匠能够加工坚硬的半宝石并创作更为复杂的印章纹样。

（乔治娅·弗拉达）

127

Seal

Middle Minoan ⅡB (1750-1700 BCE)

Lapis lazuli

L. 1.7 cm, w. 0.8 cm

Palaikastro

Archaeological Museum of Heraklion, Σ-K1678

Seal in the shape of a narrow, compact rectangular rod of lapis lazuli. Of interest is the symmetrical arrangement of the motifs on the two sealing surfaces: they are set in squares on either side of a vertical band incised with a rhomboid mesh. Quatrefoil rosettes in combination with a cruciform pattern are depicted on one face, and a combination of lilies with a sigmoid that has curled-up ends on the other.

The introduction of the lapidary lathe to Crete in the 18th century BCE has totally revolutionised seal manufacture, as it allowed seal craftsmen to work on hard semiprecious stones and produce more elaborate seal motifs.

References

CMS II.2, 286. Krzyszkowska 2005, 87-88.

(Georgia Flouda)

128

印章

米诺斯中期ⅡB（约公元前 1700 年）

尼西罗斯岛伊雅利的黑曜石

高 1.2 厘米，底部直径 1.1 厘米

发现于克里特岛马利亚穆区的“印章切割工坊”

希腊伊拉克利翁考古博物馆藏，编号 Σ-K1801

带装饰性钮的印章，底部雕刻有未完成的双刃斧纹样。这种能将坚硬的火山石材——黑曜石精雕细琢成小型印章的技术，充分展示了克里特工匠在印章制作技艺和相关工具方面所取得的显著进步。

（乔治娅·弗拉达）

128

Stamp-seal

Middle Minoan ⅡB (Ca. 1700 BCE)

Obsidian from Gyali, Nisyros

H. 1.2 cm, diam. base 1.1 cm

Malia, Quartier Mu, "Seal-Cutter's Workshop"

Archaeological Museum of Heraklion, Σ-K1801

Ornate-handled stamp-seal (Petschaft), with unfinished double axe motif on the base. The efficient carving of obsidian, a hard volcanic material, into the tiny shape of a seal demonstrates the progress Cretan craftsmen had made in seal-making techniques and the tools required.

References

CMS II.2, 129. Krzyszkowska 2018, 7, fig.3b.

(Georgia Flouda)

129

印章

米诺斯中期ⅡB（约公元前 1700 年）
绿色滑石
高 1.4 厘米，宽 1.2 厘米
发现于克里特岛马利亚穆区的“印章切割工坊”
希腊伊拉克利翁考古博物馆藏，编号 Σ-K1831

三面棱柱形印章，其中两面雕刻着人群、陶器和一件可能是锯子的物品。这类印章上常出现单个人物或群体的形象，以及代表日常生活特定职业和活动的物品，可能象征着特定的社会群体或工匠行会。

（乔治娅・弗拉达）

130

印章

米诺斯中期ⅡB（约公元前 1700 年）
滑石
底部直径 1.5 厘米
发现于克里特岛克诺索斯普罗菲提斯–伊利亚斯的 VII 号墓
希腊伊拉克利翁考古博物馆藏，编号 Σ-K1714

大型三面棱柱形印章，其中两面雕刻着钻孔形成的同心圆纹样。

（乔治娅・弗拉达）

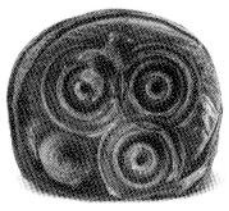

129

Seal

Middle Minoan ⅡB (Ca. 1700 BCE)
Green steatite
H. 1.4 cm, w. 1.2 cm
Malia, Quartier Mu, "Seal-Cutter's Workshop"
Archaeological Museum of Heraklion, Σ-K1831

Three-sided prism seal. Two faces are carved with groups of men together with vases and an object, possibly representing a saw. The appearance of human figures, singly or in groups, and often together with objects indicating specific occupations and activities of everyday life, may have symbolically denoted social groups or artisan guilds.

References
CMS II.2, 159. Anastasiadou 2011, 541-42 no.187.

(Georgia Flouda)

130

Seal

Middle Minoan ⅡB (Ca. 1700 BCE)
Steatite
Diam. base 1.5 cm
Knossos, Profitis Ilias, Tomb VII
Archaeological Museum of Heraklion, Σ-K1714

Large three-sided prism seal, depicting motifs of concentric circles produced by a drill on two of the three sealing surfaces.

References
CMS II.2, 55.

(Georgia Flouda)

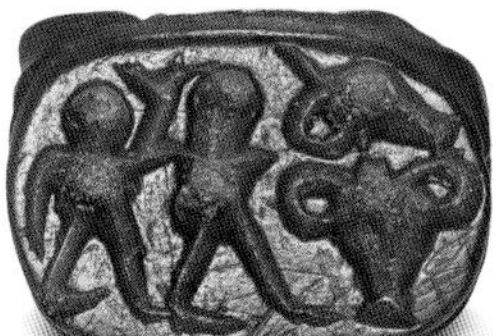

131

印章

米诺斯中期Ⅱ至Ⅲ（公元前 1700 ~ 前 1600 年）

滑石

直径 1.3 厘米，厚 0.7 厘米

发现于莫克洛斯的 XVI 号墓（西格发掘）

希腊伊拉克利翁考古博物馆藏，编号 Σ-K763

滑石圆盘状印章，有两个印面。其中一个印面上雕刻有两组带中央点的同心圆，并且带有两个孔洞。这些形状是米诺斯印章工匠使用实心钻等多种工具精心雕琢而成，展现了他们的创新精神。另一个印面上则将同心圆纹样与交叉直线网格图案结合呈现。

（乔治娅・弗拉达）

131

Seal

Middle Minoan Ⅱ–Ⅲ (1700-1600 BCE)

Steatite

Diam. 1.3 cm, th. 0.7 cm

Mochlos, Seager Excavation, Tomb XVI

Archaeological Museum of Heraklion, Σ-K763

Steatite discoid seal with two sealing surfaces. One depicts two groups of concentric circles with a central dot, as well as two hollow holes. These have been made with a solid drill, one of the various tools employed by the inventive Minoan seal craftsmen. On the second sealing surface a similar motif of concentric circles is combined with a mesh of intersecting straight lines.

References

CMS II.2, 253, 355 (on provenance and style).

(Georgia Flouda)

132

印章

米诺斯中期Ⅲ至米诺斯晚期Ⅰ（公元前 1700 ~ 前 1450 年）

金属合金

长 1.51 厘米，宽 1.1 厘米，厚 0.31 厘米

发现于莫克洛斯的 XVIII 号墓（西格发掘）

希腊伊拉克利翁考古博物馆藏，编号 Σ-K778

金属合金制“垫形”印章，上面带有七道纵贯主长轴的深刻平行切痕。类似的印章在克诺索斯和帕莱卡斯特罗也有发现，制作时间可追溯至新王宫期。

（乔治娅・弗拉达）

132

Seal

Middle Minoan Ⅲ – Late Minoan Ⅰ (1700-1450 BCE)

Metal alloy

L. 1.51 cm, w. 1.1 cm, th. 0.31 cm

Mochlos, Seager Excavation, Tomb XVIII

Archaeological Museum of Heraklion, Σ-K778

Metal alloy "cushion" seal, with seven parallel deep cuts running transverse to the main long axis. Similar seals have been found at Knossos and Palaikastro, and date to the Neopalatial era.

References

Seager 1912, 110. CMS II.3, 256. Soles 1992, 105-06. Dionisio-Jasink-Weingarten 2014, 97, 101 (Cat.M-4).

(Georgia Flouda)

133

印章

米诺斯中期Ⅲ至米诺斯晚期Ⅰ（公元前 1700 ~ 前 1450 年）

水晶

1.8 × 1.3 厘米，厚 0.9 厘米

发现于莫克洛斯（西格发掘）

希腊伊拉克利翁考古博物馆藏，编号 Σ-K757

杏仁形印章，采用“护身符风格”，其上刻有双圆环和枝条图案。这些图案是通过使用空心钻工具以及雕刻或切割工艺来完成的。“护身符风格”的印章最初被认为是护身符，因为其图案非常抽象。近期研究认为，这种风格是其制作技术所致，制作者刻意保留了旋转工具的痕迹，并未试图将其打磨或修饰。

（乔治娅 · 弗拉达）

133

Seal

Middle Minoan Ⅲ – Late Minoan Ⅰ (1700-1450 BCE)

Rock crystal

1.8×1.3 cm, th. 0.9 cm

Mochlos, Seager Excavation

Archaeological Museum of Heraklion, Σ-K757

Amygdaloid seal in the "talismanic style", with a composition of double circles and branches, the result of using a hollow drill and carving or cutting respectively. Seals of the "talismanic style" were originally considered to be charms due to their abstract images. Recent research has reconsidered their style as the result of manufacturing technique, in which the marks of rotary tools are left visible, without an attempt to model or smooth them away.

References

CMS II.3, 266. Onassoglou 1985, 165, pl.LXIV 39. Kenna 1969, 32.

(Georgia Flouda)

134

印章

米诺斯中期Ⅲ至米诺斯晚期Ⅰ（公元前 1700 ~ 前 1450 年）
安山岩
直径 2.3 厘米
发现于克里特岛罕德拉斯的西提亚
希腊伊拉克利翁考古博物馆藏，编号 Σ-K126

透镜状印章，上面刻有两头狮子纹样，分立于抽象形式柱子的两侧。狮腿纤细，采用新王宫期的特殊切割圆盘制作而成，关节处采用钻孔雕刻工艺来表现。

（乔治娅・弗拉达）

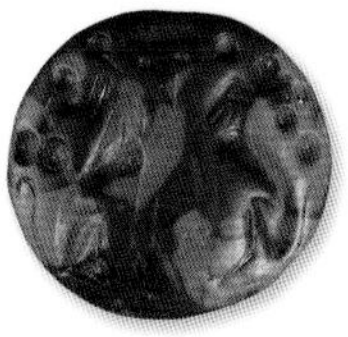

134

Seal

Middle Minoan Ⅲ – Late Minoan Ⅰ (1700–1450 BCE)
Andesite (lapis lacedaemonius)
Diam. 2.3 cm
Chandras, Siteia
Archaeological Museum of Heraklion, Σ-K126

Lentoid seal depicting two lions, one on either side of a pillar rendered in abstract form. The thin legs of the lions are executed by special cutting discs used during the Neopalatial era, while their joints, rendered with holes, have been carved with a drill.

References

CMS II.3, 306.

(Georgia Flouda)

135

印章

米诺斯晚期Ⅰ（公元前 1600 ~ 前 1450 年）
黑色赤铁矿
高 2.15 厘米，宽 1.3 厘米，厚 0.7 厘米
发现于克里特岛克诺索斯卡托-吉普萨迪斯的得墨忒耳神庙
希腊伊拉克利翁考古博物馆藏，编号 Σ-K2107

黑色赤铁矿杏仁形印章，带有垂直钻取的挂绳孔。此印章属于“护身符风格”，主要特点为采用抽象图案。印章上刻有较深的纵向和斜向切线，另外还可见两个钻孔以及一个椭圆形浅凹槽，可能是在描绘一种动物面具或纸莎草图案。

（乔治娅・弗拉达）

135

Seal

Late Minoan Ⅰ (1600–1450 BCE)
Black haematite
H. 2.15 cm, w. 1.3 cm, th. 0.7 cm
Knossos, Kato Gypsades, Sanctuary of Demeter
Archaeological Museum of Heraklion, Σ-K2107

Amygdaloid seal of black haematite with a vertically drilled string-hole. It belongs to a special group of seals of the "talismanic style", which are distinguished on the basis of their abstract motifs. It depicts either an animal mask or a papyrus motif by means of deep vertical and oblique cuts, two drilled holes and a shallow oval hollow.

References

CMS II.3, 80. Onassoglou 1985, 52, 55-56, 229, pl.XX 1.

(Georgia Flouda)

136

印章

米诺斯晚期 I（公元前 1600 ~ 前 1450 年）
红玉髓
2.3 × 1.7 厘米，厚 0.9 厘米
发现于克里特岛帕莱卡斯特罗
希腊伊拉克利翁考古博物馆藏，编号 Σ-K564

“护身符风格”杏仁形印章，其上刻有两条在海中游曳的抽象鱼形图案。鱼头用空心钻雕刻出圆环和新月形，海洋则通过交叉网格图案和平行刻线表示。

（乔治娅・弗拉达）

136

Seal

Late Minoan I (1600-1450 BCE)
Carnelian
2.3×1.7 cm, th. 0.9 cm
Palaikastro
Archaeological Museum of Heraklion, Σ-K564

Amygdaloid seal of the "talismanic style", depicting two stylised fish floating in the sea. The fashioning of their heads with circles and crescents is effected by the use of a hollow drill, while the sea is indicated by a cross-hatch net pattern and parallel incised lines.

References

CMS II.3, 284. Onassoglou 1985, 91-96, pl.XXXIV 4.

(Georgia Flouda)

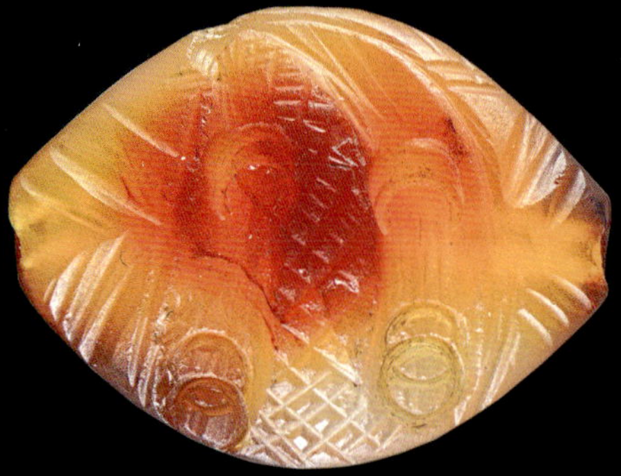

137

印章

米诺斯晚期 I（公元前 1600 ~ 前 1450 年）
黑色赤铁矿
直径 2.3 厘米
发现于克里特岛克诺索斯的皇家大道
希腊伊拉克利翁考古博物馆藏，编号 Σ-K2096

黑色赤铁矿透镜状印章，其上刻有一只卧姿野猪，周围点缀有植物图案。

（乔治娅·弗拉达）

137

Seal

Late Minoan I (1600-1450 BCE)
Black haematite
Diam. 2.3 cm
Knossos, Royal Road
Archaeological Museum of Heraklion, Σ-K2096

Black haematite lentoid seal with a recumbent boar among plant motifs.

References

Unpublished.

(Georgia Flouda)

138

印章

米诺斯晚期 I（公元前 1600 ~ 前 1450 年）
蛇纹石
直径 1.5 厘米，厚 1.5 厘米
发现于克里特岛圣特里亚达
希腊伊拉克利翁考古博物馆藏，编号 Σ-K1417

透镜状印章，其上刻有一头卧姿公牛，其头部向左偏转（在印模中呈现），其后还有另一头抽象公牛，仅能看见牛首和牛颈的背部轮廓。

（乔治娅·弗拉达）

138

Seal

Late Minoan I (1600-1450 BCE)
Serpentinite
Diam. 1.5 cm, th. 1.5 cm
Hagia Triada
Archaeological Museum of Heraklion, Σ-K1417

Lentoid seal depicting a recumbent bull with head turned to left (in the impression) and a second, abstract bull in the background, of which only the back of the head and neck are visible.

References

CMS II.3, 119.

(Georgia Flouda)

139
印章
米诺斯晚期 I（公元前 1600 ~ 前 1450 年）
蓝玉髓
直径 1.4 厘米
发现于克里特岛克诺索斯普罗菲提斯–伊利亚斯的 VII 号墓
希腊伊拉克利翁考古博物馆藏，编号 Σ-K1719

蓝玉髓透镜状印章，上面精心雕琢一头被长矛刺中的公牛，展现出工匠的高超技艺。蓝玉髓是米诺斯印章切割工艺中使用的最坚硬的原料之一。

（乔治娅·弗拉达）

140
印章
米诺斯晚期 I（公元前 1600 ~ 前 1450 年）
红碧玉
1.6 × 1.2 厘米，厚 0.55 厘米
发现于克里特岛梅萨–拉西提
希腊伊拉克利翁考古博物馆藏，编号 Σ-K642

“护身符风格”的“垫形”印章，由硬质半宝石红碧玉雕琢而成。这种风格的发展得益于印章工匠发明的新型专业工具，使得工匠们能够创作出装饰性和抽象性的图案。

工匠们熟练操作带有不同切割和研磨头的金属钻、锯片和刀片，创造出直线、深孔、圆形、半圆形和圆润棱纹等简单的几何形式。这枚印章是创作者即兴之作。制作者将圆形、半圆形与纵向刻线相结合，形成了一个相对自由的抽象布局，最终呈现出独特的主题。

（乔治娅·弗拉达）

139
Seal
Late Minoan I (1600-1450 BCE)
Blue chalcedony
Diam. 1.4 cm
Prophitis Ilias, Knossos, Tomb VII
Archaeological Museum of Heraklion, Σ-K1719

A lentoid seal depicting a bull wounded by a spear, carved with great skill in blue chalcedony, one of the hardest raw materials used in Minoan seal-cutting.

References

Unpublished.

(Georgia Flouda)

140
Seal
Late Minoan I (1600-1450 BCE)
Jasper
1.6 × 1.2 cm, th. 0.55 cm
Mesa Lasithi
Archaeological Museum of Heraklion, Σ-K642

A cushion seal made of hard semi-precious jasper, cut in the “talismanic style”. A prerequisite for the development of this style was the invention of innovative and specialised tools by the seal craftsmen for creating compositions of decorative and abstract motifs.

Through the skilful manipulation of metal drills with different kinds of cutting and grinding heads as well as drills and saws/blades, simple, elementary forms such as straight lines, deep holes, circles, semicircles and rounded ridges are produced. This seal demonstrates a typical improvisation on the part of its creator: circles and semi-circles combined with vertical engravings make up a relatively free abstract arrangement, resulting in a completely original theme.

References

CMS II.3, 291. Onassoglou 1985, 99-102, 257, pl.XL 59. Dionisio-Jasink-Weingarten 2014, 33, 57, 65 (Cat.105).

(Georgia Flouda)

141

金粒装饰的棱柱形印章

米诺斯晚期Ⅱ（约公元前 1450 ~ 前 1400 年）
红玉髓，带金粒装饰
带金粒长 2.4 厘米，直径 1.9 ~ 2 厘米
发现于克里特岛克诺索斯维尼泽里奥的 3 号墓
希腊伊拉克利翁考古博物馆藏，编号 Σ-K1658

三面棱柱形印章，表面圆滑且带弧度，仅有两面刻有图案。孔洞边缘镶嵌有金粒。

这枚印章出自该时期随葬品最多的墓地之一。印章的一面刻有一头向左奔跑的公牛和一棵分枝的树；另一面刻有一头回首的狮子，狮子身上中了一支标枪和三支箭。尽管印章的雕刻面积仅有数平方厘米，但却充分展现了米诺斯艺术家精湛的技术水平。

（克莱奥·察纳基）

141

Prism seal with granulation

Late Minoan Ⅱ (Ca. 1450-1400 BCE)
Carnelian with gold granulation
L. with granulation 2.4 cm, diam. 1.9 - 2 cm
Knossos, Venizeleio, Tomb 3
Archaeological Museum of Heraklion, Σ-K1658

Three-sided prism seal with rounded and curved surfaces. Only two of the sides are engraved. Gold granulation adorns the edges of the perforation.

The sealstone comes from a tomb of one of the wealthiest cemeteries of this period. A bull running to the left and a tree with branches are engraved on one side of the seal. On the other side, a lion is depicted seated with its head turning backward while being wounded by a javelin and three arrows. The impressive carving on sealing surfaces no larger than a few centimetres in diameter demonstrates the high technical skill of Minoan artists.

References

CMS II, 3, 75 (no 64). Hood–de Jong 1952, 273. Krzyszkowska 2005.

(Kleio Tzanaki)

142

印章戒指

米诺斯晚期ⅠB至Ⅱ（公元前1500～前1400年）

黄金

戒面长2厘米，戒面宽2.1厘米

发现于克里特岛阿尔哈内斯-富尔尼的A号圆顶墓

希腊伊拉克利翁考古博物馆藏，编号X-A989

金戒指的椭圆形戒面上刻有一幅崇拜圣树与圣石的场景。画面右侧，一名瘦削但健壮的男性正用力摇动一棵从带有交叉图案的三叉木制围栏中央生长出的树干。男子的艰苦努力通过其动作生动地表现出来，他高高地抬起弯曲的右腿，同时用左腿支撑身体以施加更大力量。在画面另一端，一位体型相似的青年双膝跪地，双臂紧紧拥抱着一块长柱形石头。画面中心是一位占据主导地位的女性，她站在铺砌的地面或平台上，右手抬至右肩，左手自然垂下。这位女性身着一袭典型的米诺斯风格褶裙，似乎在这场仪式中扮演着主导角色。跪拜者附近悬浮着柱子和蝴蝶符号，象征着女神即将显形，这也是仪式的最终目标。

该场景展现了一场米诺斯宗教仪式的画面，其中包含拥抱自然石块和摇动一棵神圣树木这两个并行或交替进行的祭祀行为。此外，画面还描绘了一位一边舞动身躯、一边协调祭祀的高级女祭司。两性的参与、高度戏剧化仪式动作的模糊内容以及神灵显形的神圣象征，都表明了仪式表现的狂热性质以及与所崇拜神灵相关的神话的存在。

（斯特拉·曼达莱基）

142

Signet ring with cult scene

Late Minoan ⅠB – Ⅱ (1500-1400 BCE)

Gold

Bezel l. 2 cm, bezel w. 2.1 cm

Archanes Phourni, Tholos Tomb A

Archaeological Museum of Heraklion, X-A989

Gold ring with scene of tree-worship and baetyl-worship on the oval bezel. At the right of the scene a slim, muscular male figure is vigorously shaking the trunk of a tree emerging from a tripartite wooden enclosure with crisscross decoration on the raised central section. The arduous effort is clearly depicted in the movement of the figure, as the man lifts his bent right leg high and stands on his left to apply more force. At the other end of the scene, a second youth of similar build is kneeling to embrace a long, cylindrical stone with both arms. The centre of the scene is occupied by a dominant female figure bending her right hand to her right shoulder and lowering her left. She is wearing the characteristic Minoan flounced skirt and appears to be playing a leading role in the events, which are taking place on a paved floor or podium. Floating symbols (a pillar and butterflies) near the kneeling worshipper indicate the imminent epiphany of the goddess, the ultimate goal of these ritual acts.

The scene pictured here is a recognisable Minoan religious ceremony involving two parallel or alternating cult acts: embracing a natural stone and shaking a sacred tree. This version also depicts the coordination of events by a high priestess, who may be dancing. The participation of both genders, the obscure content of these highly theatrical ritual motions, and the symbolic representation of the epiphany, all indicate the ecstatic nature of the performance and the existence of a myth associated with the deities being worshipped.

References

Crooks, S. 2013, 45-46, fig.39. Μανδαλάκη 2004, 17-18, fig.6. Μανδαλάκη 2015b, 101-02. Marinatos 1990. Marinatos 1993, 184-8, fig.188. Niemeier 1990, 168. Σακελλαράκης-Σαπουνά-Σακελλαράκη 1997, Vol.II, 654-60. Warren 1990, 196.

(Stella Mandalaki)

143

印章

米诺斯晚期ⅢB1（公元前 1300 ~ 前 1250 年）

玛瑙

直径 1.9 ~ 2 厘米，厚 0.9 厘米

发现于克里特岛古尔尼斯墓地的 2 号墓

希腊伊拉克利翁考古博物馆藏，编号 Σ-K1249

玛瑙透镜状印章，纵向钻有穿孔。图案刻画了一头转身面向幼崽的母牛，这是米诺斯印章雕刻中常见的主题之一。在同一墓地的另一座墓中也发现了一枚描绘类似场景的印章，可能出自同一工匠之手。

（乔治娅·弗拉达）

143

Seal

Late Minoan ⅢB1 (1300-1250 BCE)

Agate

Diam. 1.9-2 cm, th. 0.9 cm

Gournes Cemetery, Chamber Tomb 2

Archaeological Museum of Heraklion, Σ-K1249

Agate lentoid seal with a vertical string-hole drilled through. Representation of a cow turning to her calf, a favourite subject of Minoan seal carvers. A seal with a very similar rendering of the scene has been found in another tomb in the same cemetery, and is probably the work of the same craftsman.

References

CMS II.4, 160.

(Georgia Flouda)

古罗马诗人维吉尔赞叹代达罗斯在神殿之门上的雕刻栩栩如生。不知是代达罗斯从克里特人的艺术天赋中获得启迪，还是他反过来影响了克里特人的雕塑技艺。

考古发现表明，在新石器时代和米诺斯文化早期遗址中，已出现造型抽象的女神雕塑和风格简朴的祭祀者陶俑。大概在外来艺术和宗教信仰影响下，克里特岛逐渐出现一些附有陶土或石头肢体的大型木雕，尽管如此，米诺斯雕塑家们始终青睐小型作品。到米诺斯文化兴盛阶段，克里特人习惯在宫殿祭所、山顶神殿、山间洞穴、家庭神龛里放置男女全身或四肢、躯干陶塑，虔诚献祭给祖先和神灵。

这些雕像融合埃及、近东风格，介于抽象与写实之间，虽然外形依旧粗犷，却表现了克里特雕工对人体结构的掌握，对人物神态的拿捏，对动作姿势的塑造，可谓形神兼备、匠心独运。古希腊写实雕塑艺术由此肇始，经历古风时期的发展，在古典时期与希腊化时期登上巅峰。

The ancient Roman poet Virgil praised Daedalus for his lifelike carvings on the temple gates. It is not known whether the Cretan artistic talent inspired Daedalus or otherwise Daedalus influenced Cretan sculpture.

Archaeological sites from the Neolithic and early Minoan civilization already found sculptures of abstractly shaped goddesses, as well as simple, austere terracotta figurines of dancers and ancestors. Minoan sculpture always favored the small scale, although examples of large-scale wooden statues with added stone and clay parts and limbs have also been created, probably under the influence of foreign art. By the time the Minoan civilization flourished, the Cretans were accustomed to placing terracotta figurines of men and women with their whole bodies or limbs and torsos in their palaces and shrines, hilltop shrines, mountain caves, and household shrines to make devotional offerings to their ancestors and the gods.

These statues, blending Egyptian and Near Eastern styles, strike a balance between abstraction and realism. Despite its rough appearance, this Cretan sculpture reveals the artist's mastery of anatomy, expressive power, and dynamic posing skillings, achieving a remarkable fusion of form, spirit and ingenious creativity. The art of ancient Greek sculpture thus began, evolved through the Archaic Era, and reached its peak in the Classical Era and the Hellenistic Era.

144

简化人形雕像

米诺斯早期Ⅲ至米诺斯中期ⅠA（公元前2300～前1900年）

灰绿色石材

高67.5厘米，肩宽17厘米，最大厚度6.5厘米

发现于克里特岛佩迪亚达地区萨姆巴斯的拉可斯遗址

希腊伊拉克利翁考古博物馆藏，编号Γ1107

雕像呈细长板条状，三面为斜边，底部较窄，角度锐利。雕像向上逐渐平滑，肩部角度圆润。颈部高耸，线条略微凹陷，头部接近圆形。从侧面看，雕像略微凸起。雕像截面呈圆形。颈部与头部体积较大，曲度因此更为突出。雕像正面非常光滑，背面则较为粗糙。

这类萨姆巴斯型人形雕像对称性极佳，平凸表面进行过高度打磨处理，是大型简化人形雕刻艺术的巅峰之作。这也表明前王宫期当地石匠在大型石像制作方面拥有精湛技艺。这种独特造型可能借鉴了某种未知的木雕形态和技艺，并在此基础上将原版雕塑放大至纪念碑大小。这些雕像最有可能作为墓碑使用，但也可能只是普通的拟人化雕像。但无论其功能如何，这类雕像都清晰反映出早期大型抽象宗教人物雕像的制作传统。

（迪米特里斯・斯法基纳基斯）

144

Schematic human figure

Early Minoan Ⅲ– Middle Minoan ⅠA (2300-1900 BCE)

Grey-green stone

H. 67.5 cm, w. at the shoulders 17 cm, max. th. 6.5 cm

Sambas Pediada, Lakkos site

Archaeological Museum of Heraklion, Γ1107

Elongated, plank-shaped torso, with sharp angles at the narrow lower end – bevelled in three dimensions – and a smooth widening towards the rounded shoulders. High neck with slightly concave outline and almost round head. The figure is slightly convex in profile in its side view and rounded in cross-section. The neck and head are larger in volume and with a corresponding accentuated curvature. The front surface is smooth, the reverse less so.

The slender trunk of the Sambas-type figurine, with its symmetry and the advanced treatment of its plano-convex, smoothed faces, probably represents the zenith of a long tradition of large-scale schematic human sculpture. It also testifies to the technical proficiency of the local stoneworkers in the production of large stone figures in the Prepalatial era. Its distinctive shape seems to mimic the morphological elements and techniques of an otherwise unknown woodcarving tradition on a monumental scale. Irrespective of the function of these objects, either as grave markers – which is most likely since they are associated with burials – or as anthropomorphic effigies for wider use, figures of this type are the clearest evidence of an underlying tradition of making xoana: large-scale, abstract cult figures.

References

Σαπουνά-Σακελλαράκη 1983, 46ff., fig.1, pl.23. Krause 1992, 99, 287-88.

(Dimitris Sfakianakis)

145

雕像残件

米诺斯中期ⅡB至ⅢA（公元前1750～前1650年）

陶土

前臂和手长16厘米，脚长13.8厘米，下躯干长12.7厘米

发现于克里特岛佩迪亚达的马马卢库科弗山顶神庙

希腊伊拉克利翁考古博物馆藏，编号Π33195 a、b、c

这些陶土雕像残件包括一只中空右脚（从踝关节起），一只实心右臂（一半上臂、前臂和手），以及中空下躯干的前半部分，推测来自一尊高度在70厘米以上的大型雕像。雕像脚部穿着鞋子，鞋底上的痕迹表明它曾固定在基座上。鞋底可以看到一个圆形竖孔和一个纵向的椭圆形开口，用于将雕像固定在木框架上。鞋尖呈尖状，足部轮廓曲线也值得注意。上臂表现出肌肉线条，前臂也有肌肉凸起。肘部弯曲，与上臂呈锐角。手部呈握拳状，指缝有沟槽，拇指凸出。手掌内侧有一个半圆形的宽沟槽，可能用于抓握长圆柱形物品。下躯干雕刻设计大胆，展现出大腿上部的凹陷特征，并且带有一个宽而深的纵向沟槽，用于连接下体盖片。躯干上有一个便于烧制的通风孔，所用陶土与四肢稍有不同。

三块残件均出土自同一地点，表明这些肢体可能属于同一雕像。凭借肢体部分可以确认，这是位于山顶神庙的一尊双臂交叉胸前的男性立像，其创作于新旧王宫之间的过渡时期。这件马马卢库雕像可能是现存最大的山顶神庙雕像。这尊雕像与科菲纳斯出土的多件大型雕像一同为米诺斯陶土雕塑艺术的研究提供了新的资料。

（迪米特里斯・斯法基纳基斯）

145

Parts of a figure

Middle Minoan ⅡB–ⅢA (1750-1650 BCE)

Clay

L. forearm and hand 16 cm, l. foot 13.8 cm, h. lower trunk section 12.7 cm

Mamaloukou Korfi peak sanctuary, Pediada

Archaeological Museum of Heraklion, Π33195 a, b, c

The hollow right foot from the ankle joint on, the solid right arm – half of the upper arm, the forearm and the hand – and the front half-section of the hollow lower torso, all probably belonged to a large figure which would have been at least 70 cm tall. The foot, shod, would have stood on a base, judging by the traces of its attachment on the sole, on the surface of which there is a round vertical opening and an elongated one, along the sole. These show how the statue was fixed to a wooden frame. The shoe is pointed at the toes, while the curving outline of the foot is worthy of note. The upper arm is shaped to display the musculature. The forearm, which also exhibits modelled swellings of muscle, is bent at the elbow, at an acute angle to the upper arm. The hand is a closed fist, with grooves separating the fingers and a protrusion for the thumb. A wide groove of semicircular cross-section is preserved on the inner face of the hand, indicating that it probably held a long cylindrical object. The lower torso, with its bold moulded hollows defining the upper thighs, features a wide, deep vertical groove to accommodate the added codpiece. The clay of the trunk, which has a vent hole for firing, differs slightly from the clay of the limbs.

The three pieces were found in the same area, making it likely that the limbs belong to the trunk. In any case, the extremities alone confirm the existence of a large standing male figure, in the familiar gesture of the arms folded across the chest, in a peak sanctuary, dating from the transitional period between the old and new palaces. The Mamaloukou figure is perhaps the largest example, confirming the presence of large-scale figures at the peak sanctuaries. Together with the large figures from Kophinas, it adds new data to the study of Minoan coroplastic art.

References

Unpublished. Personal communication from the excavator Giorgos Rethemiotakis.

(Dimitris Sfakianakis)

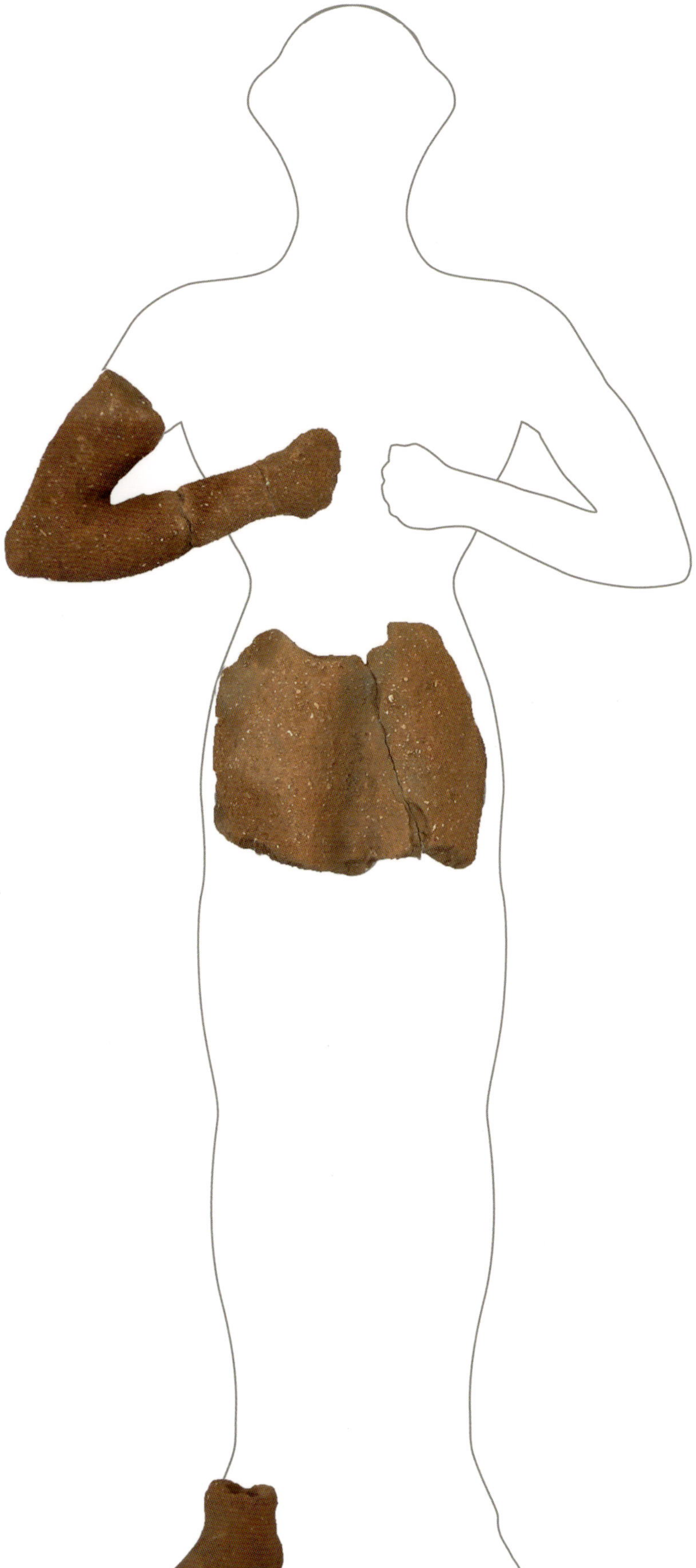

146

佩戴匕首的男性雕像

米诺斯中期ⅡB至Ⅲ（公元前1750～前1600年）
陶土，带红色颜料痕迹
高13厘米
发现于克里特岛佩佐法斯的山顶神庙
希腊伊拉克利翁考古博物馆藏，编号Π28351

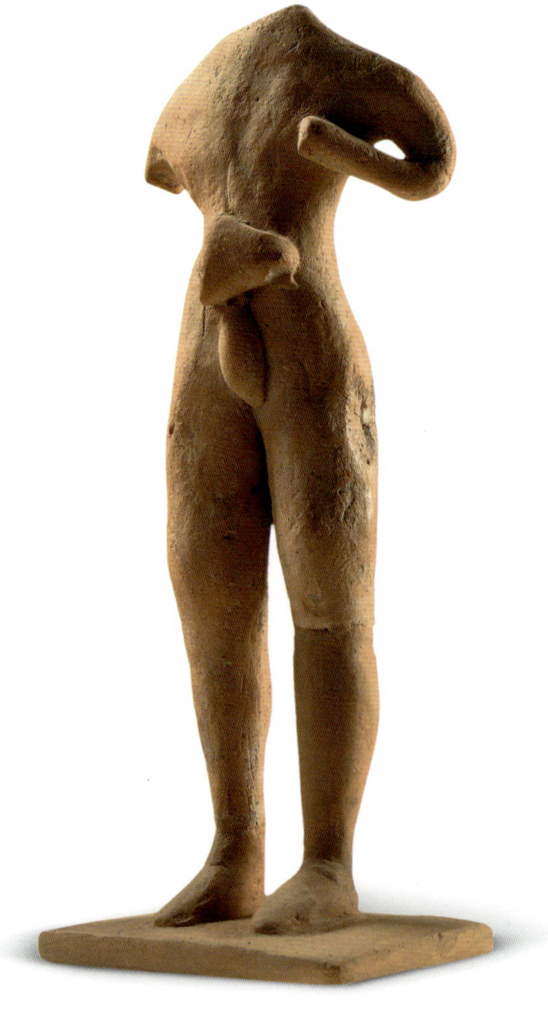

陶男性立像，双手置于胸前，腰间佩戴着一把匕首。雕像的头部、右臂、匕首的一部分、左小腿以及双脚均已遗失，而缺失的双脚在这里被修复为固定在矩形基座上。相较于上半身，雕像的腿部较长，表现出肌肉和关节的造型。相比之下，雕像的手臂则显得较为随意且略显萎缩，弯曲地贴在胸部的两侧。躯干部分呈三角形轮廓，两侧平整，略微向后倾斜。身前的缠腰布和腰间遮挡前腹的匕首均为后期复原并添加上的。

值得注意的是，工匠在下半身和腿部的刻画上投入了极大的精力。雕像的腿部比例协调，肌肉线条精致，缠腰布和匕首等元素的加入，都是佩佐法斯山顶神庙雕塑中的常见元素。这件雕像在身体塑造及其配饰（如衣物和匕首）的个性化表现上，展现出了令人瞩目的写实技艺。这些技艺在小型乃至大型雕塑中都形成了共同的范式语言。

（迪米特里斯·斯法基纳基斯）

146

Male figure with dagger

Middle Minoan II B–III (1750-1600 BCE)
Clay with traces of red paint
H. 13 cm
Petsophas, peak sanctuary
Archaeological Museum of Heraklion, Π28351

Clay standing male figure with hands on chest. He sports a dagger at his waist. The head, right arm, half the dagger and the shin of the left leg are missing, as are the feet, which have been completed here as resting on a rectangular base. The legs, long in relation to the upper body, show modelling in their representation of muscles and joints. The arms, in contrast, are rendered completely indifferently and rather atrophied, bent at the sides of the chest. The torso is triangular in outline, flat on both sides, with a slight backwards inclination. The codpiece and the dagger that obscures the front of the waist are modelled and added.

Notable here is the artisan's focus on the lower torso and legs: the proportions of the legs, their careful musculature, the loincloth and dagger are common elements in the sculptural tradition of the Petsophas peak sanctuary. The individual characteristics of the physical portrayal of the body, as well as its accoutrements (clothing, dagger), reveal remarkable achievements in the realistic rendering of the human body. These achievements form a common modelling vocabulary between small and sizeable or even large-scale sculpture.

References

Rutkowski 1991, 63, pl.IX, fig.1-3 (cat. no.1.1.15).

(Dimitris Sfakianakis)

147

男性雕像

米诺斯中期Ⅲ至米诺斯晚期Ⅰ（约公元前1700～前1450年）

青铜

高12.5厘米，宽4.31厘米

发现于克里特岛提利索斯

希腊伊拉克利翁考古博物馆藏，编号X1832

青铜男性礼拜者雕像，实心铸造，站立于一块长方形底座上。雕像佩戴双层腰带，身裹缠腰布，呈现出该时期雕像的两个典型特征，一是身体明显后仰，二是整体采用礼拜姿势。雕像右手置于胸前，左手向下伸展并握拳。这些礼拜姿势是一种身体实践和交流方式，旨在让礼拜者融入宗教仪式，与神灵实现互动。

参与此类仪式的人士会通过各类供品展示和强调自己的身份。提利索斯的这尊青铜雕像象征着一定的地位。由于其原材料珍贵且制造过程需要投入大量精力，因此供奉此类物品能够彰显出奉献者较高的社会或政治地位。

虽然这尊男性雕像缺乏具体的考古背景，但青铜人形雕像通常出现在洞穴遗址，聚落中则较为少见。有类似青铜器物出土的山顶神庙也只是少数，在这些神庙中，人形和动物陶像更为常见。

（卡特琳娜·阿塔纳萨基）

147

Figurine

Middle Minoan III – Late Minoan I (Ca. 1700-1450 BCE)
Bronze
H. 12.5 cm, w. 4.31 cm
Tylissos
Archaeological Museum of Heraklion, X1832

Bronze figurine of a male adorant, solidly cast and standing on an oblong base, featuring a double belt connected to a loincloth with two common characteristics of figurines of this period: the pronounced backward bend of the torso and a typical gesture of worship. The right hand rests on the chest, while the left is extended downward with a clenched fist. These worshipping gestures, as embodied practices and modes of communication, engage the worshipper in ritual performance and interaction with the divine.

Participants in these rituals signalled and reinforced their identities through distinct types of votives. The dedication of prestige artifacts, such as the bronze figurine from Tylissos, reflects the acquisition of valuable raw materials and the labour invested in its manufacture, demonstrating higher social or political status.

Although the specific archaeological context is lacking for this male figurine, bronze human figurines are typically found in cave assemblages. They are less commonly found in settlements, and only a few peak sanctuaries have yielded such artifacts. Instead, human and animal clay figurines are the artifacts most frequently found at these sites.

References

Hazzidakis 1934, 94-95. Verlinden 1984, 202.

(Katerina Athanasaki)

148

雕像头部残片

米诺斯中期Ⅱ至Ⅲ（约公元前 1800 ~ 前 1600 年）

陶土

最长 8.5 厘米，最宽 8.3 厘米

发现于克里特岛佩佐法斯的山顶神庙

希腊伊拉克利翁考古博物馆藏，编号 Π4841

大型人像头部残片，呈梯形，来自头部中空部分。人像左眼得以保留。左眼长 3 厘米，以高浮雕形式呈现，椭圆形眼球略显平坦但凸出，眼睑对称，眼角处有一小切口。三角形鼻子立体感十足，鼻长 6 厘米，两侧近乎平坦。鼻孔边缘和下部有些许缺损，内部有一定深度。脸颊部位有明显的弧形雕塑痕迹，鼻梁上端用浮雕凹槽勾勒出鼻弓边缘。残片内表面粗糙不平，保留了成型过程中的不规则印痕。

残片呈平凸形，但缺乏任何明确的加工边缘，因此尚无法确定其是大型雕像头部的中空部分，还是一张人脸面具。不过，截至目前，尚未发现山顶神庙陶塑存在面具形式。由于未发现其他与之匹配的部分，有学者推测这枚残片可能来自一件“人首形陶奠酒器”，也有学者认为该陶质头部可能曾安装在易腐材料（如木材）制成的躯干上，但没有留下任何痕迹。

由于该残片面部特征独特，很难将其归入米诺斯晚期ⅢB–C时期，也难以划分进大型陶塑类别。鉴于其风格独特、对称性强，并且表面带有褐红色涂层，表明它可能属于米诺斯文明中期，这一时期正是山顶神庙文化的鼎盛阶段。

（迪米特里斯・斯法基纳基斯）

148

Part of head of a figurine

Middle Minoan Ⅱ–Ⅲ (1800-1600 BCE)

Clay

Max. l. 8.5 cm, max. w. 8.3 cm

Petsophas, peak sanctuary

Archaeological Museum of Heraklion, Π4841

Trapezoidal fragment of a face from the hollow head of a large human figure. The left eye (l.3 cm) is preserved, in high relief with an ellipsoid rendering of the somewhat flat and prominent eyeball and the symmetrical eyelids, separated at the corners by a small incision. The voluminous triangular nose (h. 6 cm) has almost flat sides. Some chips are noted in the lower portion and the sides of the nostrils. The holes of the nostrils are visible to some depth. A distinct modelled curve marks the apple of the cheek. A relief notch on the upper end of the nose indicates the edge of the nasal arch. The inner surface of the fragment is uneven with irregular impressions from its modelling.

The plano-convex shape of the fragment and the absence of any true and intentional edges do not allow a safe interpretation as to whether the piece is the roughly hollowed head of a large statue, or a mask of a human face. However, the latter are to date completely unknown in the coroplastic assemblages of the peak sanctuaries. The absence of any other fragment that might go with this sizeable figure has led to the hypothesis that it is a "clay rhyton in the shape of a human head" or even a clay head that was fitted onto a body of perishable material that left no traces (wood, for instance). The facial features raise doubts about its dating in the Late Minoan ⅢB-C period and its inclusion in the widespread tradition of large clay figures. Its stylistic individuality and symmetry, as well as the composition of the clay with the brownish-red coating, constitute the main arguments for placing it rather into the Middle Minoan chronological horizon, the heyday of the peak sanctuary.

References

Myres 1902-03, 375-76, pl.XII.34. Πλάτων 1951, 121-22, n.61 (cult figure). Rutkowski 1991, 80, pl.XXII.2, 3 (rhyton in the shape of a human head).

(Dimitris Sfakianakis)

149

足部残件（一对）

米诺斯中期Ⅲ（公元前 1700 ~ 前 1600 年）

陶土

脚长 12 厘米

发现于克里特岛马利亚王宫“带长椅的南部神庙”的 XVIII 1 号房间

希腊伊拉克利翁考古博物馆藏，编号 Π8630

一对从脚踝往下的人类足部陶塑。雕塑脚上穿有一种独特的鞋子，厚实的鞋底前端向上翘起，形似没有毛球装饰的希腊传统鞋。鞋尖部分遗失，现已复原。小腿部分为圆柱形，没有穿孔，脚背未表现出明显的紧绷或倾斜状态。鞋底附近的陶土略有膨胀，可能是在刻画鞋底的厚度。这双足部陶塑存在许多随机裂痕和指印（特别是鞋底处），并且由于烧制前与其他物品有过接触，表面可见不少压痕和凸起。两只脚上均有燃烧痕迹，右脚鞋底外侧留有烧痕，左脚烟熏痕迹更为明显，分布于小腿和鞋面平整区域。

这对足部陶塑的发现地点位于南部神庙的中央大厅，该厅是通往宫殿的重要区域，根据出土环境和与之一同发现的宗教物品推断，这些足部陶塑可能曾是木雕人像的基座。厅中可见大量烧焦痕迹，足部陶塑上的燃烧痕迹可能与木质人像主干被烧焦碳化有关。无论南部神庙与宫殿或南部聚落之间有何关联，这对足部陶塑的出土都有着重要意义，能够证明克里特岛在新王宫期的早期便已存在木质人像。

（迪米特里斯・斯法基纳基斯）

149

Pair of feet

Middle Minoan Ⅲ (1700-1600 BCE)

Clay

L. foot 12 cm

Malia, palace, "Complex of the South Sanctuary with Bench", Room XVIII 1

Archaeological Museum of Heraklion, Π8630

A pair of human feet from the ankles down, of clay, shod – a specific type of shoe with a strong sole which turns upwards at the tip, in the form of a "*tsarouchi* without a pom-pom". The pointed ends of the shoes were lost and are now restored. The shin is cylindrical without holes, while the instep does not display any particular tautness or slope. A relative swelling in the clay can be seen around the sole, probably portraying the thickness of the shoe here. The legs bear many random chips and also finger-marks (especially on the soles), as well as evidence of both flattening and protrusions in their contact with other objects before firing. Traces of burning are found on both feet: on the right foot, they are preserved along the outside of the sole, while on the left, where the traces of soot are even stronger, they are visible on the shin and the top flat surface.

The find context, in the central hall of the "South Sanctuary", a particularly important area providing access to the palace, in association with a number of cult objects, strengthens the hypothesis that the feet formed the "base" of a *xoanon*: these are large wooden human figures. The traces of charcoal in this particular room, and especially the traces of burning preserved on the legs, may be attributed to the charred wooden trunk of the statuette. These feet from the "South Sanctuary with Bench" of Malia, regardless of the relationship between the site and the palace itself or the settlement to the south, constitute one of the strongest arguments for the existence of effigies of this type in the early phase of Neopalatial Crete.

References

Chapouthier-Demargne 1962, fig.3. Gesell 1985, 106, plan 46, fig.177.

(Dimitris Sfakianakis)

150

足部残件

米诺斯中期Ⅲ至米诺斯晚期ⅠA（约公元前 1650 ~ 前 1500 年）
陶土
长 14.5 厘米，高 9 厘米
发现于克里特岛斯克拉沃坎博斯的乡村别墅南入口（从上层掉落）
希腊伊拉克利翁考古博物馆藏，编号 Π8966

右足陶塑，包含脚踝往下部分，脚上穿着鞋子。陶塑由两部分拼接而成，断裂处位于脚背上部。脚趾较小侧和脚跟周围有些许缺损。裂痕边缘以及胫骨部位的平坦表面均可见陶土流失痕迹。脚底略带弧度的自然轮廓和脚踝塑造得十分生动。该陶塑没有附着孔。发掘记录中提到，脚趾前端缺失部分原本向上翘起，使脚底呈现出独特的形状。

斯克拉沃坎博斯的陶足出土于一座乡村别墅的南入口，位于崇拜物品堆积层中，根据地层分析，陶足由上层掉落。发现地点位于建筑的主要入口，这可能与其用途有关。在其他建筑主要入口处的仪式场所也发现了类似陶塑（如马利亚发现的一对陶足，参见本书图版 149）。此外，依据陶足且没有悬挂孔判断，其并非供奉用悬挂式足雕。从脚部的细节比例和写实的自然轮廓表现可以推断，这可能是一尊大型人像的“局部塑造”元素。

（迪米特里斯·斯法基纳基斯）

150

Foot

Middle Minoan Ⅲ – Late Minoan Ⅰ A (1650-1500 BCE)
Clay
L. 14.5 cm, h. 9 cm
Sklavokambos, villa, south entrance (fallen from the upper floor)
Archaeological Museum of Heraklion, Π8966

Separate, right human foot of clay, from the ankle down, shod. It has been joined together from two parts (broken across at the height of the instep). There are chips around the smaller toes and on the heel. A loss of clay is observed at the edges of the fractures, as well as around the flat surface at the shin. The curves of the natural contour of the bottom of the foot and the modelling of the ankles are dynamically rendered. It does not have an attachment hole. The excavator notes that the lost part of the toe-end was pointing upwards, giving the sole its distinctive shape.

The foot from Sklavokambos was found in a context with cult objects at the main south entrance of the rural villa. According to the stratigraphy, it fell from the upper floor. The relevance of the find location at the main entrance of the building may be significant in terms of its purpose, since other specimens are also found in corresponding cult spaces at main access points to buildings (cf. the case of Malia, cat. no.149). Furthermore, its size and the absence of a hole show that it was not a votive (suspended) foot. The naturalistic rendering of many details of its proportions and outline supports the hypothesis that it was an "acroplastic" element from a large human figure.

References

Μαρινάτος 1939-41, 72-73, 87, pl.3, 4. Gesell 1985, 20, 135, cat. no.124.

(Dimitris Sfakianakis)

8966

151

足部残件

米诺斯中期Ⅲ至米诺斯晚期ⅠA（约公元前1650～前1500年）

陶土

高度15.8厘米，保存部分长度15.8厘米

发现于克里特岛古尔尼亚聚落

希腊伊拉克利翁考古博物馆藏，编号Π5590

右足陶塑，从小腿中部向下延伸。脚趾部分完全缺失，脚后跟区域有一层陶土脱落，位于脚底后半部分。脚部有两个穿孔，一个位于胫骨平面中央，另一个位于脚踝外侧上方，二者相连形成一个倾斜的弧形孔洞。脚部造型具有一定特殊性。小腿下部横截面呈椭圆形，前后有明显的锐角，呈现出近似菱形的形状。连接脚背与脚底垂直壁的纵向边缘也呈现出相似的棱角线条。

脚部造型刚硬且带有少见的贯穿孔，表明其可能是制鞋用的鞋楦。脚的高度与许多克里特–迈锡尼文化中描绘的靴子高度完全匹配，但其小巧的尺寸却又与这一说法相矛盾。在同一聚落还发现了两件类似的足部陶塑，其中一件与本件大小相同，另一件则更小。因此，两件相同尺寸的陶塑可能原为一对。此外，这些足部陶塑的小腿部分呈楔形且具有菱形截面，与阿涅莫斯皮利亚发现的一对足部陶塑结构相似，可能具有相同功能。目前考古界对古尔尼亚足部陶塑知之甚少，唯一能够确定的是这些陶塑并未与其他宗教物品一同出土，但这可能是遗址中各种后期干扰因素所致。

（迪米特里斯・斯法基纳基斯）

151

Foot

Middle MinoanⅢB – Late MinoanⅠA (1650-1500 BCE)

Clay

H. 15.8 cm, l. of preserved foot 15.8 cm

Gournia, settlement

Archaeological Museum of Heraklion, Π5590

Right human limb, from about mid-shin height downwards, of clay, shod. The entire toe section has been lost. A layer of clay has become detached in the heel area, on the back half of the sole. It has two holes that join to make a single oblique, curved perforation: the first pierces the centre of the flat surface on the shin and the second is at ankle height on the outer face. The foot presents certain peculiarities in its modelling: the lower part of the shin is ellipsoidal in cross-section with sharp angles to front and back, giving it an almost rhomboidal shape. Corresponding angularities in the lines of the contours are observed at the longitudinal edges connecting the instep with the vertical walls of the sole.

The rigidity in the plastic rendering of the dynamic curves of the foot and the unusual through-perforation have led to the interpretation of the object as a cobbler's last, used in shoemaking. Indeed, the height of the foot perfectly matches the height of the boots found in many representations of the Cretan-Mycenaean cultural cycle. However, the small size of the foot is an argument against this interpretation. Two more specimens of feet were discovered in the same settlement, though the exact findspot is unknown: one is the same size as the one described, while the other is smaller. Therefore, it cannot be ruled out that the two equal-sized examples were an actual pair. The "wedgelike" shin with a rhomboidal cross-section is structurally similar to the pair of clay feet from Anemospilia, so their functions are probably the same too. The only information provided on the contexts of the feet from Gournia is that they were not found in association with other cult objects, but this could be attributed to various later causes of disturbance on the site.

References

Hawes et al. 1908, 32-33, pl.III, C11

(Dimitris Sfakianakis)

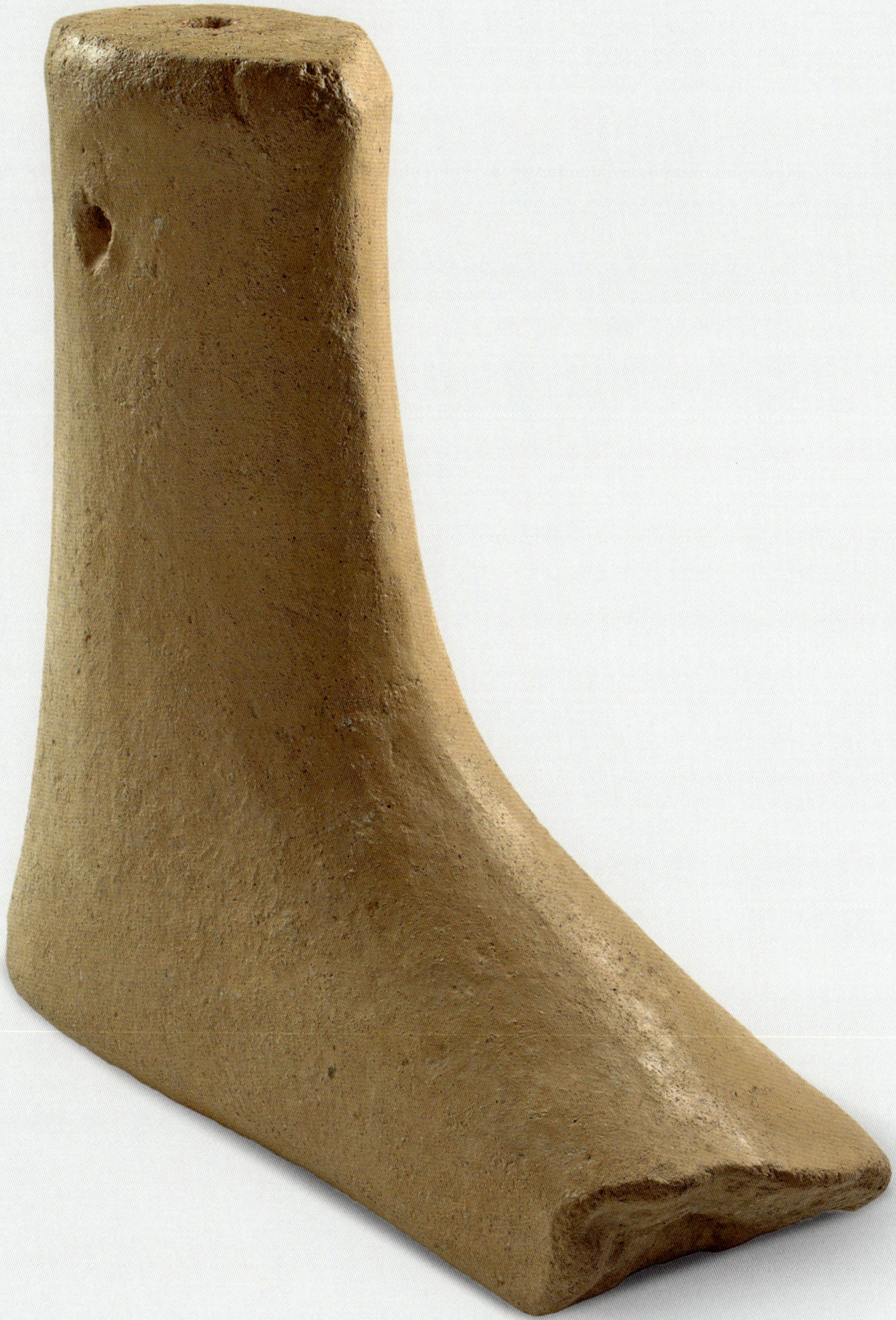

152

女性雕像

米诺斯中期ⅢB 至米诺斯晚期ⅠA（公元前 1650 ~ 前 1500 年）

陶土

高 26.3 厘米

发现于克里特岛皮斯科凯法洛的卡特里尼亚山

希腊伊拉克利翁考古博物馆藏，编号 Π9832

陶女性立像，身着长裙，头戴复杂头饰，所用姿势罕见。裙子和一只手臂已修复并根据同一地点发现的其他雕像残片进行补全。细长的头部雕刻出精致的五官，能够辨认出浅浅的眼窝、纤细的鼻子、光滑的脸颊和下巴。陶像头发盘成发髻，用发带固定，额头中间分缝，波浪状的发束对称地垂在两侧。

陶像上半身腰部纤细，胸部以浅浮雕形式呈现，腹部略微隆起，可能暗示怀孕。右手抬起至左肩，覆盖胸部之间的缝隙，左手则稍微倾斜，覆盖腹部。如果陶像的确是位孕妇，则该手势可能是在本能地保护腹部，而非通常认为的宗教或仪式性姿势。

这是一件典型的陶供品，出土于一处位于高地上的神庙，这里毗邻东克里特岛最重要的居民中心之一。这类高地神庙和山顶神庙可能是当时乡村最重要的崇拜场所。这一神庙曾出土大量陶雕像，其工艺水平即便在今天仍令人叹为观止。工匠在塑造男女自然比例时展现出的动态效果，以及面部特征的精致呈现，都体现出极高的艺术水平。有些作品甚至被认为具有肖像雕刻性质。

（迪米特里斯·斯法基纳基斯）

A standing, skirted figure, with elaborate headdress and adopting an unusual gesture. The skirt and one arm have been restored and completed; they have been modelled according to corresponding fragments of other figurines from the same site. The slender head has delicate facial features, with shallow eye sockets, a delicate nose, and smooth surfaces on the cheeks and chin. The hair is caught up in a bun secured with a headband, while the parting over the forehead lets the wavy locks fall symmetrically on either side of the head. The upper torso has a narrow waist, with the bust rendered in low relief, as well as a slight bulge in the abdomen that may indicate pregnancy. The right hand is bent up towards the left shoulder covering the cleavage between the breasts, while the left is angled slightly to cover the abdomen. If this is indeed a pregnant woman, this could be an instinctively protective gesture covering the belly, departing from the generally accepted ritual or cultic gesture.

A typical example of a clay votive offering from a sanctuary set in a high place, on a hill adjacent to one of the most important residential centres of East Crete – places that, together with the peak sanctuaries, were probably the most important places of worship in the countryside at that time. This particular sanctuary yielded a multitude of clay figurines that amaze even today for the dynamism exhibited by the craftsmen in the naturalistic rendering of the human form, both in the proportions of the individual components of the female and male bodies, and in the delicate rendering of the facial features, to such an extent that in some cases there is even talk of modelled portraiture.

References

Πλάτων – Πλάτωνος-Γιώτα 2023, 51.

(Dimitris Sfakianakis)

153

女性雕像头部

米诺斯中期ⅢB 至米诺斯晚期ⅠA(约公元前 1650 ~ 前 1525/1500 年)

陶土

高 8.1 厘米

发现于克里特岛皮斯科凯法洛的圣殿

希腊伊拉克利翁考古博物馆藏，编号 Π9823

女性陶像头部，发型十分精致。雕像面部特征以柔和的浮雕形式表现，脸部还留有白色颜料痕迹。

令人印象深刻的圆柱形发型上装饰着一条宽发带，使头部整体高度加倍。这件雕像出土于皮斯科凯法洛山顶圣殿，是信徒们供奉的众多献祭雕像之一。这些雕像以优雅的发型而引人注目，充分展示出工匠们精湛高超的技艺。

（克莱奥・察纳基）

153

Head of female figurine

Middle Minoan ⅢB – Late Minoan ⅠA (Ca. 1650-1525/1500 BCE)

Clay

H. 8.1 cm

Piskokephalo, Shrine

Archaeological Museum of Heraklion, Π9823

Clay head of female figurine with elaborate hairstyle. The traits of the face are executed in gentle relief. Traces of white paint can be seen on the face.

The impressive cylindrical shape of the hairdo doubles the height of the head and is decorated by a wide band. This is one of many votive figurines offered by the worshippers at the peak sanctuary of Piskokephalo that stand out for their elegant hairstyles and demonstrate the great depth of skill of the craftsmen who manufactured them.

References

Πλάτων 1951, pl. H, fig.1, 145. Rethemiotakis 2001, pl.2.

(Kleio Tzanaki)

154

大型木质雕像的假发

米诺斯中期ⅢB 至米诺斯晚期ⅠA（公元前 1650～前 1500 年）

黑绿色蛇纹石

高 23 厘米，宽 23 厘米

发现于克里特岛克诺索斯王宫的东翼“排水渠填埋层”

希腊伊拉克利翁考古博物馆藏，编号 Γ352

大型人形雕像的假发模型，由至少六块独立雕刻且巧妙拼接的部件组成，呈现出对称的发型。头发分为前后两层，前层为主要的塑形部分。两条弯曲的发束环绕额头，两侧对称，从中央的分缝处（以斜线刻痕表示）向下延伸至与耳齐高，覆盖头部两侧。发束末端为两个巨大的水滴状发髻。发髻位于头部两侧，略微向前倾斜，但不与后层头发接触。后层的弧形头发与前层之间以一条深刻的沟槽分隔。假发在颈部位置延伸出两个带有贯穿孔的梯形部件用于固定。假发背面平坦，带有浅刻痕，可能是用于连接第三层头发，从而确保发型完整。各部件之间以及假发与雕像头部之间通过榫孔和卯槽结构固定，连接时需要用到销钉和榫头。

这是目前在克诺索斯发现的最为完整的发型模型。这件模型属于一尊大型人形雕像，该雕像可能为木制，也可能是由其他可雕刻材料（如石膏）制成。假发背部的固定结构表明这尊巨型雕像采用立体雕刻，而非平背式雕刻。排水渠填埋层的位置非常靠近“东侧大厅”，这里曾出土过一些真人尺寸的高浮雕彩绘石膏人像，以及大型青铜发束。此类长发与东方风格的水滴状侧发相似，可能与斯芬克斯有关。根据这件假发模型所属的雕像可以推断，新王宫期东翼大厅宏伟壮观、布局成熟，能够摆放大型人形雕像，并且宫殿内大型人像还会采用多种材质塑造。

（迪米特里斯・斯法基纳基斯）

154

Wig from a large wooden figure

Middle Minoan ⅢB – Late Minoan ⅠA (1650-1500 BCE)

Black-green serpentinite

H. 23 cm, w. 23 cm

Knossos, palace, "Fill of the Drain" in the East Wing

Archaeological Museum of Heraklion, Γ352

A model wig from a large human figure. It is composed of at least six pieces that have been carved separately and expertly fitted together for the symmetrical rendition of this particular coiffure. The hair is styled in two layers, one at the front and one at the back. At the front are the most important modelled elements. Two curved pieces crown the forehead on either side of the central parting (indicated by oblique grooves) and fall to the height of the ears, covering the corresponding quarters of the head. These locks terminate in two massive, teardrop-shaped bunches, that fall at the sides of the head and slope slightly forward, without contacting the hair at the back. The rear arched layer of hair is separated from the first by a deep groove. At neck height are two trapezoidal extensions with through-holes for their attachment. The flat, incised surface of the reverse side may have been joined to a third layer of hair that would have completed the whole. Socket-holes and mortices were used to join the pieces to each other and also to affix the wig to the head by pegs and tenons.

This is the most complete representation of a hairdo found at Knossos; it belongs to a large human statue that was made either of wood or of another carvable material (plaster?). The fastening sections at the back indicate that the monumental statue was carved in the round rather than having a flat back. The "Fill of the Drain" is very close to the "Great East Hall", with which a number of over-life-sized human figures in high relief painted plaster, as well as large bronze locks of hair, are connected. The attribution of such tresses to a sphinx is due to the similarity of the drop-shaped side-locks to Eastern models. Whether in partial or full three dimensions, the figure to which the hairdo was attached reveals the large size of the human representations associated with the mature Neopalatial layout of an imposing hall in the East Wing. It is also a further indication of the variety of materials utilised to create the large human images inside the palace.

References

PM III, 419ff., fig.288, pl.XXXVI A. Gesell 1985, 92

(Dimitris Sfakianakis)

155

发束（3 组）

米诺斯中期ⅢB 至米诺斯晚期ⅠA（公元前 1650 ~ 前 1500 年）
青铜
最大长度：A) 14.5 厘米，B) 15 厘米，C) 9.5 和 10.5 厘米
发现于克里特岛克诺索斯王宫的东侧大厅
希腊伊拉克利翁考古博物馆藏，编号 X1218，1219，1220 a、b

这是三组末端呈波浪卷曲状的青铜发束。A 和 B 保存完整，C 因金属腐蚀而导致严重膨胀。虽然 C 的两部分并未相连，但很可能属于同一发束。这些物品大致呈圆锥形，主干由三个分段组成，随发束旋转逐渐变窄并延伸至末端。A 的尾部呈单点卷曲状，B 的尾部有两个分叉，末端呈螺旋状扭曲。两者的延展形态均可见明显的凹凸，很好地模仿了发束的纹理。C 上有一系列横槽，明显是在模拟发辫的波浪形态，其末端也呈螺旋状折叠。

这些金属发束再现了大型人形或其他生物（例如斯芬克斯）的额前卷发。东侧大厅曾发现多尊以石膏浮雕工艺制成的大型人形雕像，这些拳击手和驯牛者雕像均呈现出生动的姿势。据发掘者推测，这些青铜发束可能是一尊仪式用大型女性木雕的前额发型，附近大量烧焦的木材也能够佐证这一观点。发束造型的差异可能是由于 A 和 B 位于额头上方，C 则位于太阳穴处。也有观点认为，这三件青铜发束均为完整发型，分属三尊独立女性雕像，但这种推测较为牵强，缺乏其他考古佐证。

（迪米特里斯·斯法基纳基斯）

155

Locks of hair

Middle Minoan III B-Late Minoan I A (1650-1500 BCE)
Bronze
Max. l. A) 14.5 cm, B) 15 cm, C) 9.5 and 10.5 cm
Knossos, palace, Great East Hall
Archaeological Museum of Heraklion, X1218, 1219, 1220 a, b

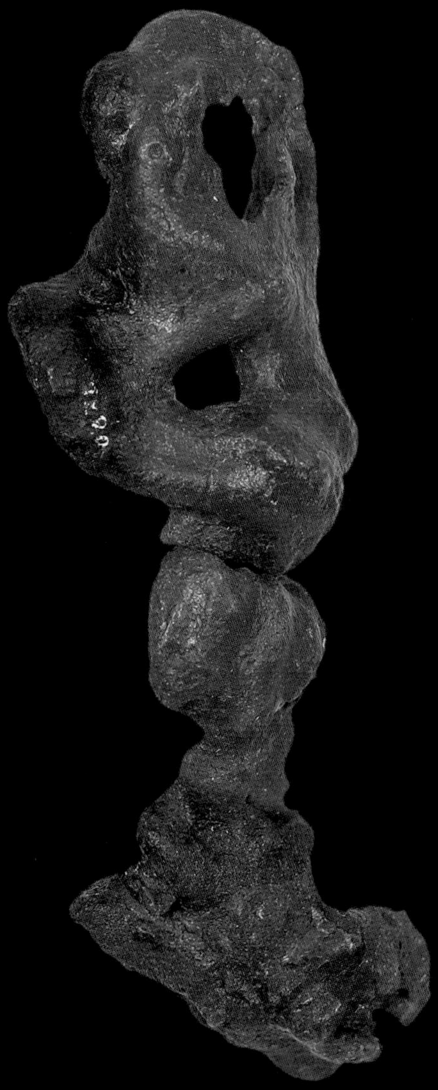

Three bronze locks of hair ending in wavy curls. (A) and (B) are preserved intact, while (C) shows strong swellings from the corrosion of the metal. Although the two fragments of (C) are not connected, they probably belong to the same tress. The items are roughly conical, with the main body composed in three stepped zones, which with the twist of the hair-tress become increasingly longer and narrow towards their ends: (A) ends in a single pointed curl, (B) splits into two points, with a spiral twist at its end. Both, in their elongated twisted body, display hollows and ridges in imitation of a lock of hair. (C) bears a series of transverse grooves, apparently imitating the wave of a braid of hair, up to its very end which is folded into a spiral.

These are metal representations of fringes springing from the forehead in small curls, coming from a large figure, either human or some other creature (sphinx?). The Great East Hall yielded a number of large human figures in stucco relief, captured in dramatic movement (boxers, bull-leapers). The excavator hypothesised that these pieces are a typical portrayal of locks on the forehead of a "giant, female" wooden statue, probably cultic. This is supported by the amount of charred remains of wood found with them. The variation in the shape of the locks is due, according to their original reconstruction, to the fact that (A) and (B) form part of the hair above the forehead, while (C) comes from the region of the temples. Their interpretation as complete, solid wigs of three individual female figures is considered fanciful and lacks comparanda.

References

PM III, 521-25, figs 365, 366. Hägg 1983, 547-49, figs 9 and 10 (interpreted as wigs of three individual female figures).

(Dimitris Sfakianakis)

156

代表头发的镂空片和扭曲线（3组）

米诺斯晚期Ⅰ（公元前1600～前1450年）

青铜

发现于克里特岛克诺索斯王宫的东侧宝库

希腊伊拉克利翁考古博物馆藏，编号X1429

A. 最大长度6厘米

三块钩状青铜镂空片，末端卷曲。其中一块保留有一颗横向钉子，用于将青铜片固定到其他物体上（可能是木制品）；另两块仅可见钉孔痕迹。在同一块青铜片的内表面，还留有碳化木材痕迹。

据发掘者推测，这些青铜片可能代表斯芬克斯或狮子的鬃毛。这些青铜片也可能出现在其他大型塑像上，因为在克里特-迈锡尼文化的人形陶塑中，垂下的卷发（尤其是前额的流海）是一种标准特征。

B. 长度5厘米

细长青铜片，轮廓呈波浪状，末端卷曲成三个紧密的“环状发束”。这是同一填埋层发现的一系列金属片中的另一种形态，这些片材可能是一尊大型雕像的流苏状毛发，如狮子或斯芬克斯的鬃毛。

C. 最大长度4厘米

多根扭曲的青铜线，表面残留鎏金痕迹。它们是出土于克诺索斯王宫东翼东侧宝库象牙堆的杂技演员头雕上发环的一部分。此外，还发现了几片细长的金箔，推测同属发环装饰；另外还发现一些略宽的金属片，可能来自雕像的其他部位（如缠腰带）。多根金属线均呈现出一定的弯曲角度，可能是为了表现杂技演员飞扬的头发。

（迪米特里斯·斯法基纳基斯）

156

Cut-out sheets and twisted wires representing hair

Late Minoan Ⅰ (1600-1450 BCE)

Bronze

Knossos, palace, East Treasury

Archaeological Museum of Heraklion, X1429

A. L. of largest piece 6 cm

Three bronze cut-out sheets, in the form of a hook ending in a curled-up tip. In one of them, a transverse nail is preserved – in the other two, just traces of the nails are visible – for fastening them to another, presumably wooden, object. A piece of charred wood is preserved on the same inner surface.

These are a series of bronze sheets representing hair, probably a mane, of a sphinx or a lion according to the excavator. Their presence on other large-scale plastic works should not be ruled out, since dangling curls of hair, especially in a fringe above the forehead, are standard in Creto-Mycenaean anthropomorphic coroplastic.

B. L. 5 cm

Oblong bronze sheet with a wavy outline and looped over, terminating in three "ringlets" that finish in tight curls. Second type of shape among a series of sheet-metal objects from the same fill that yielded a fringe of hair from a large effigy, possibly the mane of a lion or a sphinx.

C. L. of largest piece 4 cm

Pieces of twisted wire with traces of gilding. They are parts of the ringlets from a series of acrobat heads of the Ivory Deposit from the East Treasury of the East Wing of Knossos. Along with these were found several elongated pieces of gold leaf that presumably belong to the ringlets, and also wider pieces from other parts of the figurines (loincloths?). Many of the wires are bent into angles. Although this cannot be stated with certainty, the existing, angular state of the ringlets may be intended to portray the acrobats' flying hair.

References

Evans 1901-02, 71, figs. 35, 36. PMⅢ, 413-14, fig.276.

(Dimitris Sfakianakis)

1429

157

人首形容器

米诺斯晚期ⅢB（公元前 1300 ~ 前 1200 年）

陶土

高 14.5 厘米（不含把手）

发现于克里特岛斐斯托斯宫殿

希腊伊拉克利翁考古博物馆藏，编号 Π5831

带有底座和把手的奠酒容器，整体造型为男性头部形状。液体填充孔位于头顶平面，倾倒孔则位于底部。双眼采用凸起的浮雕形式，鼻子、嘴巴、山羊胡和耳朵等部件是单独粘附在主体上的。眼睛、前额卷发、鬓角和山羊胡以棕红色彩料突出显示。这件来自斐斯托斯的奠酒器很难准确分类，因为它同时具备容器和雕像特征。此器物是克里特岛最早的手工塑造人形器物之一，出现于米诺斯晚期ⅢB，主要用于仪式活动。到米诺斯晚期ⅢC，此类器物已较为常见，早期希腊时期也有发现。据推测，米诺斯人的设计灵感可能来源于叙利亚-巴勒斯坦地区类似的容器。

（伊万吉立亚・西克拉）

157

Vessel in the shape of a human head

Late Minoan ⅢB (1300-1200 BCE)

Clay

H. 14.5 cm (without handle)

Phaistos, Palace

Archaeological Museum of Heraklion, Π5831

Libation vessel (rhyton) with base and handle, modelled in the shape of a man's head. The filling and pouring holes are in the flat top of the head and the base respectively. The eyes are rendered in high relief. The nose, mouth, goatee and ears are added separately to the main body of the vessel. The eyes, the forehead curls, the sideburns and the goatee are highlighted in brownish-red paint. This rhyton from Phaistos is difficult to define, as it combines features of both vessels and figurines. This is one of the earliest plastic anthropomorphic vessels to appear in Crete in Late Minoan ⅢB. They are common in Late Minoan ⅢC and continue into the Early Greek period, and are used for ritual purposes. It has been argued that the Minoans drew their inspiration for these vessels from similar vessels from the wider region of Syro-Palestine.

References

Carinci 1997, 13-27. Pernier-Banti 1980, 180, 507-512, fig.103b, 288. Ρεθεμιωτάκης 1998, 38-39, 77-79, pl.35γ, δ.

(Evangelia Sikla)

158

圆柱形人形像

米诺斯晚期ⅢC 至亚米诺斯时期

（公元前 1190 ~ 前 1000 年）

陶土

高 20.5 厘米

发现于克里特岛普里尼亚斯（1907 年由意大利考古学院组织发掘）

希腊伊拉克利翁考古博物馆藏，编号 П7653

陶女性人像，手臂紧贴躯干。身体呈圆柱形，底部略微展开。手臂以抽象方式表现，与娇小躯体相连，但和身体及头部不成比例。左臂垂直贴在身侧，如立正姿势一般，右臂对角放置在腹部上方。圆柱形颈部相较于身体而言比例偏大，头部同样呈圆柱形，顶部敞开，形成一个杯形容器。眼睛和鼻子经过手工塑形，双眼凸出，并用红色线条勾勒，鼻部挺拔，两侧有捏制痕迹。嘴唇和头发以红色笔触呈现，嘴唇呈水平线状，颅侧为波状卷发。陶像颈部和躯干保留有红色条带状彩绘装饰。

陶像的几何造型和圆柱形下身是米诺斯晚期Ⅲ和亚米诺斯时期的典型风格。另一方面，陶像的杯形头部表明它可能是某种奠酒容器。此类陶像常与适合倾倒的管状陶器一同出土，进一步证实了其在奠酒仪式中的用途。

（迪米特里斯・米洛纳斯）

158

Cylindrical human figurine

Late Minoan ⅢC – Subminoan period (1190-1000 BCE)

Clay

H. 20.5 cm

Prinias (Italian School of Archaeology excavation, 1907)

Archaeological Museum of Heraklion, П7653

Clay female figurine with arms attached to the body. The body is cylindrical, opening out slightly at the bottom. The arms are abstractly rendered, attached to the small torso, and disproportionately small compared to the main body and head. The left arm is attached to the body vertically, as though held at attention, while the right is placed diagonally over the abdomen. The cylindrical neck is disproportionately large compared to the body. The head is also cylindrical and is open at the top, forming a krater. The eyes and nose are plastically rendered: the bulging eyes are outlined in red, while the nose is vertical with pinched sides. The lips and hair are denoted by red brush-strokes, the lips rendered in a horizonal line and the hair in wavy locks on either side of the face. Red painted decoration is preserved in bands on the neck and body of the figurine.

The dominant geometric shapes and the cylindrical lower body are stylistic features of the Late Minoan Ⅲ and Subminoan periods. On the other hand, the krater-shaped head of the figurine indicates that it is related to libation vessels. The fact that such figures were used for libations is confirmed by the tubular vases found together with them, of suitable shape for pouring liquids.

References

Unpublished. Cf. Rethemiotakis 2001.

(Dimitris Mylonas)

VI

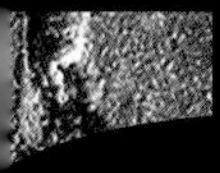

第六单元　远航

Unit 6 Voyage

米诺斯文化出色的工艺与艺术成就得益于发达的海外贸易。克里特岛四面环海，资源匮乏，定居者被迫去岛外寻觅生产资料，航海成了那里不可或缺的险业。

考古证实，早在数万年乃至十万年前的石器时代，已陆续有勇者从小亚细亚沿岸乘小船前往克里特岛。大约公元前 3000 年以降，克里特岛跨入青铜时代，外来移民持续增长，金银、铜锡、象牙、玛瑙、红玉髓、紫水晶等物资需从域外进口，本地产品和艺术风格开始受到周边影响。克里特岛也成为繁忙的出口基地，货船从林立的港口扬帆出发，将彩陶和奢侈品输送到广阔世界，将商品纳入东地中海的贸易网络。

海，是克里特人的第二家园，也是他们的精神寄寓。一些死者墓葬不但用贝壳、鹅卵石铺地，墓门也要面朝大海的方向。他们制作船的模型，刻画船的形象，正是依靠无畏的航海探险，克里特人发展了强大实力，促进了繁荣经济，造就了蓬勃艺术。启程远航，把璀璨的米诺斯文化传播到海那边的远方。

The remarkable craftsmanship and artistic achievements of the Minoan civilization benefited from its advanced overseas trade. Surrounded by the sea on all sides and lacking natural resources, the settlers of Crete were compelled to seek means of production beyond the island. Thus, seafaring became an indispensable, albeit perilous, industry for its inhabitants.

Archaeological evidence confirms that as early as tens of thousands to a hundred thousand years ago during the Stone Age, brave individuals sailed from the coast of Asia Minor to Crete. Around 3000 BCE, Crete entered the Bronze Age, with a continuous influx of immigrants. Materials such as gold, silver, copper, tin, ivory, agate, carnelian, and amethyst were imported from abroad, and local products and artistic styles began to be influenced by surrounding regions. Crete became a bustling export hub, with ships setting sail from numerous ports, transporting painted pottery and luxury goods to a wide world, integrating these commodities into the trade networks of the eastern Mediterranean.

The sea was a second and spiritual home for the Cretans. Some Cretan burial sites were adorned with shells and pebbles, with tomb entrances facing the sea. They crafted ship models and depicted maritime scenes, as it was through fearless seafaring that the Cretans built their strength, fostered economic prosperity, and cultivated vibrant art. The Cretans set sails and spread the brilliant Minoan civilization to distant shores.

159

船只模型

米诺斯早期Ⅱ（公元前2600~前2300年）
陶土
最高7厘米，长22厘米，最宽5.3厘米
发现于克里特岛帕莱卡斯特罗埃利尼卡的Ⅱ号墓
希腊伊拉克利翁考古博物馆藏，编号Π3911

陶土船模，船底平坦、吃水浅，船舷几乎垂直。从俯视图看，船体呈水滴形：较窄的一端有一根倾斜约70°的圆柱状高杆，较宽的一端则有一个类似圆柱的凸起，位置略高于船底。船的上方横跨两根细长的圆柱形杆，可能是“横梁”，将船体分为大致相等的三个部分。

如果横梁数量具有实际意义而非仅作为象征，那么帕莱卡斯特罗的这件船模可能是以一艘小型双桨或四桨船为原型。这件船模是已知唯一的基克拉泽斯“长船”立体模型，这种加长版“独木舟”靠多人划桨驱动，不使用桨架辅助划行。

这件模型并非精准、细致的复刻品，而是凭借印象对这种船型进行塑造。虽然从基本特征上可以识别该船的类型，但由于缺乏更多细节，特别是缺少对舵的描绘，目前无法弄清有关这艘船的装备及操作的一系列问题。

船底的平坦设计可能表示水线而非船体下方的真实构造。船壁与高耸的圆柱形船头间的连接方式可能表明船体内部有一条贯穿船底的中梁，这条中梁主要作为龙骨，用于固定船壁的木板。

帕莱卡斯特罗的船模表明，该地继承了早期青铜时代爱琴海地区的造船传统，而帆船技术要到青铜时代末期才会传入克里特岛。

（迪米特里斯·斯法基纳基斯）

159

Boat model

Early Minoan II (2600-2300 BCE)

Clay

L. 22 cm, max. w. 5.3 cm, max. h. 7 cm

Palaikastro, Ellinika, Tomb II

Archaeological Museum of Heraklion, Π3911

Clay model of a boat with a flat bottom and shallow draught, with almost vertical sides. The vessel is teardrop-shaped in plan: its narrower end terminates in a tall, cylindrical rod, placed at an angle of about 70°, while the wider end bears a similar round-sectioned projection, set slightly higher than the bottom. Two slender cylindrical rods, perhaps the thwarts, run transversely across the upper part of the walls, dividing the vessel into three segments of approximately equal length.

The Palaikastro model is of a small, two- or four-oared vessel – if we accept the number of thwarts as actual and not merely indicative. It is, however, the only known three-dimensional depiction of the so-called "longboat" of the Cyclades, a sort of elongated "canoe" manned by a numerous crew, propelled by free rowing/paddling, that is without the use of rowlocks.

In this case the model is not a precise and detailed one, but more of an impression of this specific type of ship. Although this example is obviously recognisable from its basic characteristics, the absence of more details, and especially of the rudder, does not allow a definitive answer to a series of questions concerning the equipping and operation of the boat.

The flat bottom probably represents the waterline against the side and is not an accurate depiction of the lower part of the hull. The way the attachment of the walls to the tall cylindrical stem is portrayed perhaps argues for the existence of a central beam that ran the length of the hull in the form of a keel, to which were fastened the planks making up the walls of the vessel.

The Palaikastro model demonstrates that the centuries-old shipbuilding tradition, that had already taken form in the Early Bronze Age Aegean, was known in Crete, before the innovation of sailing ships was introduced to the island at the end of that period.

References

Bosanquet-Dawkins 1923, 7, fig.4. Basch 1987, 77-89. Wedde 2000, 307 no.103.

(Dimitris Sfakianakis)

160
带克里特象形文字的棱柱形印章
米诺斯中期ⅡB（公元前1750～前1700年）
滑石
长2.1厘米，宽1厘米
发现于克里特岛马利亚的“印章切割作坊”
希腊伊拉克利翁考古博物馆藏，编号Σ-K1770

三面棱柱形印章，由软滑石制成，保存状态不佳。两个椭圆形印章面刻有尚未解读的克里特象形文字，其中包括标准化的“槽与箭”二符号序列，以及典型的米诺斯单桅船图案。最后一个印章面刻有野山羊图案及填充性装饰图案。

在旧王宫期末期以前，印章被广泛用于在未烧制的陶土块上印制印记，然后将这些陶土块贴附到物体上，以保护物体的完整性或用作标签。曾发现带陶土印章的行政文档，表明这些印章图案不仅象征社会地位，还代表个人或集体的身份。同时，刻在印章上的简短克里特象形文字也用于传递词汇信息，与陶土板上用于行政目的的刻文相似。

（乔治娅·弗拉达）

160
Prism seal with Cretan Hieroglyphic script
Middle Minoan ⅡB (1750-1700 BCE)
Steatite
L. 2.1 cm, w. 1 cm
Malia, "Seal-Cutter's Workshop"
Archaeological Museum of Heraklion, HMΣ-K1770

Three-sided prism seal of soft steatite, partially preserved. Two of its oval sealing surfaces bear inscriptions in the undeciphered Cretan Hieroglyphic script, as the standardised two-sign sequence "trough and arrow" and the sign represented by the typical Minoan single-masted ship demonstrate, while the third sealing surface is decorated with an agrimi (wild goat) and a filling motif.

By the end of the Protopalatial era, seals were widely used for impressing clay nodules attached to objects as a means of protecting their integrity. The seal impressions on a range of clay sealed documents from administrative contexts indicate that the seal motifs must have signified social status as well as individual and collective identity. At the same time, the short Cretan Hieroglyphic inscriptions carved on seals were also meant to convey lexical information, like the similar inscriptions that were incised on clay tablets for administrative purposes.

References

CMS II.2, 130-131. Olivier-Godart 1996, 240 (#231). Flouda 2013.

(Georgia Flouda)

161

写有线形文字 B 的泥板

米诺斯晚期ⅢA2（公元前 1375 ~ 前 1300 年）

陶土

高 3 厘米，最大宽度 7.3 厘米

发现于克里特岛克诺索斯王宫

希腊伊拉克利翁考古博物馆藏，编号 Π–N261 (KN U 736)

棕榈叶形泥板，书写线形文字 B，正反两面均有铭文。虽然板体存在部分残缺，但依旧能够证明公元前 14 世纪克里特岛有专门从事造船的工匠。泥板第一行用较大字体写着"na–u–domo/* ναυδόμος（naudomos）"，可能是主格复数或与格单数。这是一个技术术语，根据其词源可解释为造船工匠，或建造神庙的石匠（不过后者的拼写有所不同）。泥板第二行记录了词符 *181 和词汇"e–to–ro–qa–ta/*ἐντροκwᾱτᾱς"，该词可能是指某个与船桨有关的部件。

在希腊本土皮洛斯发掘出的线形文字 B 泥板 PY Na 568、Vn 865 以及 Xn 990 中也提到了十二名"naudomoi"（造船工匠）。皮洛斯位于希腊本土，拥有麦西尼亚海岸地区重要的海军力量。这一发现进一步表明该术语可能指代负责建造和装配船只的船舶工匠。这些专门工匠受宫殿直接雇佣并领取薪水，与泥板上记录的其他工匠情况相同。考古发现为了解这类工匠的装备和实践提供了实物证据。此外，通过实验考古，这些装备如今也得以重现。

（乔治娅・弗拉达）

161

Linear B tablet

Late Minoan ⅢA2 (1375-1300 BCE)

Clay

H. 3 cm, max. w. 7.3 cm

Knossos, palace

Archaeological Museum of Heraklion, Π-N261 (KN U 736)

Palm-leaf tablet in the Linear B script, with inscriptions on both sides. Despite its fragmentary condition, it testifies to the existence of Cretan craftsmen who specialised in shipbuilding during the 14th century BCE. The word *na-u-domo/* ναυδόμος* (*naudomos*) written in larger letters in the first line of the tablet could be the nominative plural or dative singular. It is a technical term, which, based on its etymology, can be interpreted either as a shipwright or a mason who built temples, although in the latter case the spelling would be different. The logogram *181 and the term *e-to-ro-qa-ta/*ἐντροκwᾱτᾱς* are recorded in the second row of the tablet: the latter probably refers to some part of the ship to do with the oars.

Twelve *naudomoi* are also mentioned in the tablets PY Na 568, Vn 865 and Xn 990 from Pylos in the mainland, which had a naval presence along the Messenian coastline. This fact reinforces the association of the term with boatbuilders in charge of the construction and assembly of the ships. These skilled artisans were dependent on and paid directly by the palace, like other specialist craftsmen recorded on the tablets. The archaeological finds offer tangible evidence for their equipment and practices, which have been recreated through experimental archaeology.

References

DMic I, 259, 278-79. Melena 1975, 51, 57. Palaima 1991, 288. Petrakis 2011, 207-08. Montecchi 2013, 209-12. Maragoudaki 2017, 238, 243-46. Melena-Firth 2019, 279, 624.

(Georgia Flouda)

ΤΑΛΩ

勇于突破极限的代达罗斯不愧是人类探索飞行的先驱，却不幸为他的致命绝技付出惨重代价，其子伊卡洛斯的折翼悲剧似乎隐喻了无数逐梦问天之士的挫折和牺牲，也启示人类在大自然面前务必遵循规律，量力而行。古希腊罗马观念中，世人常常在诸神与宿命面前孱弱无力，任由摆布，但直面命运的勇气和敢于反抗的精神不可或缺，值得颂扬。罗马诗人奥维德将代达罗斯丧子的悲剧归因于他谋杀外甥遭到的报复，虽意在讽刺，却字里行间对人造翅膀的精巧和父子二人的勇敢表露钦敬之情。

自传说的代达罗斯以来，这种挑战命运、征服自然的欲望和精神流芳百世，浸入到古希腊人的血脉里，反映到古希腊人的行动上。他们对自然规律、科学技术的兴趣、研究和探索绵延不断，成就非凡。朴素的唯物主义哲学、天文学、地理学、几何学在古希腊得到长足发展，为开拓未知领域铺设道路，为后代科技进步奠定根基。代达罗斯，无异于探索发现的精神所在！

Daedalus, who dared to push the boundaries of human limits, is undoubtedly a pioneer in the exploration of flight. Yet, he paid a heavy price for his fatal ingenuity. The tragic fall of his son, Icarus, serves as a metaphor for the setbacks and sacrifices endured by countless dreamers who strive to reach the heavens. It also reminds humanity to respect the laws of nature and act within its means. In the Greco-Roman worldview, mortals often appear fragile and powerless before the gods and fate, subject to their whims. However, the courage to confront destiny and the spirit of defiance are indispensable and worthy of celebration. The Roman poet Ovid attributed the tragedy of Daedalus losing his son to retribution for the murder of his nephew. While the account carries a tone of irony, it also reveals admiration for the ingenuity of the artificial wings and the bravery of both father and son.

Since the legendary Daedalus, this desire and spirit to challenge fate and conquer nature have endured through the ages, deeply ingrained in the ethos of the ancient Greeks and reflected in their actions. Their enduring interest in and exploration of natural laws, science, and technology led to remarkable achievements. The development of rudimentary materialist philosophy, astronomy, geography, and geometry in ancient Greece paved the way for the exploration of the unknown and laid the foundation for future scientific and technological progress. Daedalus, in essence, embodies the spirit of exploration and discovery!

古希腊神话在国内博物馆场域的跨文化转译
——基于故宫博物院“代达罗斯：希腊克里特岛的神话”展览策划与设计的深度思考

刘晓康　罗梦丹　薄海昆
故宫博物院

本文以故宫博物院“代达罗斯：希腊克里特岛的神话”特展为例，探讨国际交流展览中普遍存在的跨文化传播难题。笔者借鉴新博物馆学理论，结合展览策划实践，提出分步解决方案：首先解析文化差异对展览叙事的影响，继而探索希腊神话的本土化阐释策略，最终通过内容策划与形式设计的具体实践来验证策略的有效性。下面将对此展开详细论述，旨在为同类展览突破文化隔阂提供可操作的参考范例。

代达罗斯：文明交流中的神话隐喻与阐释困境

古希腊代达罗斯神话以迷宫建造与人造飞行的奇幻叙事为载体，承载着克里特岛青铜文明与古希腊技术伦理的深层意涵。希腊合作方提出的建议性展览框架以“迷宫”与“飞行”为母题，试图通过单线叙事展现技术崇拜与命运悖论的交织、海洋文明的多维互动以及神话重构历史的逻辑。然而对于中国观众而言，这种跨文化阐释面临多重挑战：

第一，文化符号的异质性构成首要认知壁垒。代达罗斯神话中“发明者—受难者”的矛盾形象，隐喻技术双刃剑的辩证思考，与中国传统“道器并重”的技术观形成伦理张力；克里特岛“以海立国”的生存逻辑，迥异于农耕文明的“安土重迁”思维；西方通过考古实证将线形文字泥板作为神话物证的路径，也与东方将神话纳入正史的文献传统存在阐释差异。

第二，历史语境的时空断裂加剧理解难度。米诺斯文化独特的技术成就与集权体系，既不同于同期夏商周礼法制度，也有别于后世希腊城邦形态。展览将公元前 14 世纪神话雏形与公元 1 世纪文学重构并置的层叠叙事，容易模糊文明演进脉络。克里特岛作为地中海文明枢纽的战略地位，更需观众具备基本地理认知框架。

第三，哲学观念的隐形鸿沟形成深层障碍。伊卡洛斯神话蕴含的僭越悲剧意识，与儒家“中庸”、道家“知止”理念形成价值观碰撞。代达罗斯以技术突破神权禁锢的叙事，凸显人神博弈的西方思维，区别于天人和谐的传统观念。展览之中双刃斧从工具到宗教符号的嬗变，陶器纹饰的象征演进，皆需理解西方“物即观念载体”的研究范式，而非单纯“器以载道”的道德解读。

第四，展览自身的叙事策略也构成接受挑战。中国观众对

“神话—历史”二元对立的认知传统，可能难以快速接受考古论证神话真实性的逻辑。展览将神话拆解为技术、空间、艺术维度的物证重构，要求观众具备跨学科整合能力。而“迷宫”作为建筑实体、权力隐喻与哲学命题的多重意指，更提高了符号解码成本。

明线与暗线：文化转译的双重叙事建构

为突破跨文化展览的认知隔阂，中方团队创造性采用“神话—历史”双线叙事结构。在保留希腊原有神话框架的基础上，通过增设米诺斯文化历史暗线，形成互补共生的叙事体系，构建起文化转译的双层认知系统。

在文化阐释层面，明线以代达罗斯神话的戏剧冲突搭建情感共鸣通道，暗线则通过建筑遗存、青铜工具等文物群构建技术史证据脉络。这种设计既延续了希腊策展方神话叙事的奇幻特质，又通过考古实证注入了历史纵深感，展现出合作策展中文化互鉴的共生智慧。

在叙事重构层面，双线结构实现了文化记忆的创造性转化。通过将文学想象升华为承载文明记忆的历史坐标，借助时间轴与历史地图完成神话的历史化转译，践行“批判性怀旧”的现代阐释理念。明线叙事满足观众对神话故事的情感期待，暗线则通过青铜工具、陶器、黄金首饰等器物揭示技术革新与社会权力结构的深层关联，以实证解构的方法实现跨文化认知校准，打破传统展览的单向灌输模式。

这种双轨并行的叙事架构既保持了对原始主题的尊重，又通过历史维度的拓展实现了文化再生产。故宫博物院团队在希腊伊拉克利翁考古博物馆提供的框架内，用神话魅力衔接历史认知，印证了跨文化展览中文化尊重与在地化阐释的动态平衡哲学，为破解认知壁垒提供了创新性解决方案。

解构与重构：内容转译与空间叙事的协同创新

在跨文化展览策划中，空间逻辑与内容逻辑的深度协同是实现文化转译的关键。故宫博物院策展团队基于希腊方提供的原始框架，在建构双线叙事的总体策略引导下，通过“解构—重构”方法，将神话叙事、历史实证与空间体验熔铸为有机整体。这一过程不仅解决了神武门展厅的物理局限，更开创了“内容—形式同步策展”的新范式，使展览成为跨学科协作的文化转译实验场。

（一）解构：原始框架的适应性转化

1. 单元次序调整

希腊合作方提出的展览方案以代达罗斯神话为单一叙事主线，根据相对独立的故事片段较为自由地划分单元，以全面呈现神话情节，却有意弱化了对克里特岛地理概况、米诺斯文化发展脉络及工艺美术成就的逻辑性系统阐释（表 1）。这种叙事方式对西方观众而言可能易于理解，对中国观众却存在认知障碍，不但难以捕捉“神话是米诺斯文明现实折射”的核心命题，还可能误将展品与神话人物直接对应。

因此，中方策展团队决定在保留原有神话框架的基础上构建双线叙事结构，通过调整单元次序与简化标题（表 2），形成“神话—史实”的互文体系，在具体操作中落实这一策略。每个单元仍以神话元素切入，如：

第四单元 巧匠

代达罗斯为国王米诺斯设计迷宫，为公主阿里阿德涅建造舞池。他是绝无仅有的天才，是智慧机敏的匠师，是发明创造的能手。

不管代达罗斯是否确有其人，考古发现的众多精美之器证明克里特岛米诺斯时代果真拥有丰富的物产、高超的技术、出色的审美。陶瓶朴拙，彩色纹饰勾勒奇趣之美；金光灿灿，项饰耳坠闪烁贵人华彩；石皿莹润，天然纹理包罗浩渺苍穹；印章玲珑，微雕细刻凝缩大千世界。

杰出工艺让人看到米诺斯文化发达的生产力和旺盛的消费需求，数千年前爱琴海青铜时代的岛民们已经享受了品质卓越的劳动成果。精巧的生产技术当归功于数千载勤劳实践，代达罗斯神话恰是克里特史前经济的文学投射。更有可能，并非代达罗斯造就了工艺，而是百工千艺塑造了大师。

巧匠，何止代达罗斯一人；巧匠，是千千万万隐匿于历史烟尘的劳动者。

各大单元文字说明都立足这种模式，整体构建出清晰的文明发展逻辑：从神话传说催生考古发现，到遗址揭示迷宫与牛头怪的史实原型；通过建筑遗存追溯米诺斯三千年兴衰历程，解析集权制度、城邦建设与青铜技术的文明根基；继而展现依托航海贸易网络发展的实用工艺品、宗教雕塑与壁画艺术，最终揭示代达罗斯神话所凝聚的技术创新精神对古希腊文明的深远影响。这种重构既保持神话叙事的吸引力，又系统呈现了米诺斯文明的考古实证与历史价值。

2. 单元权重平衡

针对希腊合作方建议性展览大纲中单元文物体量失衡问题（如“作为巧匠的代达罗斯”单元展品达139件，而“在‘幽蓝之海’上航行”“迷宫与建筑艺术”单元分别仅有6件、8件），策展团队以双线叙事为轴心进行结构性重组。通过将38件青铜器从原“作为巧匠的代达罗斯”单元剥离，在“迷宫”与“巧匠”单元之间新增第三单元“青铜”，使原单元展品量级回归合理区间。此次调整进一步厘清了展览的历史叙事逻辑：青铜单元既作为“迷宫”单元展示的米诺斯文化生产力注脚，又为“巧匠”单元的精工技艺提供物质基础支撑。重组后六个单元形成均衡的三三制空间布局——神武门展厅一层承载序言及前三个单元，二层容纳后三个单元及尾声，实现内容体量与空间配比的双重平衡（表3）。

3. 单元展品调配

在初步平衡单元体量后，针对仍存在的部分单元展品单薄问题，策展团队实施二次优化，即将“巧匠”和“青铜”单元中与米诺斯王宫遗址直接关联的文物重新定位。例如克诺索斯

单元	章节	文物数量
序厅	展标、中英文前言	0件/组
神话	神话的起源	5件/组
	神话的形成	8件/组
作为巧匠的代达罗斯	米诺斯陶器：艺术、工艺和独创力	30件/组
	金属制品：对金属的赋形与重塑	38件/组
	黄金加工：珠宝与首饰	25件/组
	硕石回响：米诺斯石质器皿工艺巡礼	30件/组
	小石头大印象：印章世界的微小奇观	16件/组
在“幽蓝之海”上航行	传说代达罗斯发明了帆	6件/组
迷宫与建筑艺术	传说代达罗斯为米诺斯王修建了迷宫	8件/组
雕塑的诞生	传说代达罗斯教会克里特人制作雕塑	15件/组
流芳	代达罗斯的前瞻性发明（代达罗斯为其子伊卡洛斯用羽毛和蜡制作的翅膀，表达了人类早期的飞行梦想；代达罗斯亦被视作灵感之源）	0件/组
	放映厅（希腊方计划提供关于代达罗斯故事的视频）	
尾厅	代达罗斯与今日世界	0件/组

表1

单元	章节	文物数量
序厅	展标、中英文前言	0件/组
神话	代代相传	5件/组
	寻踪溯源	8件/组
迷宫	通过克诺索斯王宫、美斯托斯王宫等遗址讲述克里特岛青铜时代的城镇发展史	8件/组
巧匠	彩陶绘奇趣	30件/组
	青铜熠熠辉	38件/组
	金饰竞璀璨	25件/组
	美石琢巧器	30件/组
	小印铃万千	16件/组
雕像	雕像折射的克里特米诺斯文化的宗教信仰	15件/组
远航	发达的航海贸易拓宽了克里特人的视野	6件/组
流芳	代达罗斯的前瞻性发明（代达罗斯为其子伊卡洛斯用羽毛和蜡制作的翅膀，表达了人类早期的飞行梦想；代达罗斯亦被视作灵感之源）	0件/组
	放映厅（希腊方计划提供关于代达罗斯故事的视频）	
尾厅	代达罗斯与今日世界	0件/组

表2

单元	章节	文物数量
序	展标、中英文前言、克里特岛概述	0件/组
神话（文学与考古）	代代相传（神话的流传）	8件/组
	寻踪溯源（神话的来源）	10件/组
迷宫（建筑和政治、社会、艺术）	迷宫与建筑艺术	19件/组
青铜（工具和生产力）	金属制品：对金属的赋形与重塑	32件/组
巧匠（经济）	彩陶绘奇趣（米诺斯陶器：艺术、工艺和独创力）	23件/组
	金饰竞辉光（黄金加工：珠宝与首饰）	23件/组
	美石琢巧器（硕石回响：米诺斯石质器皿工艺巡礼）	23件/组
	小印铃万方（小石头大印象：印章世界的微小奇观）	18件/组
雕像（宗教信仰）	雕塑的诞生	13件/组
远航（贸易）	在“幽蓝之海”上航行	4件/组
尾声（影响力）	代达罗斯的前瞻性发明（代达罗斯为其子伊卡洛斯用羽毛和蜡制作的翅膀，表达了人类早期的飞行梦想；代达罗斯亦被视作灵感之源）	0件/组
	放映厅（希腊方计划提供关于代达罗斯故事的视频）	

表3

1. 展厅入口处的主形象标题墙
2. 一层展厅内的米诺斯廊柱装饰
3. 一层展厅墙面上的“百合花王子”与“米诺斯廊柱”呼应
4. 展柜内的理性风格设计
5. 一层展厅鸟瞰图
6. 一层展厅西端的意象化“迷宫”场景

王宫出土的彩陶器、青铜模具，斐斯托斯王宫石雕器皿等生产类文物，被调入展品数量偏少的“迷宫”单元展示，通过实物佐证该单元阐释的“王宫复合职能论”——既承担政治宗教功能，亦是手工业与贸易中心[1]。同时，将“青铜”单元中3件记录青铜生产信息的线形文字B泥板提前至首单元“神话”的“寻踪溯源”板块，与另2块泥板共同向中国观众详细阐述何为线形文字B，进而诉说其中一块线形文字B泥板上书写的代达罗斯神殿信息。通过这种跨单元文物迁移，既强化了薄弱单元的历史实证厚度，更使各板块形成“实物呼应论述，展品引导逻辑”[2]的深层互动，最终实现内容密度与叙事节奏的全局性平衡。

（二）重构：空间与内容的耦合设计

为平衡新增历史叙事线索对神话主题的消解，展览通过形式设计强化视觉叙事倾向，即通过营造神秘氛围延续核心神话脉络，并在空间建构中凸显内容结构调整后的历史叙事层级。

1. 神话叙事的剧场化空间转译

展厅通过沉浸式空间设计强化悲剧性神话氛围。入口处以克诺索斯王宫标志性牛形立体浮雕为主视觉，搭配泛光灯带与灰黑底墙的中英文前言及地图，塑造庄重神秘的第一印象。

一层展厅围绕神话溯源、考古发现与迷宫解析三重内容，将克诺索斯王宫遗址元素与米诺斯迷宫意象交织于空间设计中：右侧墙面的巨幅克诺索斯王宫“百合花王子”壁画引出“宙

[1] 亚瑟·伊文思（Arthur Evans）：《克诺索斯的米诺斯王宫》（*The Palace of Minos at Knossos*）第1至4卷，1921至1935年。其早期发掘报告提出王宫作为权力与仪式的核心场所。

[2] 该表述源自艾琳·胡珀-格林希尔（Eilean Hooper-Greenhill）的博物馆叙事理论，其著作《博物馆与视觉文化阐释》（*Museums and the Interpretation of Visual Culture*，2000）提出展品组合应构建“物证—阐释”的对话关系，强调物质载体与策展话语的互文性建构。

斯的故乡”序言区；三根立柱经包裹处理形成复原的克诺索斯柱廊，其间的独立展柜重点陈列绿泥石牛首形来通杯与特殊王宫风格海洋生物纹陶扁壶，营造文物现身废墟的时空交错感；展厅西端特设镜面迷宫空间。墙面满贴镜面，地上铺设罗马马赛克迷宫纹地毯，配合代达罗斯迷宫主题短片投影，在多重镜面反射中构建虚实相生的戏剧化叙事场景。

2. 柜内陈列的韵律化营造

柜内展品陈列设计通过形式语言强化历史叙事，构建出具有韵律感的空间节奏。设计策略主要体现在三方面：

首先，文物排布兼顾历史逻辑与空间美学。依据内容关联性与物理关系进行组合，通过高低错落、大小穿插、疏密对比形成内在节奏，尤其注重残损/小型文物的视觉重构。例如将五块线形文字泥板横向排列于黑色展板，嵌入门型框架形成视觉单元，配合图文解说增强信息厚度，同类手法应用于印章、金饰等小件文物，有效提升单体表现力。

其次，门型框架作为重复性设计元素，既构成小型文物的展示载体，又形成展线上的节奏节点，通过模块化组合打破线性陈列的单调性。

第三，通过双层背板压缩展台进深结构，在缩短观展视距的同时，利用前后层次叠加形成空间纵深感。内容展板采取韵律式间隙布局，其断裂形态抽象化呈现克诺索斯王宫遗址意象，使观众在观展动线中形成历史空间断层感知体验。

整体而言，柜内理性严谨的陈列逻辑与柜外戏剧化氛围形成二元对话——前者通过科学编排凸显历史叙事的客观性，后者则以情感共鸣激活观展体验，两者共同构建完整的叙事场域。

3. 文化转译的视觉语言编辑

展览设计的色彩体系以双线叙事为逻辑框架。展柜外部采用暗红立柱、深蓝克里特岛地形墙、灰白立体地形、土金“迷宫”景观外墙及多种绚丽壁画等高饱和度色彩组合，通过强烈的视觉表现力营造神话沉浸氛围，同时激活观展者的空间想象力。转入展柜内部，色彩系统切换为黑、深灰与土金构成的低明度基调：黑色系既凸显文物本体美感，土金色调则隐喻米诺斯遗迹的废墟质感，共同强化历史叙事维度。空间材质刻意保留粗粝肌理，通过材料本身的沧桑属性，构建跨越时空的历史语境。

（三）协同创新：内容与形式的共生逻辑

本次展览策划突破传统“内容先行—设计跟进”的线性模式，构建跨学科协作机制，形成“空间立体策展”方法论。策展团队初期即对神武门展厅进行空间踏勘，将建筑结构、展线

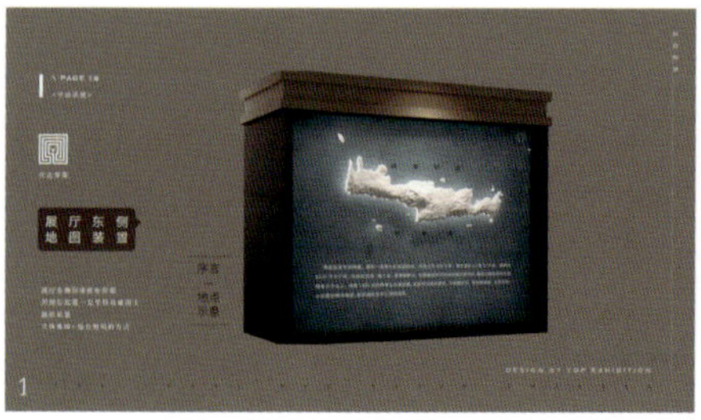

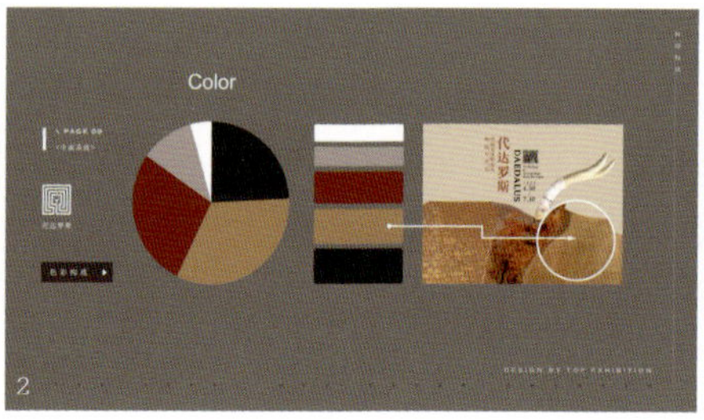

1. 克里特岛立体地理模型
2. 展览空间内的色彩构成饼形图
3. 意象化“迷宫”近景

容量等物理条件前置整合至大纲框架中，确保内容创作与空间逻辑同步生成。

执行过程中，展览文本与形式设计始终并行推进：大纲初稿完成时，展厅平面布局与柜内陈列方案已同步产出。通过双向验证机制，团队能够快速识别文物排布失衡、图文呼应错位等问题，继而针对性优化大纲内容与展陈细节。在此动态调整中，学术叙事持续校准空间表达，设计形式反复呼应内容精神，两者形成螺旋上升的适配关系。

这种协同机制最终实现内容与形式的深度契合——神话与历史脉络转化为空间节奏，文物组合构成视觉语法，墙面图文与展品阵列形成密切对话。双线叙事强化了学术信息的空间转译效能，又通过具象化的展陈语法消解文化认知壁垒，使展览成为跨文化传播的有效媒介。

深挖与扩展：考古实证与历史语境的延伸

策展团队以知识考古学方法论为指导，通过深挖与扩展策略，将这次展览展示的碎片化文物转化为文明史叙事载体，具体方法是围绕单个展品进行说明牌微观描述，围绕成组展品进行知识链接中观描述，围绕单元展品进行单元说明宏观描述。这一过程不仅是对米诺斯文化的深度解析，更是对当代博物馆“以物记事，以事叙史，以史启思”[3] 阐释思想的具体实践。

（一）内容深挖：从文物证史到历史启示

1. 关键知识领域的界定

展览以神话叙事为双线逻辑框架，表层勾连神话意象，深层切入米诺斯文化的四大核心脉络——技术史、艺术史、社会史与思想史。通过技术革新揭示物质基础，艺术流变解码文化表征，社会结构展现组织形态，精神体系勾勒价值内核。文物说明牌、知识链接与单元说明构成三级阐释系统，将器物实证、关联网络与文明框架逐层整合，最终破除神话表层叙事，呈现技术、艺术、社会与思想维度交织作用的文明演进机制。

2. 知识链接的梯度设计

为了厘清叙事逻辑，展览各个单元的知识链接有意做了梯度设计。下文以其中三个主题单元为例，说明知识链接如何通过因果推导与历时性分析构建认知框架。

“神话”中的“代代相传”分单元知识链接以克里特岛纳入希腊文化圈（公元前 11 世纪起）为切入点，解析阿芙洛狄忒与阿波罗等神像展品的符号隐喻，揭示地方神话纳入泛希腊信仰的文化转译机制。然后结合考古遗存与文献对证，追溯代达罗斯传说在希腊罗马时期的叙事层积，最终形成从地域传统到经典神话的成熟情节。

“迷宫”单元知识链接通过双重视角解构历史：一方面以克诺索斯王宫实证数据消解迷宫传说，剥离代达罗斯的建筑师神话属性；另一方面以米诺斯文化分期为轴，通过前王宫期、旧王宫期、新王宫期与后王宫期的历时演变，重构克里特青铜时代的社会发展过程。

“巧匠”中的“彩陶绘奇趣”分单元知识链接沿技术社会学路径，分析米诺斯陶器从早期形制到卡马雷斯陶器，再到王宫风格陶器的演化，最终揭示迈锡尼东扩引发的陶艺风格突变，完整展现工艺变迁与社会结构转型的互动逻辑。

各单元知识链接均通过问题链牵引，在历史语境中完成从现象描述到系统解释的知识再生产，实现认知跃迁。

[3] 一言、单嗣平、薄海昆：《时代答卷：“何以中国”策展笔记》第52页，浙江大学出版社，2024年。

（二）知识扩展：多维度叙事中的时空定位

本次展览通过制作设计中国、希腊历史对照表及可视化时间轴，多维度解析米诺斯文化的历史坐标：横向定位其与中国新石器晚期至商代中后期的同期性，纵向厘清其在希腊文明谱系中承启新石器时代与黑暗时期、古风时期的枢纽地位。结合文物图像与时间线设计，观众得以直观建立跨文明时空认知，深化对米诺斯文化历史及其价值的理解。

表达与图示：文学性与视觉性的转译共振

在跨文化国际展览中，文字表达与视觉图示并非简单的信息载体，而是建构认知框架的文化转译器。本次展览通过“史诗化叙事语言”与“图谱式视觉设计”的双重策略，将晦涩的文明史知识转化为可感知的美学体验，在诗意与实证的张力中实现米诺斯文化的在地化阐释。

（一）文学性表达的诗学转译

1. 史诗语体与学术严谨的平衡

展览的核心文本尝试采用“古典主义”写作范式，借鉴《荷马史诗》文风，在保证学术准确性的前提下植入文学感染力，如最重要的前言文本如下：

海皇挥舞三叉戟劈开爱琴碧波，浪花飞溅处诞育三千岛屿，宛若美神阿芙洛狄忒抛下的璀璨宝石。克里特，正是那永恒生辉的祖母绿。

它风光旖旎，被视作众神之王宙斯的故乡；它玄秘莫测，萌生出代达罗斯修建迷宫的奇想。瑰丽神话，驱使考古学家用鹤嘴镐击碎时光岩壁；不懈努力，让失落已久的史前遗迹重现天颜。

听啊！闪烁荣光的文明清泉从克里特及周边岛、陆汩汩涌出，汇聚成河，于公元前三千纪冲破青铜时代的闸关。冒险者以舟为箭射穿海上迷雾，为贸易远涉四方眺望星汉。

视野开阔的岛民熔炼外域文化，制作了精美器皿，营建起壮伟宫殿，创造出瑰丽艺术。一个崇尚自然、多姿多彩、兼收并蓄的文明在欧、亚、非三洲交汇处绽放绚烂，为古希腊文明结成夏果献上第一波春日芳妍。

当神话挣脱虚幻的桎梏，便化作鎏金密钥，去开启尘封已久的历史匣龛。

欣逢故宫博物院百年华诞，这里展示来自希腊伊拉克利翁考古博物馆的珍贵文物，让克诺索斯王宫的柱廊与紫禁城的丹墀互映辉光，向您解读代达罗斯神话背后的古希腊之源，昭示伟大文明间应有的和合之美、交流互鉴。

前言通过荷马式比喻与排比句式，唤醒观众对地中海文明的诗意想象，增加可读性，营造历史氛围。即便用这样诗意的语言，前言内容字斟句酌，高度概括了展览内容、线索与米诺斯文化特征，是以学术严谨性为前提的。其他几个单元的文字也都采用了这种语言风格。占展览文字内容主体的知识链接和说明牌文字则完全是简单叙事化的语言，两种风格语言交替阐

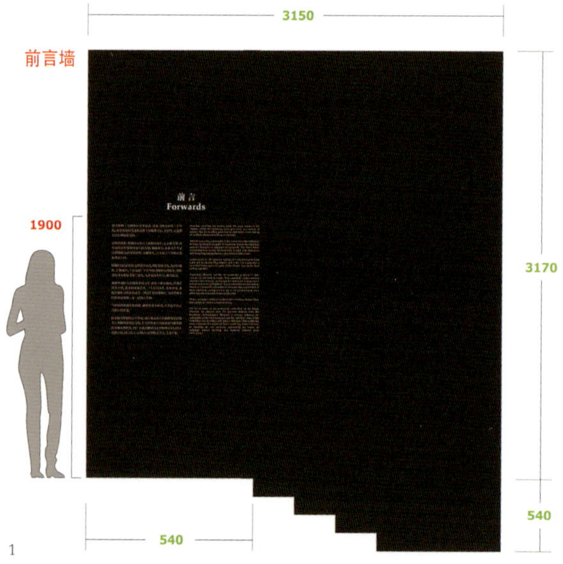

1

述是为了避免过多的文学化语言带来的疲劳感。

2. 陌生化修辞的认知润滑

针对中国观众的文化盲区，展览采用“隐喻移植”策略降低理解门槛，例如将“线形文字 B”戏称为“地中海甲骨文”，通过文字载体的功能类比建立认知桥梁；把“双刃斧祭祀”解读为“爱琴海青铜时代的玉琮礼天”，以礼器象征性触发文化共鸣；用“米诺斯陶轮”对应“景德镇拉坯技艺”，通过技术共性消解工艺陌生感；将“代达罗斯”戏称为“青铜时代克里特岛的鲁班”，用相似身份解读陌生人物的历史地位。

（二）图示系统的认知重构

1. 平面图谱的视觉转译

为提升展览信息传达效能，策展团队在希腊合作方大力支持下研发了 10 类原创图示系统：

（1）时空定位图

以手绘水彩地图呈现克里特岛地理位置、爱琴海文明源流、青铜时代航线、锡拉火山影响范围及迈锡尼文明版图，严格遵循地图报审规范。

（2）遗址平面图

通过克诺索斯、斐斯托斯、扎克罗斯、马利亚等王宫遗址平面图，揭示米诺斯建筑的空间组织逻辑。

（3）功能解析图

动态展示“跳公牛”仪式流程，可视化双刃斧祭祀装置的结构特征。

（4）文明对照图

并置米诺斯青铜工具与江西新干商代青铜器，建立跨文

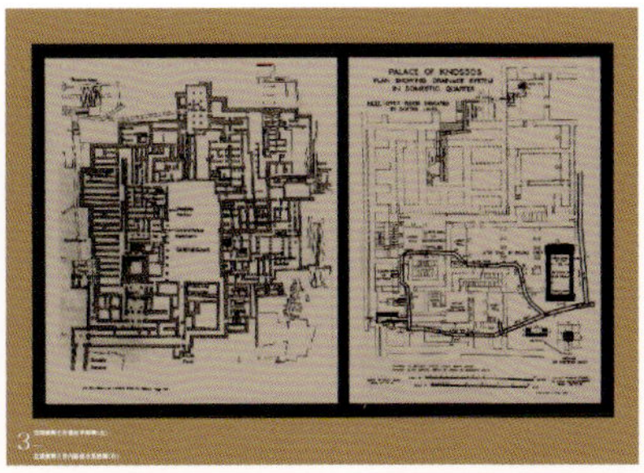

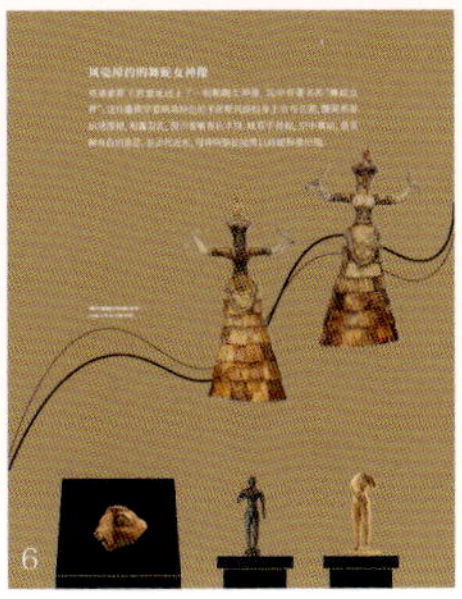

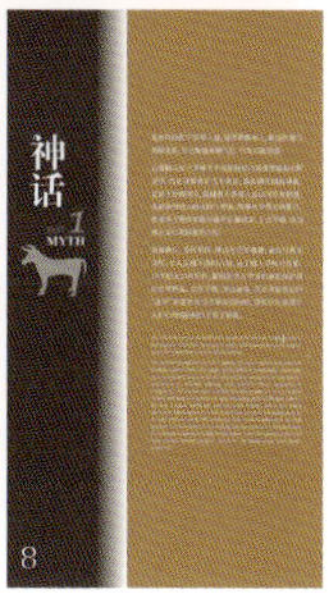

1. 前言墙施工图
2. 罗列米诺斯王宫风格陶器纹样的图示
3. 克诺索斯王宫遗址平面图
4. “跳公牛”过程示意图
5. 展柜内图文与展品的空间关系
6. 舞蛇女神像图示
7. 江西省博物馆藏新干大洋洲商代青铜工具
8. 第一单元“神话”单元展板上的“神牛”小图标

明时空对话。

（5）文物补充图

增设伊拉克利翁考古博物馆藏精品图片，如斐斯托斯圆盘、金蜂挂坠等，另通过金饰、印章等小件文物图像丰富展柜层次。

（6）交流实证图

展出克里特岛出土的基克拉泽斯雕像与古埃及文物图像，佐证文明互动。

（7）微观呈现图

设置重点文物和微小文物放大图，辅助观众观察细密纹饰与微型雕刻。

（8）纹样谱系图

系统梳理卡马雷斯陶器、王宫风格陶器等纹样演变脉络。

（9）工艺复原图

参照古埃及壁画线描重构克里特石器制作工序。

（10）史料辅助图

配置伊文思考古照片、克诺索斯王宫遗址航拍图等历史影像资料。

2. 平面设计的空间赋能

在确保图文内容充足的前提下，平面版式设计成为提升文化转译效能与信息传达效率的关键。设计师通过三项核心策略突破传统呈现方式：其一，在维持整体版面肃穆基调的基础上，巧妙植入装饰性辅助线条，通过几何韵律打破静态空间结构，形成具有呼吸感的视觉动线；其二，构建系统化色彩管理体系，对彩色平面素材进行跨媒介色调校准，确保多元素在统一色谱逻辑下和谐共生；其三，采用黄金比例网格系统规范图文布局，建立内容模块间的视知觉关联，通过严谨的负空间规划强化信息层级。这套复合型设计策略既保留了文化传播的庄重感，又借助动态视觉语言激活受众的阅读兴趣。

结语

故宫博物院“代达罗斯：希腊克里特岛的神话”特展开创了博物馆国际交流展览文化转译的第三路径：在文明互鉴的坐标轴上，以批判性对话重构文化认知的语法。展览突破“全盘移植”与“单向阐释”的传统窠臼，通过学术考辨与美学转译的双重奏，让克里特岛米诺斯文化在紫禁城的展示空间中获得了主体性的言说能力。

这场文化对话实践呈现出三重创新维度：其一，在策展机制上构建平衡话语权，以“时间轴对照”创造文明比较的认知界面，使平行时空产生互文性张力；其二，在阐释方法上引入考古实证与神话解构的双重视角，用事实证据刺破神话叙事的浪漫主义面纱，揭示文明演进的多维图景；其三，在转译策略上实现“物—文—境””的共振转化，使物质载体升华为可感知的文明景象。

展览昭示着全球化时代文化转译的新范式——真正的文明对话既非镜像复制亦非权力解构，而是在保持文化主体性的前提下，通过创造性转码建构共通的意义场域。当克里特陶罐的螺旋纹样与太和殿的蟠龙藻井形成美学共鸣时，博物馆已超越物理空间局限，成为文明基因解码与精神图谱重绘的超级实验室。这种转译智慧，或许正是破解文明冲突论的文化密钥。

The Cross-cultural Translation of Ancient Greek Mythology in the Field of Domestic Museums: In-depth Reflections Based on the Exhibition Planning and Design of "Daedalus: Legends of Crete" in the Palace Museum

Liu Xiaokang, Luo Mengdan, Bo Haikun

The Palace Museum

Abstract: Under the tide of globalization, international exchange exhibitions have become crucial vehicles for civilizational dialogue. The Palace Museum's 2025 exhibition "Daedalus: Legends of Crete" developed in collaboration with the Hellenic Archaeological Museum of Heraklion, establishes an interpretive framework balancing cultural authenticity and audience accessibility through dual narrative structures and spatial-poetic translation strategies. Grounded in precious artifacts and thematic frameworks provided by the Greek institution, this Sino-Hellenic collaboration transcends being merely a display of cultural treasures – it represents a pioneering exploration in cross-cultural exhibition methodology. By respecting the foundational academic context of Greek partners while employing an innovative "content-form synchronized curation" model, the exhibition transforms an obscure ancient Greek myth into a tangible dialogue between civilizations.

Key words: International exchange exhibition, Daedalus, ancient Greek mythology, museum context, cross-cultural transcreation

故宫博物院
THE PALACE MUSEUM

展览策划

娄　玮　王跃工

展览统筹

刘　辉　孙　淼　张　亮　王　博

展览涉外协调及翻译

李绍毅　罗梦丹

策展团队

薄海昆　康晓慧　郑欣荻

展览设计

徐晓婧　刘晓康　胡　博

展览执行（按姓名拼音首字母排序）

薄海昆　胡　博　康晓慧　李怀玉　刘晓康　田少飞　熊　铎　徐　翔　徐晓婧　赵　航　郑欣荻

展览支持

院办公室　文化产业管理处　文物管理处　器物部　数字与信息部　社会教育部　出版编辑部
故宫世界遗产监测部　保卫处　消防处　安全技术处　开放管理处　行政处

图录主编

薄海昆

图录撰稿

薄海昆　李怀玉　刘晓康　罗梦丹

ΑΡΧΑΙΟΛΟΓΙΚΟ ΜΟΥΣΕΙΟ ΗΡΑΚΛΕΙΟΥ

Authors of entries

K.Athanasaki G.Flouda I.Galli M.Kyrimi S.Mandalaki D.Manidakis

D.Mylonas I.Nikolakopoulou L.Platon D.Sfakianakis K.Sidiropoulos

E.Sikla P.Stamataki K.Tzanaki E.Tziraki

Translation of entries

Rosemary Tzanaki

Scientific editing of entries

Georgia Flouda Paraskevi Stamataki